THE EXTRA-DIMENSIONALS

COMING SOON FROM TAMA
(THE AGE OF MASS AWAKENING) BOOKS:

THE CLEAR-HEARERS
True Tales and Concepts of the Great Voice

THE EPHEMERALS
True Tales and Concepts of Ghosts and Seers of the Dead

THE RETURNEES
True Tales and COncepts of True Death Experiences (TDE's)

Extra-Dimensionality is the key to understanding everything......

By everything, we mean all the areas in which we have been deceived to believe the physical world is the beginning and end of all things. "The Extra-Dimensionals" is the stark revelation of where Alien Visitors are actually coming from and to where they are returning. Understanding Extra-Dimensionality is the way to unfold the truth of the paranormal, the spiritual and even the physical world. These Visitors have been with us since time immemorial and their messages to us are everywhere around us. The truth will eventually explode into our field of vision. If we refuse to listen then we are only delaying the inevitable to a time when an alarm will be sounded that is so loud that it will consume everything upon the Earth. Once the black swans arrive, once we awaken to numerous mile long shadows cast by these ancient ships—hanging over our major cities, soundless, motionless, maddening; it will be too late.

It is in these final moments that we can still, with open minds and clear hearts, decipher that which has been intentionally hidden from humanity for so long—the truth of Extra-Dimensionality. That comprehension will, in turn, illuminate every hidden truth of our material existence. Then, we will find that for the first time, we will finally have the key to understanding everything.

John DeSouza

THE EXTRA-DIMENSIONALS

JOHN DESOUZA

TAMA
Publishing

The Age of Mass Awakening

*This work is dedicated to all those who look up at the sky at night and know that something **unbelievable** is coming.*

CONTENTS

PRESENT EXTRA-DIMENSIONALITY

THE EXTRA-DIMENSIONAL AGENDA

FINAL WARNINGS

THE AGE OF MASS AWAKENING

We are in it already. The circle of Mass Awakening has opened because of the expansion of what people believe. Despite what mainstream society tries to tell us, belief determines everything in life and beyond. Faith and belief are the only things that can transform everything. Eventually, we will no longer recognize the universe we live in. This may take a decade or an entire age—time is irrelevant in Ultimate Awakening because it originates from and concludes outside normal time and space. It is happening right now. The "Mass" in Mass Awakening only means breaking the six percent barrier in the population of any town, city, nation or planet. All over the world, we are bursting through that six percent barrier. People are awakening as never before in the history of humankind. The barrier is splintered, cracked and showing gaps. Escapees are increasing daily. Transcension is at hand.

We promote this awakening through transformation of the language of the Paranormal. It is vital to replace the labels and language of Newtonian scientists and 1950's pilots that still haunt these areas. We are still not sure what "Unidentified Flying Object" really means because it means almost nothing. It's a horribly neutral term popularized only to convey a sense of uncertainty and vagueness. I also don't know what a "Near-Death Experience" is any more than we know about "Near-Pregnancy." A person is either dead or they are not. The people who had this fatal experience—were Dead-Dead. Then, they returned to tell the living about how "the real world" appears on the other side of the veil. This verbal mislabeling is no accident. The paranormal is loaded down with coded language meant to convey fogginess and drowsy confusion. It is time to lift that fog.

Awakening progresses and if we change our words and our language; a new way of thinking will follow. Imprisoned minds will go free and the old non-solutions forced upon us will no longer seem viable. As the Author says: *"**We** will become the disclosure we wish to see."*

Goldie Serrano, Chief Editor, TAMA PUBLISHING

OLD PARADIGMS
DECOMPOSE

The giant leap forward for mankind didn't happen on the moon, it happened in your mind and it's happening right now.

I

A CALL THAT SHOOK THE PLANET

Late one night, in the fall of 1997, a national radio talk show host discussed "Area 51." This is the informal name of a United States military base at Edwards Air Force Base. Area 51 is in Southern Nevada, 83 miles northwest of downtown Las Vegas. Officially, the base's purpose is to support development and testing of experimental aircraft and weapons systems. The United States government didn't even acknowledge the existence of Area 51 until July 14, 2003. Over the years, Area 51 has been the subject of numerous alleged whistleblowers over the years that have periodically come forward to expose the secret activities of this base.

The show cleared its phone lines and invited former or current employees at Area 51 to call in. The segment was mostly unmemorable. The caller lines were plagued by people espousing vague, third hand stories about a friend of a friend, who once knew a guy, who once had an uncle that "maybe" worked at Area 51. There was nothing solid or even interesting uncovered.

Then something happened.

A call got through on the air from a young man with a quavering voice. The panicky caller said he didn't have much time. The host questioned the man on whether he is an employee of Area 51. The host tried to elicit clear statements for the audience. The young man responded that he was a former employee who was discharged about a week prior. Panicky Caller said he'd been on the run across the country since that time (implying he was being chased). He said "they" would triangulate on his position very soon. Ignoring what that meant (since this language and technology were not commonly known in 1997) the host urged the man to get his information out quickly. Panicky Caller made several jarring statements about the true nature of extraterrestrials and their relationship to the human rulers of our planet. There was a ring of authenticity in his statements. His tone, inflection and choice of words conveyed an urgent desire to warn humanity of terrible, *unspeakable* things. What he managed to get out was so shocking that news of what he said traveled all over the planet in a matter of hours. Anyone who heard the incident occur live on the air will never forget it. Most who were told about the call afterward, sought out more information about it (very easy to find even today on Internet); but anyone who actually knows what really happened that night—*has never revealed it.*

Even while still in the midst of making "the call" Panicky Caller realized that he'd crossed a threshold that he might not survive. He broke down into sobs. Yet, he labored to continue. He began to answer the question of the nature of the association between Alien Visitors and the human overlords of Earth—there was a buzz, a high-pitched squeal, then...

n o t h i n g.....

All the boards and screens read the same message:

TRANSMISSION LOST...

There was an unprecedented catastrophic failure of the live satellite feed. There was dead air...bumper music. When the show resumed; it was chaos. The host didn't know if he was on the air. He was in the act of grilling some new oblivious caller on whether any of the Panicky Caller's comments got out onto the airwaves. The host got nowhere fast.

In the ensuing days and weeks, Panicky Caller made news around the world. There were rumors, overblown paraphrasing and exaggerations throughout the English-speaking nations. Some blowback from all this landed squarely back on the host of the radio program; who became the focal point of global angst over whether this call was "real." Arguments have raged about this call even to this day. Voice, spectral and technological analysis done on "Panicky Area 51 Caller's" voice, inflections and use of language during the course of his call—always came to the same result—the caller was being truthful and he was scared, *very scared.*

However, there were others who were also frightened: the Elite Powers In Control (EPIC), the Global Powers who disrupted a global radio show that transmitted in analog, digital and satellite systems all simultaneously. The amount of power and technology that was required to knock a satellite out of its transmission position, to shut down the analog transmission system and also disrupt the digital signal—at the same moment—was an Earth-shaking amount of energy. Even today, the nations don't *overtly* have the tech to accomplish this sort of thing in the conventional world—and they certainly didn't in 1997.

An out of work actor, sometime later, called the host on this same radio show claiming that he had hoaxed the call but rudimentary analysis casts serious doubt on his oddly worded confession. Most revealing was that this person never identified himself in any way in order to profit from this globally successful "hoax." The failure to actually take credit under a true identity was the strongest indicator that it was a "paid for" confession—a far more common phenomenon than most would think. The host didn't press the point because he was desperate to put the whole affair behind him. The "hoaxer" was dismissed without any cross-examination—***case solved and put to bed***. At least it was solved for the unawakened mainstream seeking ways to stay safely ensconced inside their comfortable box of false reality.

Even if "Panicky Area 51 Caller" did start out intending to be a fraud, I believe it ended up as genuine because he tapped into something real. The EPIC (Elite Powers In Control…of the institutions of the Earth) would also agree because they activated and directed electro-magnetic power on a vast, almost unimaginable scale to temporarily disable a satellite transmission from high above the Earth's orbit.

What explosive comments did "Panicky Caller" unleash on that particular evening so many years ago to cause so much global and institutional response?

He said that our space program, or rather, an early precursor of the full space program, came across unexpected Alien Entities. Thereafter, those beings attached themselves to members of our space program, returned with them and infiltrated our military and thereafter, our government. They injected themselves like a virus throughout Area 51. These entities told our governments of great disasters that are coming and where upon the Earth would most impacted by these impending catastrophes.

As Panicky Caller began to cry uncontrollably, he sputtered that the national governments know of safe areas where they could be moving people but that the coming massive loss of life throughout the Earth fits perfectly into the genocidal agenda of Earth's *human* overlords. They want Earth depopulated. That way, the remnants will be easier to control. Yet this devastation will have no effect on the alien entities because they *are not* what people think they are. They are not *physical* extra-terrestrial beings from this or any other star system. They pretend to be from our physical reality but they aren't. They are beings that traverse here from other realms of reality.

They are Extra-Dimensionals.

2

THE COSMIC GAME CHANGER

The Extra-Dimensionals—*non-terrestrial, intelligent life forms who are visiting our dimension of time and space as transitory beings from outside our plane of physical time and space—e.g. from outside our existence.*

This definitional sentence may seem like just another divergent viewpoint but it is far more. Once accepted and even embraced as truth, it is a *Cosmic Game changer.*

Such acceptance would disentangle us from the old mind-traps of the fossilized materialist-scientific paradigm. It would deflate numerous energy sapping systems that are used to keep Earth's nations embroiled in deceptive pursuits that give no substantive return on the constant infusion of global energy, treasure and will. Once we were to understand that those non-terrestrial beings are constantly visiting humanity are *from outside* our plane of existence, we might no longer heartily support a system of ongoing space exploration that is looking for something purely physical.

Extradimensionality is a closely associated to the Inter-Dimensional Hypothesis. This hypothesis proposes that the UFO phenomenon is caused by materialization of visitors from alternate realities or parallel universes that coexist apart from our own. I'm not certain who is the originator of the InterDimensional hypothesis but, in the modern era, its strongest proponent was the brilliant thinker and writer, Jacque Valée. He believed this phenomenon squarely rejects the possibility that Alien Visitors could be coming from our own physical reality or our own outer space. Others point to many instances of UFOs appearing and dematerializing as proof that the InterDimensional Hypothesis must be true. Jacque Valée related that this hypothesis also explains other phenomena that routinely seem to appear and disappear such as instances of supernatural beings, crypto-creatures, ghosts and demons. To us they seem to appear and disappear but if these phenomena have permanent existence of any sort, then they must be coming from and going to *somewhere else.*

Every bit of commonsense, experience and prior knowledge of sentient being behavior, shouts out to us that UFOs and Alien Visitors do not behave like physical phenomena from our physical reality. If they *were* from our physical reality, they would simply make open contact with our race, openly commune with our leaders and consummate trade with humanity. So why isn't any of this accomplished by our Alien Visitors?

It's because they can't.

They aren't fully physical. At least not the way we are. Neither our Visitors nor "their craft" are fully physical in our universe because they are not a part of our material universe. They probably can maintain a type of physicality for short periods and they probably were fully physical in our universe somehow eons ago (this is apparent from the superhuman megaliths all over the Earth and structures on the Moon and Mars from prehistory periods). Somehow they cannot achieve that same physicality again in our reality—yet.

Once we accept the InterDimensional Hypothesis, it leads to the truth that such Alien Visitors are themselves Extra-Dimensionals. A natural follow up query is: *who knows about this* and how does it guide their actions?

If we are let in to the "inside truth" that the nations are not in outer space seeking alien life, we might openly ask the questions that cannot be answered by the national governments. Why does NASA only show us pictures of the Moon and Mars in stark colors with poor contrast so that it's almost impossible to detect all the intelligently designed structures and the outlines of previously built facilities? Why is it so important to keep us from knowledge of the remnants of ancient civilizations on other planets in our solar system? If those ancient civilizations are extinguished and there really is no other physical Extra-Terrestrial life, w*hat exactly are they looking for out there?*

If the nations are merely seeking out artifacts and ancient devices from these former civilizations, why do they not simply share these bold exploration purposes with the rest of us? The logical conclusion that presents itself is that they have no intention of sharing such incredible discoveries with the general population, just as past discoveries have not been shared.

Such paradigm shifting questions (and logical answers) would all lead toward the same possibility—massive cracks in the monolith of the materialist/purely physical prison that holds over 95 percent of humanity. Such splintering in the globe spanning, ancient prison could even cause many to wonder if there might be even more answers to the great conundrums of humanity outside of our plane of physical existence— outside of our current time and space.

Ufology, and therefore the future of humanity, has been essentially stuck in the same holding pattern for over sixty years. Those still mired in the obsolete scientific-materialist worldview will reflexively reject such a hypothesis and it may be time to leave them behind as we enter the Age of Mass Awakening. If we can't prepare those who wish to stay in slumber, *at least we can prepare each other.*

Many in ufology say that there have been great advances in the field of UFO's. In truth, there has been a grand total of...**one:** *UFO's are real, they are paranormal and they are coming from somewhere other than physical Earth.*

Mainstream culture, after many decades of tireless labor and agitation by awakened souls; has grudgingly acknowledged that paranormal UFO's do exist, they are a real and growing phenomenon. Only in the field of ufology can acceptance of self-evident facts, proven repeatedly, ad-nauseam during many centuries; be considered a major leap forward. Yet, we have merely ascended one floor from the old level of uncertainty to a new level of uncertainty —*who is behind it and why.*

The only place we will find the answers we have sought for so long is in the minds of the non-terrestrial beings themselves. We should no longer entertain the time and energy wasters of the old paradigm—do they exist, are they real, *what solid proof can we show all the debunkers, critics, scientists and "objective" skeptics?*

That is a game that the Awakened can never win. This game was created to maintain genuine spiritual, paranormal and supernatural topics inside the material prison EPIC set up for its prisoners. But it serves a double purpose. It holds the prisoners in but also saps the strength, energy and will of the tiny awakened minority trying to break everyone else out of that prison—trying to shake their cherished ones and fully awaken them. It is designed to draw the Awakened into the Grand Valley of False Hope—hope that they can change the old playing field, hope that will occupy them and consume them. Then, at the most opportune moment of exhaustion, that familiar avalanche of naysayers, cynics and debunkers, come crashing down on them to wear them down—*and wear them out.*

It's time for the Awakened to win at this game, by never playing at all. We are already entering the Age of Mass Awakening. It's time to dismiss the mind-traps of the last few centuries. We have spent over six decades looking for answers in the dusty archives. We keep examining airbrushed, censored and edited space photos. Even many of the Awakened continue begging national governments to disclose something—looking for the next level of answers in all the wrong places. The search for the truth behind UFO's is an elusive mystery that requires radical thinking and a new way to find these answers. As The Awakened tire of: choking on the dust of declassified government documents, taking affidavits from former government officials who are *now ready to tell what really happened* and of reviewing alien remnant samples sent back by laboratories only to read "UNDETERMINED SUBSTANCE;" they must finally resolve to move forward into a new paradigm. Let us give thanks to all those in the old paradigm who tolerated our presence for so long. Thanks for expending our energy and hope. Thanks for letting us roll the dice at your rigged table. *Thanks for nothing.*

3

HE'S AWAKE

(I grew as a child in a rundown tenement building in Manhattan, New York City, somewhere along the Hudson River. I contended with all manner of supernatural phenomena in that building. Yet, worse than the phenomena, was the fact that my family belonged to a very strict religious sect that made no allowance for anything outside their doctrine.)

When I was nine years old, an incident occurred which, in retrospect; I now know were Extra-Dimensional contacts. One night I had been practicing "nocturnal clock watching." This is a practice of very young boys wherein they attempt to stretch their powers to stay awake longer and longer each night as a kind of game. Young boys believe it is mysterious and wonderful to stay awake for no particular reason. We lived in a small apartment in New York City and I was in a bedroom right next to my parents' bedroom. There was little in my bedroom besides the cot I slept on and a clock with glowing tritium numerals and arrow hands. It was the clock on which I had learned to tell time. One night I had broken my personal best and gone well past 2:00am in the morning. It had been 2:45am when I last checked. My mind reeled as I approached the magical barrier of 3:00am. I was quite sure there was no little boy in New York City who had ever broken that record.

I suddenly felt a cold mist go through my body and I became rigid. I lost sensation in my body and became like a wooden plank. Yet, I sensed activity all about me. Several beings were skittering about the apartment in our bedrooms and although I could not see or hear them, *I could sense them.*

The entities continued to scurry about in my parents' bedroom and in my bedroom but I could not turn my head to look at them. I could only see straight up to the white plaster ceiling ten feet above my bed. I felt what seemed like cool gloved hands on my feet and head. I couldn't even see the cold appendages that were lifting my suddenly ephemeral body. Somehow my rigid body had become as light as a balloon half-filled with helium. I was light as air and yet my body had a measure of stability. They slowly moved with my body upward, toward the ceiling. Although I was terribly drowsy, I could barely open my eyes to see the ceiling coming closer and closer.

Then, I felt a thud. As the entities were attempting to bring me through the ceiling *with them*, the surface of my forehead and body proved somewhat solid—unable to pass through the barrier as the entities carrying me were easily passing through. There were more thuds as they kept trying to push, pull and force my body through the ceiling that they themselves were easily passing through. They were still trying to do it gently so as not to wake me but their consternation grew. Like floating engineers faced with an unexpected problem, they seemed to stand upon nothing and scratch their heads. Their frustration and the constant bumping of the front of my body against the ceiling dissipated the preternatural drowsiness that had gripped me. I was now fully conscious and was even able to turn my head a little. They lowered my still floating body midway between the floor and ceiling and left my plank-like body at this new location as they floated upward to analyze the ceiling that was obstructing them.

With great effort I turned my head sideways and in my peripheral vision I caught sight of my parent's bed from through the top of the open door. There were two entities each holding their hands over my parent's bed. Somehow, I could see partially through the wall. My mother and father each writhed side to side as they lay in sweaty nightmares from which they could not awaken. The creatures looked like pale rubber action figures to me but I could see from their fluid movements that they were alive— *kind of.* They had large heads but tiny bodies. The most prominent feature seemed to be the large black eyes that seemed to wrap around their heads. The entities seemed to be having some trouble maintaining the stasis field especially over my father. My father was a fighter and the entity holding its hands over him seemed to waver back and forth as if getting great resistance. It seemed uncertain of its ability to keep him under. I did not hear any words but I felt their consternation.

"*What's the delay?*" said the two on the ground, without using words, to the two creatures that were testing the ceiling above me by passing back and forth through it. The two above me responded again without words again yet I could hear them clearly.

"*Something's wrong.*"

Still floating stationery several feet above my bed, I wondered to myself if I was possibly just a spirit floating above my own physical dead body. With great effort I twisted and twisted my head to the side and finally got enough angle to see beneath me. I was fully expecting to see my physical body laying in the sheets below me. Nothing was in my bed except sheets strewn about. I felt a great sense of relief.

I wasn't dead.

I still couldn't move my body but my neck was becoming more flexible. Again my face and body were brought up to the ceiling. There was another thud as my body failed to pass through the barrier. Again they lowered me a few feet. These two seemed like very limited beings with no real creative imagination for problem solving. They simply tried the same method that didn't work, *over and over again*. This time, I turned my head all the way to see the other two entities holding my parents in stasis. They were both facing me this time. I saw them and they saw me. Two pairs of those deep soulless eyes peered at me and yet were unable to look into the deepest part of me. I perceived them signaling again to the two who held me. These were the last words I would ever hear from Extra-Dimensional beings:

"He's Awake"

My body descended and slammed into the bed. I was solid. I was heavy again and no longer frozen. I got up and looked at the ceiling and all around my bedroom. The two creatures that had been carrying me were gone. I perceived telepathic silence throughout the apartment. I looked through the doorway leading into my parent's bed. The entities were gone. They were all gone. My parents, despite laying in sopping wet pools of sweat, now slumbered peacefully. The fidgeting and flailing had stopped and they seemed settled in now. I called out to them—not too loud. I was unwilling to believe they could truly be sleeping through the attack that had just occurred on our household. They did not awaken and I finally lay down on my own bed to think what I could do to wake them up without incurring my father's wrath. My mind was racing and I was bursting with excitement. I imagined all the extraordinary, sophisticated conversations I would have with the adults about this phenomena in the morning—the same adults who hadn't believed me so many times in the past when I tried to tell them about my other experiences in that building. I sat up knowing for a certainty that I would never sleep again after what I had just experienced. Then, I fell asleep.

I awoke late in the morning to the sounds of several adults shuffling around in the living room of our apartment, only a few feet away from my bedroom. It was all my aunts, uncles and my parents speaking in somber tones about some grave matter. They all had worried looks when I came ambling into their midst in my pajamas. My father spoke first. He asked me if I had any strange dreams last night. It all came back to me. I began babbling about the events of the previous night, about the creatures making me lighter than air, about them moving me around like a floating plank, about my hearing their thoughts as they communicated to each other, about them holding my parents hostage in some kind of field as they slept, about how weird the creatures looked like nothing I'd ever imagined, about how they tried to push me through the ceiling, about how they couldn't figure out the problem and how I was finally released from the spell and saw them face to face and heard them call the operation off and depart. I related that what happened to all of us wasn't any dream—*it was real*, far more real than standing around with my worried relatives trying to figure out what to do next.

My aunt, the one who knows and conveys everyone's business to everyone else, was the first to reply to my meandering monologue: "See. I told you guys—demonic attack."

As I opened my mouth to protest, my father cut me off.

"We don't know that. Don't anyone go telling that we have had a demon attack on our household when we don't know that for sure." He was on guard against the antics of the neighborhood gossip.

Every adult who lived in my apartment: my mother, father, aunt and two uncles had, during the night, experienced shared nightmares in which creatures similar to my descriptions had taken them to alien landscapes and strange places, against their will all connected to each other by some sort of rope tied to each one. They were being herded toward a great gleaming black metallic structure. The captors they described were exact in appearance *and* number (there were four of them) to the gray creatures I had seen in our bedrooms. By all accounts, all five of my adult relatives marched in a single file toward their horrible fate. As usual, only my father was somehow able to fight, pulling against the rope that held them but it was to no avail as the bonds only became tighter and their movement continued. They were prodded to get closer and closer to the structure. They all recounted a feeling of horrible dread and desperation as if they knew what awaited them in that black structure.

Then something happened.

The alien skyline suddenly grew dark. Unbearable booms shook and rattled the landscapes. It seemed like a terrible storm without rain. The great sonic booms even seemed to frighten their small inhuman captors who kept looking up for the source of the crashing thunders. The booms seemed to follow a rhythm—*three times, pause, then a fourth* and it kept that beat at a volume that threatened to shatter existence. The prisoners crouched and held their ears against the incredible noise. As the thunder grew nearer, the frightened gray captors released my relatives. They ran together toward a growing portal of light. They entered the light and ended the dream.

"That noise was me." I stated to my relatives. My aunt bent down to look into my eyes.

"What do you mean?"

"The noise, it was my head as they were trying to put me through the ceiling and they couldn't. They kept bumping me three times, pause, then a fourth time just like you said about the thunder. The bumping *was* the crashing, thunder explosions you heard. To me it felt and sounded like just a little bumps against the ceiling but where you guys were it probably was magnified into a major booming thunderstorm. That's what allowed you to escape. Those weren't demons, *they were aliens.*" My aunt stood up. She was unimpressed.

"O.K. that settles it—*demonic attack.* We all know what to do."

They ignored my explanation and anything else I said on the matter. For the next two days a top to bottom search was done on the apartment for a "guilty trinket." Among highly religious sects, demon attacks can only occur when someone brings something or someone into a residence that is an item of demonic influence. This idea harkens back to the ancient ideology of evil being unable to enter into a person's residence unless it is invited in. Tiles were pulled up. Cabinets were torn out. Sofas were ripped apart. The search was devastating but absolutely necessary—according to my gleeful aunt.

Finally, a small Celtic rune symbol dangling from a thin silver chain was found as the culprit. My family rejoiced. It was like we found the rifle that killed Kennedy (not the planted "Oswald rifle," but one of the several that really killed him) It had been under the linoleum floor in one of my Uncle's bedrooms.

No one ever admitted to bringing it into the apartment but my relatives made a big show, in front of me, of having solved the mystery, burning the demonic trinket in a paint can and then cleansing the apartment with burning herbs and numerous blessings and prayers appropriate for the occasion.

Thinking back, I'm pretty certain my father bought the trinket and planted it in order to resolve the mystery and put an end to his apartment being torn to pieces. Religious beliefs and primitive filters had been vindicated. *Case solved…everyone back to sleep*.

§

At times, abductions are sought and even instigated by the abductees. People can volunteer for activities when they don't know the full scope of what potential harm awaits them. The activity may begin as voluntary but by the time they find out what the entire process entails; it's too late to turn back. There are currently individuals even in the Awakened Community who are encouraging and facilitating what is known as "direct channeling and ET outreach." These people are "Outreachers" submitting themselves for voluntary abduction. They are sometimes taken and returned safely after the experience is over—*sometimes*.

This is a delicate area for investigation because it goes to the core values that people hold dear. Good decent people want to believe that it's always a positive thing to reach out to our space brothers with a hand of friendship, in love and peace. What could be wrong with that? *Here's the problem*: they aren't our brothers, they aren't from space (not ours anyway) and some of them don't want anything good for us.

There are astral predators out there in the Ekashic wilderness. If you go out on astral safari thinking there are only deer running out there, you may get a nasty surprise. Just ask any True Abductee (the kind that doesn't want to talk about what happened to them) or any rancher who gets his cattle supernaturally mutilated on a regular basis.

4

NEW LOOK AT FIRE IN THE SKY

(Recently we had the 40ᵗʰ year anniversary of the event of that occurred to Travis Walton—perhaps the most witnessed and authentic "alien abduction" in history. After listening to Mr. Walton in person and re-examining this event—shocking new conclusions have been revealed.)

Travis Walton was a 22 year old working as a logger in Apache-Sitgreaves National Forest in Arizona forty years ago. On the evening of November 5th, 1975, Travis and his logging crew finished their work for the day and they got into a truck for the drive home. They traveled on a road along the outskirts of the National Park. Travis and the men spotted a large golden disc hovering above a clearing and shining brightly. The disc appeared to be approximately ten feet thick and about 20 feet in diameter. Against the contrast of the clear night sky, the bright golden, light-filled disc was a stunning sight. The otherworldly craft came to rest about ten feet above the tree lines. It hung dead in the air, motionless and soundless with nothing holding it up.

The driver stopped the truck and Travis leapt out and ran toward the disc. The 22 year old said he was afraid it would disappear and so wanted to get the closest possible look. Travis came to a spot directly below the bright yellow object when the disc came to life. It began making a loud sound similar to a jet plane preparing for takeoff. Then, a beam of blue-green light emanated from the disc and struck Travis in the chest and head. The energy bolt seemed to engulf him and Travis rose a foot into the air with his arms and legs outstretched. He was then projected back through the air about 10 feet and landed on the ground. His body lay limp. To all witnesses it appeared he was certainly dead. The witnesses, being in great fear, departed the scene only to return a short time later and note that the body was missing and was nowhere to be found along with the great golden disc.

*(**Author's Note:** I forego discussion of the human interactions which make up ninety percent of the "Travis Walton Abduction" story: Travis' friends and family response to the*

abduction, the town's negative behavior towards the crew and all the emotional chaos surrounding Travis. All this is distraction from the ED-human interaction at the core of this story.)

As soon as Travis' body disappeared, a massive police and civilian search ensued in the following days and nights throughout that forest, roads and even out to the surrounding areas. All known police methods *and tracking* techniques were utilized to find Travis, all to no avail. Friends, family and even the public were enlisted in a meticulous search for Travis Walton—without any positive result. Five days later, Travis somehow materialized. He came wandering out of the previously searched forest; naked, starving, exhausted and dehydrated. Travis called his brother-In-law to come pick him up from a payphone at a roadside gas station.

Here is what happened to him during those five days immediately after "his body" disappeared. Travis woke up in a groggy, painful state. His body felt like it had been through major trauma and his head felt as if he'd been struck with a heavy object. He lay on a raised table of the sort you would be placed upon in a hospital. Three individuals were milling around him who he assumed to be doctors. As his senses cleared, he realized he had a metallic device on his chest that wrapped around his torso. It was about five inches thick and appeared to be made of dark metal or alloy. He had never seen anything it in this world. This otherworldly device was Travis' first clue he was not in a hospital but nothing could have prepared for what he saw next. He now stared at three smallish, nonhuman creatures that had the appearance of what we know as "Greys"—small grayish beings with slight bodies, large black almond shaped eyes and oversized heads. One of the creatures came right up to Travis' face and put his own face just inches from the frightened human. Travis lashed out at the creature. His blow drove back the creature directly into the body of a second creature. Travis said the creature felt spongy or fatty with no muscle tone at all. Although Travis was in a greatly weakened condition, the lightness and frailty of the creatures gave his efforts greater results than he normally would have had. The device that had been attached to his chest fell to the floor and the three creatures made a concerted effort to approach him with arms outstretched. Travis found a cylinder (perhaps a medical instrument) and swung it at them as he cursed at them to stay back. They hesitated but never spoke a word either to Travis or each other. They may have been incapable of speech as we know it. Yet as Travis was getting ready to spring at them, they scurried away out of the room.

A short time later, Travis also left the room. He began exploring the ship or where ever he was in a desperate search for an exit. He came upon a sort of planetarium room with a command chair in the middle of it. He sat in the chair and began pushing buttons and flipping levers; which made the room "disappear" to be replaced by stars and galaxies in deep space all around him. It was disorienting so Travis got out and went to the edge of the room when he saw what he took to be a human being motioning for him from a doorway. Although not known to Travis at that time, this was a typical "Nordic Visitor"—they are tall, very attractive, well-developed (muscular for the men and shapely for the women), often blonde humanoid creatures. Except for their inhuman perfection, they could pass for just very tall and attractive humans. In earlier decades these Visitors were known for bringing long flowing messages of peace and destruction-avoidance to human Contactees. These messages of a potential utopia on Earth if humans would follow their instructions, were always very peace-centered and filled with good wishes and gentle goodness. Yet, despite all this history and Travis' repeated, vociferous communications with this being, there was no verbal or speech response at all. The creature did wear a transparent bubble helmet but that would not have obstructed any attempt to be heard by the human.

So Travis followed the Nordic. As they moved together throughout what may have been a ship, Travis continued to try to elicit any communication from the creature, to no avail. After a long and winding trip, the humanoid brought Travis to a room where two more Nordics sat a table waiting—one male and one female both with the same attractive Nordic appearance as the first humanoid. Like the first Nordic in the helmet, the man was tall and muscular with perfectly symmetrical features and the "female" had very generous "womanly" proportions. These two even wore the same tight, velvety, blue uniform as the first Nordic but these two had no helmets. This lack of uniformity was one small clue that connected these three Nordics to the previous three Greys, but it would not be the last. These last two Nordics, the tall attractive man and woman in the velvety blue skin tight uniforms also appeared not to be able to speak or verbalize anything despite Travis' repeated exhortations. This is very rare for Nordics who always appear with preachy poetic flowing speeches for humans (in perfect English or by telepathic language) about the peaceful future of man with the assistance of Alien Fathers. For decades, the Nordics have appeared to many Contactees around the planet Earth with the same Modus Operandi—again, except for this single unique incident. Travis only got silence, both telepathic and verbal from all three as they gently but firmly wrestled him down onto a table quite similar to the one the three greys tried to get him settled onto. But these three were much larger and stronger than even an ordinary human being. They had little problem holding down the wiry Travis onto the table and forcefully putting an otherworldly device over his mouth to take away his consciousness. Then, he was transported back to the previously searched forest for his reappearance among humanity.

Investigative Conclusion #1—There have been two new Earth-shaking epiphanies concerning this famous episode of "Alien Abduction." *The first is that this was NOT an abduction at all.*

Modus Operandi is a way in which law enforcement identifies reliable actors who commit the same deeds again and again—they are identified by the reliable repetition of their methods and behavior in committing the same deeds over and over. Whenever there is an extreme deviation in the normal operating procedures of a group of actors, it means a mistake was made or something entirely different is going on. Previous to and since the Travis Walton Incident 40 years ago—there has never been another Alien Abduction case that occurred in the same way as it happened to Travis Walton. During thousands of reported Alien Abduction cases around the world and during the entire known history of the world—this precise pattern of the Travis Walton incident has never been duplicated. Under the most basic rules of investigation, this can only mean one of two conclusions can be true:

1. Either Travis Walton is lying and made the whole thing up (not possible due to the weight of testimony and reliable authentic evidence in this case).
2. Or *this was never an "alien abduction."*

Several other strong clues may be added to lead to this same investigative conclusion. Travis foolishly rushed into an area directly beneath the craft just at the moment it was building up its energy field in order to depart.

"I was afraid it would fly away and I would miss my chance…"

"I entered a dim halo of light reflecting to the ground."

"I was bathed in a yellow aura."

Travis was standing upright inside a plasmic energy field build up just like a person standing outside in a plain grassy field during an intense lightning storm directly over the individual. As the person refuses to take shelter, an electric field builds up around that foolish person as the worst gets ready to happen.

"I was startled by a thunderous swell in the volume of the vibrations from the craft."

"I jumped at the sound, like turbine generators starting up."

As a lightning bolt takes shape to strike, the individual who refused to seek shelter will feel a strong tingling sensation, their hair will stand on edge and their muscles will contract. Travis experienced all these and then he was struck by what he described as a bolt that felt like high voltage electrocution. His experience was nearly identical to that of many individuals when they are struck by lightning. Some of these individuals survive being struck by lightning but many die from it—as I now believe Travis died. Travis Walton was the victim of an accidental discharge of plasmic energy because he strode into the middle of this field as the golden disc was increasing its energy for departure. Such high energy plasmic fields tend to have instability even under the best circumstances—especially as they built to enormous levels of explosive energy. The natural instability of such a field would be greatly agitated by a tall human lightning rod bursting into the middle of the field at the worst moment of energy crescendo. The blue green spotlight may not have been the actual discharge. We have seen this spotlight many times in other incidents and it has never caused ill effects. The blue green spotlight may have been an automatic scanner function whenever a living organism gets too close to the vehicle. The spotlight was probably coincidental with the plasmic discharge that struck Travis Walton. After the real plasmic strike, Travis was either dead or dying.

"They killed him."

"he looked dead when he hit the ground."

"my body lay limply spread on the ground."

So if it was an accidental discharge of plasmic energy, *why wouldn't the vehicle just take off anyway?* Anyone who has studied the Grey Visitors like the three that Travis first encountered knows that they are very limited and programmed creatures. So it is likely that harming or killing a human on the ground was outside their programming. When they became aware of what had accidentally occurred to Travis, they picked his body up only in an attempt to revive him and bring him back to life. Greys have no particular concern or empathy for human life but they cannot act or by omission cause events that are clearly outside their mission parameters. If they are responsible for a substantial matter that occurs outside those parameters, they probably must act to return the situation to a status quo. This was not an abduction—*this was a rescue operation.*

Recently, Travis Walton was quoted on these new conclusions regarding the incident:

"I now think they may have saved my life."

When he first woke up, the device he had on his chest was quite non-intrusive. It just wrapped around his chest and torso. Travis was able to push it off himself easily. It is very likely that this device was being used, after they revived him, for nothing more than to monitor the stability of his vital functions. Also, Travis did not experience many of the horribly invasive procedures that many abductees report. This was probably because such procedures might cause a relapse in his condition. Finally, the three Greys that Travis encountered seemed to be quite unprepared, scattered, unsure of themselves when they encountered resistance from their human guest. They were completely unprepared to do a standard Alien Abduction. In abduction scenarios, the Greys are always prepared and in control of the situation to the point in which no resistance by the subject is possible. That is because this "abduction" was initiated unexpectedly, by Travis Walton's actions, not by the plans of Visitors.

Investigative Conclusion #2: *The first three Greys encountered by Travis Walton are the exact same entities he encountered with the second group of three Nordic beings.* The Greys simply left and changed form into the guise of Nordics much more suited to handle this unexpected resistance. The commonalities are several. The first group were exact in number to the second group—three. The first group of Greys was highly disorganized and unprepared as evidenced by their lack of control over the subject followed by their retreat when Travis offered resistance. The later three Nordics were also disorganized and unprepared. One of them wore a helmet while the other two did not—despite the fact that they shared the exact same space so why would the third one need a helmet on his head? He did not. This showed a failure to coordinate between the three Nordics before they presented themselves to Travis. Finally, the three Grey's were unprepared to communicate with a human at all…not even telepathically. They could not even attempt any communication to calm Travis down. Similarly, these three Nordics failed to live up to the standards of every Nordic Contactee experience. Like the previous three Greys, they could not speak or communicate in any way with the human Travis Walton. Yet, the strongest clue was that both groups had the exact same overarching mission pursued in the exact same way—to force the human subject down on that table in order to continue his course of treatment and final resolution. The three Greys, because they changed into the Nordic identity very hastily, failed to load the standard communication program that is such a well known part of the Nordic "identity."

The similarities between the two groups are dispositive of the conclusion that this was a simple change of costume by ED entities from Greys to Nordics. Most humans would never suspect the truth of this investigative conclusion simply because there could be no two alien races more unlike each other than Greys and Nordics.

In chapter 37, Theory of Alien Races, I further develop the idea that "Alien Races" are nothing more than a convenience (pretend appearance) for ED entities to present themselves to humanity in accordance to the needs of each particular case. Solid form of a race may be nothing more than a human interpretation of non-solid realities. For Alien Visitors, changing forms may be as easy as changing an overcoat is for humans.

5

SIGNATURES AND SHIFTS

Investigative Connection and Empathy can determine what is happening in the mind of the Non-Terrestrial Beings who are involved in the affairs of our planet. The knowledge gained through Investigative skills must then be joined to clues and understandings derived from behavior patterns. One of the ways in which these patterns become obvious are through examinations of Modus Operandi (M.O.) and more importantly, over long periods of continuous activity—shifts in Modus Operandi. Those shifts cause many cracks in the solidity of the M.O. so that new truth is exposed. As in the Travis Walton case, that shift becomes the game-changer.

MODUS OPERANDI: a method of procedure; a distinct pattern or method of operation that indicates the work of a single individual *or a single group* in multiple continuing misdeeds.

Non-Terrestrial Aliens represent a concerted, hidden enterprise that has continued with the same basic characteristics for thousands of years. Investigators must approach elusive mysteries with the same tools they use for criminal enterprises. They look for qualities in the commission of ongoing deeds, which fit a pattern that points to a single actor or group of actors.

The M.O. is a usually a series of actions that fit together in a consistent pattern from these same actor or actors, sometimes over an extended period of time. The components of the M.O. are two: the "pattern actions" that wrap around the center and at the center is "the signature." While the M.O. pattern actions can change based upon the killer's experience or opportunity, "the signature" is the perpetrator's calling card. The signature tends to remain constant even if the M.O. pattern actions change.

A serial-killer may always kills young blonde women because they are the ones that remind him of his hated mother but if the killer arrives at a period when only brunettes present themselves; he may break down and designate a brunette as one of his victims. However his central "signature," leaving the victim tied up in a splayed, vulnerable position for the police to find, will remain the same because that final action is at the center of his symbolic triumph over his hated mother. It remains his signature.

Jack the Ripper terrorized London, England. His victims were prostitutes who resided in the Whitechapel area of the city of London. The qualities and characteristics of his victims were part of his patterns but his signature was strangulation and then removal of internal organs with tremendous surgical accuracy and skill.

The alteration in the M.O. is the strong clue that something has shifted in the personal life of the actor and the circumstances surrounding his deeds—his needs, his desires, his personal evolution or his overall agenda. When authorities are confronted with actors who commit their deeds successfully over long periods of time, often the awaited M.O. shift is the only signal that great changes are taking place that can make it much more likely that the actor can be caught and stopped. Due to the superior intelligence and strategic thinking of serial killers (superior to the average criminal and even law-enforcement) the M.O. shift often presents the first and sometimes only chance for law-enforcement authorities to stop the serial killer.

This alteration tends to be the Game Changer. Amelia Dyer for over twenty years terrorized the city of London killing innocent babies and gaining the moniker of Baby Butcher in the process. Dyer became one of the most famous serial killers in history. Her modus operandi was simple. She would advertise in the paper and offer adoption services to unmarried women charging them a certain amount in return. Once she adopted these babies she would completely neglect them, which caused their deaths. After many years, her M.O. shifted, as the thrill of letting the babies die from neglect was no longer enough to quench her personal hunger for horror. She started strangling the children eventually also used opium injections to kill them. Caught in 1896, and sentenced to death; it's estimated that she had killed 247 babies. As usual in such matters, the real number and the real horror could be much greater.

There is nothing more frustrating to investigators and police forces world-wide than serial killers and long-term criminal actors who are greatly successful in carrying out their deeds over a span of many years—sometimes decades, without even leaving any significant clues for the authorities. When a police force cannot prevent its own population from being murdered sporadically by criminals whose M.O. is *already known*; this creates tremendous political pressure on them for the capture.

Enterprise M.O.'s can apply to large, diverse groups who have general traits in common but only share a narrow signature trait. La Cosa Nostra (LCN), a long-running criminal enterprise gang made up of many families and groups; tended to have a general M.O. of involvement in every aspect of racketeering—control and regulation of prostitution, drug-running, illegal gambling and extortion. LCN killers, for many years, tended to use a .22 caliber bullet shot into the victims head from a "sweet spot" just behind the left or right ear. The relatively small bullet tended to enter the skull and ricochet several times inside the skull tearing up the brain to ensure a quick and efficient death. This was a proven, reliable method to kill a person with a minimum of mess and a maximum of certainty.

There is a signature for radical jihadist terrorists a globally diverse group whose general M.O. tends to be the killing of civilians in soft non-military targets for maximum terror with explosives or firearms. The more specific *central signature* of their M.O. is the use of the Shahada declaration (the religious proclamation that "There Is No god But Allah and Mohammed Is His Prophet") and the utilization of the Q'uran as justification for acts of terrorism. A wild diversity of groups throughout the globe carrying forth numerous grim deeds of violence has almost nothing in common except for the utilization of the Q'uran and the Shahada.

In the Travis Walton incident, the crucial shift revealed what we thought was an "alien abduction" was actually a rescue operation. So it will be in the future also. The next Great Shift in the Modus Operandi of ED entities is here now. It is nothing more than a massive explosion in their activity upon the Earth. This massive increase is becoming more and more visible every day and it signals a change. They are no longer gathering data and collecting soul prints. They are, instead, now forming a ubiquitous, constant and inescapable presence everywhere in human society as they prepare for the Next Shift yet to come.

6

SHINING SHIELDS IN THE SKY

Patterns of Extra-Dimensional with human contacts were many years, decades and even eons in becoming established. Before recorded history even began, peoples were making records of unidentified, supernatural and non-terrestrial powers in the sky. Some of these records are apparent to us today, in prehistoric etchings, in ancient tales, in sacred texts and even in carvings on Megalithic structures throughout the Earth.

- Cave paintings and etchings all around the world, estimated at about 20,000 years old; depict what appear to be flying saucers in the sky and creatures in spacesuits that resemble what we know today as "Greys."

- Sumerians left records on stone texts, from about 3,500 BC, describing "Annunaki" who came to earth and these beings traveled about in "flying palaces" depicted as flying circular discs with wings.

- In 1480 BC, Egyptian Pharaoh Tutmos III recorded his impressions of circles of fire in the sky which were *sometimes numerous and shone with the brightness of the sun.*

- Written about 590 BC in the Bible, the book of Ezequiel describes "wheels within wheels in the sky...when the creatures rose from the ground, the wheels rose along with them, *because the spirit of the living creatures was in the wheels.*"

- About 400 BC, Vedic text from India: "Mahabharata" describes Vimanas as double-decker, circular aircraft with portholes and a dome. *"They fly with the speed of wind."*

- Also about from about 4th century BC, Vedic etchings also show some of their religious figures, princes and kings zipping around the sky in bullet-shaped, capsule-like vehicles (Vimanas) presumably provided to them by the Alien Visitors.

- In 329 BC, Alexander described great shining silvery flying shields spitting fire around the rims and diving toward his troops at the Jaxartes River. Alexander postponed the crossing of the river as a result.

- During the Siege of Tyre by Alexander in 332 BC, the great flying shields aided Alexander by shooting lightning flashes to destroy the protective walls of Tyre so that Alexander's troops could enter and destroy the city. For some reason, these great shining shields at first appeared to be working against Alexander's troops but then suddenly changed course and decided to assist Alexander's victories over a major city opposing him. As we know, shortly after that assistance was rendered, Alexander conquered the entire known world and changed the course of human history for all the ages to come.

Several factors confirm these records of paranormal realities are true and accurate. During pre-history, the media used for recording these events were the most expensive and labor intensive forms of scholarly recordation available. These were done by the most skilled artisans of the era and carefully preserved for future generations of man. Among these are stone etchings on tablets, stone carvings on and around Megalithic super-structures and even wood-mixture carvings that were preserved in ways modern society can't even duplicate today. Human nature, even across eons, dictates that these processes were reserved for only the most *serious known realities* of the time— not to record fanciful myths or superstition. *These observations demonstrate real events portrayed as they literally happened.* The shift during the 3rd and 4th centuries BC (direct interference in the affairs of men) represented a natural progression towards greater levels of interference in human affairs later.

7

HUMAN HARVESTINGS

(Unlike the unique Travis Walton incident, the Betty and Barney Hill abduction became the establishment of the standard "alien abduction" Modus Operandi.)

In the evening of September 15th, 196l, Betty and Barney Hill were returning from a Niagara Falls vacation along a major highway in New Hampshire. Betty observed a bright point of light which she thought was a falling star until it began to move upward and grew bigger and brighter. They stopped the car for a closer look at a scenic picnic area just off the road. Betty Hill using binoculars, observed an "odd-shaped" craft, flashing multi-colored lights travel across the face of the moon. Barney saw the same but believed it was a commercial airliner. Then, the craft rapidly descended in the couple's direction, causing Barney to understand that it was not a plane. They quickly returned to the car and drove toward a narrow mountainous stretch of road. As the craft came closer they observed that it was at a disc shaped affair measuring at least sixty feet across and it seemed to be illuminated with lights that were somehow rotating. The craft seemed to be pursuing them.

"It seemed to be playing cat and mouse with us."

Suddenly, the object rapidly descended toward their vehicle causing Barney to stop directly in the middle of the highway. The huge disc craft silently hovered about 100 feet above the Chevrolet car. Carrying a pistol in his pocket, Barney stepped away from the vehicle and moved closer to the object. Using the binoculars, Barney saw about 8 to 11 figures peering out of the craft's windows. He believed they were looking at him. Barney had a recollection of humanoid forms wearing glossy black uniforms and black caps. Barney "felt" a message from one of those beings on the craft telling him to *"stay where you are and keep looking."* Barney said these were the only words he received but something more may have come through because he went running back to the car and shouted at Betty.

"They are going to capture us!"

He saw the object again shift its location to directly above the vehicle. He drove away at high speed, telling Betty to look out for the object. Although Betty saw nothing, the Hills heard a rhythmic series of beeping or buzzing sounds. The car vibrated and a tingling sensation passed through the Hills' bodies. The Hills said that at this point in time they experienced an altered state of consciousness that left their minds dulled. A second series of beeping, buzzing sounds later returned the couple to full consciousness. They had traveled 35 miles south but had only vague, spotty memories of this section of road. They recalled only vague travel, unplanned turns and a fiery orb in the road. They arrived home around dawn and numerous indicators pointed to "lost time" for them both.

- Their watches had been stopped and neither watch would ever work again.

- The strap on Barney's binoculars was broken although he did not remember that happening to him.

- His shoes were terribly scuffed without reason that he could recall.

- They were both compulsively showering and scrubbing down to remove "possible contamination."

- The dress Betty had worn had a weird pinkish powder all over it and the dress was torn, soiled and ruined.

- There were shiny, concentric circles on their car's trunk that had not been there the previous day.

The Hills uncovered previously "screened" memories of lost time and what happened to them from the time Barney and Betty tried to escape from the hovering disc during that fateful drive. Hypnosis sessions produced more reliable and consistent information than the vivid dreams they experienced. The dreams may have been partially "screen memories."

Under hypnosis Barney reported that the binocular strap had broken when he ran from the UFO back to his car. Even as he drove away the car stalled and three men approached the car. The leader told Barney to close his eyes. Barney recalled terrible, all black, wrap around eyes that "pushed into his eyes."

He and Betty were taken onto the disc-shaped craft, where they were separated and he was made to lie on a small rectangular exam table. A sperm sample was taken, spinal exam was made and his skin was scraped. They peered in his ears and mouth. A thin tube or cylinder was inserted into his anus and removed. Betty reported a conversation with the "leader" in English but Barney said it seemed to be telepathic since their lips did not move as they communicated. Finally, Barney recalled being escorted from the ship and taken to his car. In a daze, he watched the ship leave.

Betty's recall of her examinations caused her considerable agony so she was unable to go into much detail of those. However, after her examinations, Betty was then given something no other abductee has ever received—*the home address of her captors.*

Betty was shown a holographic star-chart that she later recreated, to the point of highly accurate astronomical detail. This recreation was a perfect match to the Zeta Reticule star system—from a point of view of someone *hundreds of light years away from Earth.* Numerous books, movies and television programs have been made of the Hills' experience. Except for elements of the news media and the usual assigned cynics, the Hill's veracity was never questioned and they maintained their version of events (without deviation) right through the day they died. Most of Betty Hill's notes, tapes, and other items have been placed in the permanent collection at the University of New Hampshire. In July 2011, the state of New Hampshire, at the Division of Historical Resources, marked the site of the craft's first approach with a historical marker.

Similar instances have exploded since the Hills experience but the patterns of alien abductions were established by this single authentic incident.

- The beginnings of descriptions of typical Greys (developed further in later abductions and contacts)
- The use of Extra-Dimensional craft to pursue and acquire human subjects
- The execution of an organized preplanned strategy for human abduction
- The complete command and control over humans throughout the episode
- An intention to induce terror and fright in the subjects (perhaps to be absorbed as energy or simply to make handling of the subjects easier)
- The stoppage of clocks, watches and timepieces (almost as if time itself were paused in the target vehicle or residence)
- Use of medical facilities and medical exams using technology that is beyond human
- A complete lack of empathy or care for the subjects' pain or discomfort
- Telepathic communication with the subjects in a limited fashion
- *The collection of various samples: human tissue, blood, sperm, ova and many varieties of human material*

Regardless, this single incident established the standard model for "Alien Abductions" which would be followed quite closely in thousands of other such incidents up to present day. The enterprise Modus Operandi of Extra-Dimensionals has remained fairly consistent for many decades since Betty and Barney's experience. There is only one problem this Modus Operandi.

It's a fraud.

It may be more accurate to call it "a cover." There are ten items in the above M.O. but it is my final Investigative Conclusion that the first nine items are distraction and diversion from the true overarching purpose and mission of this process—the final item: **the collection of various samples: human tissue, blood, sperm, ova and many varieties of human material.**

This collection is the true single purpose of these engineered events. If they chose to do so, the Extra-Dimensionals could easily go directly to the final item that is the true goal—the collection of human samples and do without the rest. The Extra-Dimensionals could easily dispense with the ships, the dramatic approach, the theatrical capture, control elements for abduction, the terror induction of the subjects and all the many variables that must be accounted for in this full scenario. They could instead, materialize unconscious subjects to the place of their choosing, collect the all-important samples and discard or return the humans to their origination point. But this "Abduction Theater" is important because the Extra-Dimensionals are building a narrative that will serve their purposes later. The narrative requires the theater they have built around the true purpose of "Alien Abductions." These incidents are not really "Alien Abductions" because that is not their true purpose.

They are Human Harvestings.

8

BRAZILIAN HYBRIDS

(Brazil has one of the highest averages of Extra-Dimensional contact. This particular story is an even more blatant example of Human Harvesting)

There was a young man named Boas. He was 23-year-old Antonio Villas Boas, born October 16, 1957, in Brazil. Antonio was plowing a field on the family farm when the engine of his tractor cut out; at the same time, an object with purple lights descended from the sky. Such a sight would have sent most field workers running for shelter. However, Antonio was no ordinary Brazilian field worker. He was acutely above average intelligence and, by accounts of everyone who ever knew him—a young man of great personal integrity.

As Antonio stood his ground in that field, an otherworldly craft appeared in front of him and what seemed like doors were opened. Humanoids in spacesuits emerged from the object and took him into their craft, subjecting him to what seemed like a medical examination. There were no formal greetings or attempted salutations. They just herded him quickly to an inside area of their spacecraft. They stripped him of all his clothing, spread a strange liquid over him and took a sample of his blood.

He was left alone in a room for what seemed a long time, until a beautiful, fair-haired woman arrived. She was naked and Antonio was instantly attracted to her. She seemed like a normal (very naked) human female in every respect except she apparently could not speak. Without speaking or kissing, they had sex, during which she growled like a dog. During the sexual act she also gave him a playful little bite on his chin. Perhaps because the alien liquid had aphrodisiac-like properties, Antonio was soon ready for a second sexual session. Later, he said: "Before leaving she turned to me, pointed to her belly, and smilingly pointed to the sky." It appeared that she was part of a plan to be bred by this young man specifically to produce offspring.

Before letting him go, his captors gave Antonio a guided tour of the spaceship. The young man later told the complete story of what had happened to him to anyone who would listen. Antonio went on to become a very successful lawyer and still stood by his story, despite incredible opposition and pressure to recant his story from innumerable naysayers and debunkers for many decades after the event.

Antonio never had a shred of direct physical evidence of his encounter yet despite dogged attempts over three decades to debunk or back him off his story by the usual assailants of belief; he *never* wavered or changed any detail of his story. Human behavior after a traumatizing event tends to be the best determinant of the authencity of a witness' assertions better than any accumulation of evidentiary material. His story, even today, is widely believed in the Awakened Community partly because it coincides with many details other Contactees have given since that time. Yet this belief in his claims is mostly due to his personal integrity and his refusal to recant or alter his story even in the slightest to appease those around him right through the day he died.

§

The connection between evidence and witnesses is formed by truthfulness or intent to deceive. The intent to deceive can manifest through manufactured false evidence: for example, a drop gun planted on the victim's body to make it look as if the victim was a criminal trying to commit a crime. This intent to deceive is still an authentic connection to the consciousness of the deceiver and it can be discovered by entry to the gulf of Superconsciousness. Whether evidence is direct or circumstantial is irrelevant. What matters is that the person connected to the evidence gives authenticity to that evidence. Who can, beyond any shadow of doubt, corroborate the crucial authenticity of witnesses and victims?

Awakened Investigators can.

The Awakened Investigative Rule of Evidence: *the true value of evidence is in the depth of its connection to human consciousness. The connection between evidence and human consciousness is formed by truth, faith and authenticity. It is only by making this determination that we can decide the true value of evidence.*

The Awakened Rule of Evidence is not spoken of in criminal procedure classes because it cannot be proven or measured by laboratory or scientific means—*authencity of the victims/witnesses/suspects*. An Awakened Investigator or any seasoned investigator has the ability to identify truth-tellers simply by paying attention to the words, cadence and rhythm of the voice, inflections in speech patterns, choice of terminology, emphasis on syllables and body language.

If you wish to see the differences, go to the biggest Internet video database and watch any politician's (full body-shot) speech. You will see all the hallmarks of a carefully *rehearsed* speech—like when criminals prepare their stories for the police. Try to find such a politician who dares to take a question and answer session. You'll see the politician stumble around proceed to answer another question that *was not asked*. He's answering the question he rehearsed for. That is another hallmark of rehearsed (dishonest/deceptive) speech—not actually answering the question asked and instead answering a different question that was never posed.

Even the world of popular culture is rife with deception at times. I'm a film buff. I sometimes watch publicity surrounding upcoming movies that are highly anticipated so I've seen a great deal of puffery disguised as "promotion." Search for a movie that you know people had high hopes for but later turned out was a high-budget disaster. Then, find some historical interviews with the principal actors from the period when they were still doing their level best to convince potential audiences that the movie was great. To the chagrin of the principal actors, these interviews are frozen in infamy forever on public video databases. Here you can study public deception—what it looks like and how it sounds.

The principal actors (the big name stars) already know the movie is a catastrophe but they must soldier on as if it is the most brilliant cinema since "Gone With The Wind." You'll hear ambiguous phrases like: …*when I read the script, I knew this movie would be different from anything I'd ever worked on before* (…not great or even better just different).

People who come see this movie will not be sorry they came (why would anyone praising a movie bring up such negative ideas such as regret, especially to even utter a phrase like "sorry they came?")

The Director was very demanding but in the end the extra effort shows on the screen (why they bring up problems with the Director during a publicity junket, where only wildly positive statements should be allowed?).

Study their body language and the cadence of their words when they attempt to be absolute in their support of the movie. They will shift backward and forward in the chair, hands will be folded across the front of their body and although their mouths will smile, their eyes will "frown." After seeing a few of these you will know what public deception looks and sounds like. This is deception raised to the level of grandiose proclamation.

Study all these examples and then look at Betty and Barney Hill's interviews to see and hear what authenticity looks and sounds like. The contrast will be striking.

9

THE OVERTHROW

Anecdotal Evidence—Description of one, or a small number of specific instances, presumably of the same type and is considered rather weak.

Testimonial Evidence—Moderately strong but depends upon whether the source of testimony is an established or trustworthy individual.

Statistical Evidence—Moderately strong—referring to empirical analysis, or to the results of methodical or scientific experiments or investigations.

Real evidence is a thing the existence or characteristics of which are relevant and material to the proposition to be proved. It is a thing that was directly involved in the event: the bloody bloomers, the murder weapon, a crumpled automobile, the scene of an accident—all may be real evidence and yet they are all quite easy to generate by those practicing deception as an art.

True investigators did not create the "scientific evidence classifications" above because the comparisons are specious. Anyone who has spent any time working in the judicial system knows that evidence does not have assigned levels of intrinsic value in the material world. Rather it is the intention, purpose and authencity of the person connected to that particular evidence that matters. This reality is not convenient to the efficient running of a judicial system but it applies across the spectrum of criminal wrongdoing and paranormal phenomena. The lowest ranked (*scientifically that is*) evidence in the world has the highest value *if it is connected to human authencity*.

Events that enjoy ironclad connections to human authencity will withstand decades and even centuries of "debunking" or scientific cynicism under guise of objective investigation. Such claims will flourish and be believed long after the withering of accusations based on cynicism and prejudice. Not only do such claims withstand such attacks but also over long expanses of time—*they actually grow more credible.* This reality represents the overthrow of the scientific evidentiary paradigm.

EXTRA-DIMENSIONALITY RISING

"I occasionally think how quickly our differences worldwide would vanish if we were facing an alien threat from outside this world. And yet, I ask you, is not an alien force already among us?"

Ronald Reagan, United Nations General Assembly, 21 September 1987

10

THE SPACE BROTHERS

In 1951, in the California desert, an avid spiritualist named George Van Tassel was deep in meditation when his "astral form" was scooped up into a spaceship and given a tour by space brothers who later appeared to him in real physicality. He later referred to these beings as "Nordics." These Nordics were "handsome looking," tallish, human-looking creatures with longish, fine hair that blew gently in the breeze. If this sounds like the opening of a romance novel—that's no coincidence. This was the beginning of a decade long "space brotherly" love affair between humanity and the Nordics.

These entities gave prophetic messages about avoiding nuclear weapons and explained that the major figures of the Bible were actually space brothers put on Earth to try to help humanity find their proper path in this universe. According to their messages, they placed Adam, Eve and even Jesus Christ here on Earth to help humanity. Besides creating a thriving UFO/Alien cult, Tassel also constructed a massive cement, dome-shaped, structure for amplifying the power of meditation. It is called "The Integraton." It still stands even today as a monument to his commitment and authencity. Even today, the Nordic message reverberates in our popular culture as a standard message from Alien Visitors in our movies, television and even in New Age spiritualism. That message was merely a seed that has borne great fruit in the decades since through out the Earth but its final consummation is yet to come.

Even today, whenever people encounter Alien Visitors higher than Greys, such as Nordics or any of the "more articulate" races, these seem to still recite the same messages about helping humanity to avoid self-destruction, find universal peace and harmony and so on. These messages can seem like tired scripts from previous political campaigns. Also, popular culture, movies, television, mainstream Hollywood has grown the universal expectation of and comfort with this familiar message. Today, the benevolent and paternalistic message of the Nordic "alien fathers" is splashed across television fare all over the world on a continual basis. Van Tassel's love affair continues in our global culture.

Not much later, half a world away, similar developments came about. A one-armed farmer named Billy Meier became the ultimate example of the Nordic Contactee whose experiences were later converted into a modern UFO cult. Meier-related groups are still generating large amounts of interest and material even today. Although he had numerous contacts over many years from "Nordic" type aliens, his most famous alien partner is one that appears as an attractive, young, blonde female humanoid named Semjasa. Literature and even "UFO artwork" by great artists such as Jim Nichols, have beautifully illustrated the reality of Semjasa and numerous other Meier experiences.

The messages given to Meier were grimmer than the usual Nordic fare. There was talk of a world war that would devastate the planet and how the Nordics would be our planet's only hope for rescue. This was the new Nordic fist inside Van Tassel's velvet glove. This was an expansion of that first "alien fathers" peace message and it included warnings of crises, mass deaths and even apocalypse. What remained consistent with previous Nordic messages was the explicit promise that these alien fathers will be humanity's only hope for rescue.

Most in the Awakened Community believe that much of Meier's original material is absolutely authentic but several years ago, Meier fell under the dominion of outside caretakers and consequently, the newer material seemed less reliable. Yet his early material remains the gold standard of Contactee authencity and Nordic philosophy. The Nordic message of Space Brothers has evolved into a message of "Space Fathers." Through the writings of great thinkers such as Zecaria Sitchin, Erich von Däniken and Robert K.G. Temple and many more; we now have these ideas synthesized into their final form as the "Ancient Aliens" hypothesis. Proponents suggest that these "Alien Fathers" have seeded, created, shaped humanity in its present form. These Extradimensional visitors' advanced technologies were interpreted by early humans as evidence of divinity. They have shaped our human cultures, technologies, and religions. A common claim is that the beings humanity has worshipped as gods throughout history, were actually these "Space Fathers." Space brothers became Space Fathers and now are expected to be *Space Saviors*.

II

THE SMOKING GUN

(Even before the 1950s, there were already some forward thinking individuals embracing the InterDimensional Alien hypothesis. They were in the last place anyone would ever think—the U.S. government)

The United States government now makes available to the public a repository of open public documents on UFOs, extraterrestrials and unsolved mysteries. This repository is called "The Vault" and it is a festival of ancient documents that require some determination to decipher and search. But the effort can be well worth it. An FBI Special Agent with several advanced degrees actually wrote "The Smoking Gun" but it is officially titled: A MEMORANDUM OF IMPORTANCE, dated July 8th 1947.

Its target was the scientific community who after the Roswell, New Mexico, UFO incident, were desperate for any official pronouncements from reliable sources. Based on several "UFO" incidents and one confidential source, there are seven extraordinary investigative conclusions reached in The Smoking Gun document.

1. If our planes should attack these "flying saucers" they will certainly be destroyed and this must be avoided as it would cause public panic. (This may have happened many times but it would not be publicized)
2. Some UFOs carry crews but others are under remote control (PLASMAS)
3. Their mission is peaceful and the visitors contemplate settling "on our plane." (In our physical universe)
4. The Visitors are human-like but much larger.
5. The Visitors do not come from another planet as we understand but from *an etheric place that interpenetrates with our own and is not perceptible to us!* (Extra-Dimensional)
6. The bodies and craft of the Visitors materialize upon entering the vibratory rate of our dense matter. They can also dematerialize at will by entering the etheric plane and disappear from our view without a trace. (Extra-Dimensional)
7. The place they come from and go back to is not the commonly known Astral Plane. Everyone should have access to the commonly known Astral Plane if

they can temporarily adjust their consciousness to reach the Astral plane. It is the Lokas. Ancient Vedic philosophy recognizes the Lokas as numerous levels of parallel universes that exist on distinct levels at different vibrations so that these never intersect with each other under any circumstances. These are not different planets—they are different planes of existence that cannot interact. Yet they all exist at the same time. Some of these universes are at higher vibrations and others are at lower vibrations. We can normally only move between these Lokas by developing or by lowering our consciousness as we graduate or are promoted upon death. But apparently there are those who have found quicker ways to move between Lokas.

Here is the actual Smoking Gun document.

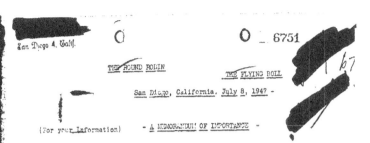

San Diego 4, Calif.

THE ROUND ROBIN   THE FLYING ROLL

San Diego, California. July 8, 1947 -

(For your Information)   - A MEMORANDUM OF IMPORTANCE -

THIS MEMORANDUM is respectfully addressed to certain scientists of distinction to important aeronautical and military authorities, to a number of public officials and to a few publications.

The writer has little expectation that anything of import will be accomplished by this gesture. The mere fact that the data herein were obtained by so-called supernormal means is probably sufficient to insure its disregard by nearly all the persons addressed; nevertheless it seems a public duty to make it available. (The present writer has several university degrees and was formerly a university department head).

A very serious situation may develop at any time with regard to the "flying saucers." If one of those should be attacked, the attacking plane will almost certainly be destroyed. In the public mind this might create near panic and international suspicion. The principal data concerning these craft is now at hand and must be offered, no matter how fantastic and unintelligible it may seem to minds not previously instructed in thinking of this type.

1. Part of the disks carry crews, others are under remote control.
2. Their mission is peaceful. The visitors contemplate settling on this plane.
3. These visitors are human-like but much larger in size.

4. They are NOT excarnate earth people, but come from their own world.
5. They do NOT come from any "planet" as we use the word, but from an etheric planet which interpenetrates with our own and is not perceptible to us.
6. The bodies of the visitors, and the craft also, automatically "materialize" on entering the vibratory rate of our dense matter. (Cp. "apports.")

7. The disks possess a type of radiant energy, or a ray, which will easily disintegrate any attacking ship. They reenter the etheric at will, and so simply disappear from our vision, without trace.
8. The region from which they come is NOT the "astral plane", but corresponds to the Lokas or Talas. Students of esoteric matters will understand these terms.
9. They probably cannot be reached by radio, but probably can be by radar, if a signal system can be devised for that apparatus.

We give information and warning, and can do no more. Let the newcomers be treated with every kindness. Unless the disks are withdrawn, a situation terrible beyond words with which our culture and science are incapable of dealing. A heavy responsibility rests upon the few in authority who are able to understand this matter.

Addendum: The lokas are oval shape, fluted length... oval with a heat-resisting metal or alloy not yet k... the front edge contains the controls; the middle portion... laboratory; the rear contains armament, which consists essentially of a powerful... energy apparatus, perhaps a ray...

How could this writer, in the year 1947, have possibly known so many unknown realities about our Alien Visitors that we have seen proven again and again in the seventy years that have followed? The writer describes the Confidential Source of his information as being "SUPERNORMAL." No further description is given. "Supernormal" is an old timey term meaning paranormal or supernatural. In this case, I believe its also means "not of this Earth" as we know it. Who or what could possibly have been the Confidential Informant that gave this writer the extraordinary revelations he left for us in "The Smoking Gun?" A close study of the document and its startling conclusions reveals the only possibility for who this confidential source must have been.

The Source was Extra-Dimensional.

12

THE ROSWELL DECEPTION

The Smoking Gun document represents a great and growing force in ufology for truth about the Extra-Dimensionals. It depicts the growing school of thought that said our Alien Visitors are not physical, are not from our physical reality and that they come from and return to an untouchable, unknowable, other dimensional plane. Global rulers have always suppressed, attacked and countered by whatever means necessary this Extra-Dimensional truth. They cannot afford for the common man to possess this understanding because it would lead them to truths in many more areas where deception is required for institutional power to continue its dominance over our planet.

Accordingly, in the same year, month and even the same week on about July 7th, 1947, in Roswell, New Mexico the anti-thesis of the Smoking Gun was perpetrated upon the populace—a psychological deception operation on a global scale. This "UFO crash and recovery of Alien physical bodies" at Roswell, New Mexico had only one major goal: to make the general populace believe that Alien Visitors are just physical beings like them, that their ships are just physical craft, like any we have, that just crash and burn on the ground.

Here is what happened.

On or about late June to early July 1947, the U.S. Air Force became aware of some sort of massive crash at a ranch near Roswell, New Mexico. There were immediate claims and eyewitness testimony from numerous reliable sources that this was the crash of one, even possibly two extraterrestrial spaceships.

The military effected a flurry of heated and secretive activity throughout the area in question but then reported that the crash was just a conventional weather balloon.

On July 8, 1947, the Roswell Army Air Field (RAAF) issued a press release stating they had recovered a "flying disc" which had crashed on a ranch near Roswell. Also that same week, the Commanding General of the Eighth Air Force Roger Ramey stated that a weather balloon was recovered by the military. A press conference was held complete with props and visual aids. There were well-lit displays featuring debris such as pieces of foil, rubber and wood. These were supposedly from the crashed object: "the weather balloon." The manipulation was complete and story lay dormant for decades.

It was later found out that in June 1947, William Brazel, a foreman working on the Foster ranch, noticed clusters of debris 30 miles north of Roswell, New Mexico. Mr. Brazel made public statements that he saw a "large area of bright wreckage made up of rubber strips, tinfoil, a rather tough paper and sticks. He gathered the material on July 4th. Brazel then involved his local sheriff, Sheriff Wilcox and the sheriff involved the RAAF, which responded and initiated the collection and transportation of these materials.

This half-hearted cover-up held for quite some time but in the 1970s and 1980s some True Investigators began a relentless pursuit of truth that unraveled the cover story. Between 1978 and the early 1990s, UFO researchers such as Stanton Friedman, William Moore and others; interviewed several hundred people who had authentic connections with the events at Roswell. In 1978, nuclear physicist and author Stanton T. Friedman interviewed Jesse Marcel, the only person known to have accompanied the Roswell debris from where it was recovered to Fort Worth where it was shown to reporters. Voluminous testimonial and documentary evidence was uncovered which had never been declassified or released before. The work these men did in their investigations was so thorough that their final three Investigative Conclusions were generally accepted as true even in mainstream society.

1. At least one alien craft had crashed in the Roswell vicinity, and advanced materials were recovered from that crash which indicated other worldly origin.
2. A government cover-up of the incident had taken place.
3. One or more alien spacecraft had crash-landed and that the bodies of several "Alien Visitors" had been recovered by the military.

CONCLUSIONS REVISITED

1. At least one alien craft had crashed in the Roswell vicinity, and advance materials were recovered from that crash which indicated other worldly origin. A government cover-up of any knowledge of the incident had taken place.

The writer of this work also agrees with this conclusion but this is only half the story. The U.S. military affected an efficient cover-up of whatever really happened at Roswell and their work was successful for many decades until the declassification period ran out and some unraveling of these carefully woven threads was bound to occur. The Roswell cover up was a "psychological operation" **designed to fail over the long run,** so that the mainstream would be greatly satisfied with the revealing of that cover up and greedily consume the Investigative Conclusions that would arise as a result of the shattering of that cover up. Once that cover up was shattered then everyone would accept that Alien Visitors are completely physical beings, that their ships are just physical vehicles that crash and burn just like ours. Therefore, these Alien Visitors and their ships are from some physical planet in or out of our galaxy just as we expect they should be.

Additionally, they "uncovered" that the bodies of several "Alien Visitors" had been recovered by the military. There was a crash provided for public consumption complete with advanced tech materials that were beyond human technology at that time. Both the tech and the bodies were Extra-Dimensional in origin but *were not themselves Extra-Dimensional or Alien Visitors.* The advanced ship materials were created and provided for the orchestrated "crash" by Alien Visitors with specific instructions that the materials and bodies were to be hidden from the public as much as possible (of course they knew very well that this was impossible and that was the main part of their plan).

The bodies, even the living one, were hybrid creatures created with partial human and Visitor DNA specifically for this "crash and recovery." The dead ones were probably just empty husks meant for cosmetic purposes only. The living creature probably didn't live or communicate for very long after recovery. Yet the DNA and remains of the bodies could have been shared among the nations and consumed for scientific experimentation but this never happened. The Alien Visitors who orchestrated this cover up knew the cover up would not stand and that revealing of the cover up was a vital part of their plan. Meanwhile, having them fall upon that false truth was the real trap all along. The Extra-Dimensional truth, the Smoking Gun document and the reality of InterDimensional Beings were all sent into the furthest possible exile after Roswell was uncovered in the 1980s. That was the ultimate plan of the Extra-Dimensional Visitors when they orchestrated the Roswell theater.

13

THE CARPET-STAIN MONITORS

Should you become one of those rare individuals who awaken and continue in that process—you will become an Awakened Investigator. You will get to the truth like a sprinter running. On the way, you will pass the great mainstream of people stultified in the tar pit of the old paradigm. Others who are also awakening will accompany you on every side. You will all be ignited by the desire to share these truths with a wider group. Then you will hit the next tier of truth-obfuscation.

That second tier of obfuscation is the fundamental nature of national governments and their bureaucracies known as the *Carpet Stain Syndrome:* the national government mentality that regards every government assignment, domain and jurisdiction as a "fiefdom protectorate." Those assigned to these protectorates are "Carpet Stain Monitors."

Carpet Stain Syndrome—*a collection of National government behaviors and responses expressed through: agencies, bureaus, military structures and various government actors aka: Carpet Stain Monitors; wherein governmental authority is used to secure the jurisdictional territory and responsibilities assigned to the monitor and reinforce the monitor's purpose: jurisdiction over his governmental carpet stain.*

The carpet stain is the governmental assignment, large or small that the governmental actor must act upon, protect, promote and when necessary, *clean up.*

These are the main duties of the monitor: protection, clean up and increase whenever needed of his carpet stain. If the carpet stain is kept at a reasonable size, the monitor gets accolades and heaps of rewards. When the stain grows too large, then the monitor has an excuse to request more funding and resources for the following year's budget. Either way, the position of Carpet Stain Monitor is a win/win proposition. The stain never disappears (the governmental need is never resolved.) If it did fade away, the monitor would have no need to exist either. That never happens.

Fittingly, a U.S. government official involved in the Global World On Terror (the GWOT) invented the Carpet Stain analogy in my presence many years ago. We were standing and conversing in a typical national security, Washington D.C. building at the time. He was complaining about all the peripheral agencies and bureaus he had to constantly placate in order to get his mission accomplished—to organize and carry forward the fight of the Western Powers against radical terrorism all over the world. After the initiation of his rant, he noticed that he and I were divided on the ground by a chocolate-colored, Rorschach splash-pattern, coffee stain on a hideous *good enough for government work*" orange carpet. The spot had long ago supported a coffee machine that had sedated throngs of jittery government drones, many of whom contributed drips and spills towards the expansive blob that remained long after the coffee machine was removed to the ash heap of history. He wagged his finger accusingly at the dark shape in the carpet.

"That's what they are! They are Carpet Stain Monitors. That's their carpet stain. Don't you get near their carpet stain. They own that carpet stain. Their whole existence is based on maintaining that carpet stain!"

He laughed an angry sort of laugh and related the list of minor agencies he is forced to deal with and treat with deference. They were Carpet Stain Monitors trying to justify their existence by filling some tiny/irrelevant niche and then connecting that niche to a true global security mission like Counterterrorism. During his rant he made it clear that all agencies except his own fit into that defined category of irrelevancy. He actually had *a vital global mission.*

What the national bureaucrat who coined the pejorative phrase "Carpet Stain Monitor" didn't understand was this: to the Executive Branch Overlords sitting around the President's office at that moment—his Global War On Terrorism (GWOT) mission was *nothing more than another carpet stain.* From their highest national perch perspective, they saw the GWOT mission as relatively minor when measured against their supreme mission: getting the President re-elected.

It's relative to who is above on the next level. Throughout the Western world, the executives sitting around the President's or Prime Minister's office managing the latest re-election believe their mission is beyond this syndrome but the global puppet masters *above them* perceive the President, the Prime Minister and all national leaders as an just an expendable commodity—as just more Carpet Stain Monitors—to be used for their benefit or erased in accordance to the convenience of the EPIC Globocrats who really issue their orders every day.

I know Carpet Stain Monitors. By way of partial-full disclosure I must reveal that I spent many years as a rabid Carpet Stain Monitor in the secret National Security structure of the Western nations. I took my own carpet stains very seriously. I was willing to take the life of another or give up my own life in the single-minded pursuit of protecting and improving my carpet stain. There are innumerable noble men and women of fidelity and integrity who are just as serious about their duty and rightfully so. They internalize their oaths and can be the most noble people on Earth. Unfortunately, most never have an inkling of the ultimate controlling EPIC agendas.

On any chessboard, the most sincere and earnest pieces are often the pawns (and of course also the most easily sacrificed). Carpet Stain Monitors tend to be managers, builders and advocates of government fiefdoms but it's the pawns that carry out the day-to-day operations of all the national governments. They make up about 99 percent of all national governments. They know essentially what the assignment is and what is involved but they focus on the daily chores of the institutions. They are the soldiers in the field, the government workers in the trenches, bureaucrats doing the best they can and they are law-enforcement doing the dangerous work in the field. They do their work for the sake of their brethren. They accomplish their mission to give support and aid to their brothers and sisters. They confront the dangers they face to protect and serve the ideals of nations they believe in. They tend to be the most professional and dedicated pieces on the chessboard.

Most will sail through their time in government service and never be touched by the repercussions of this corrosive system but for those who are affected; it is a terribly rude awakening to a world that was hidden from their eyes throughout most of their lives. Often such loyal advocates stumble across terrible injustice or even criminality committed by the very people they had always believed were most dedicated to public service. Victimized pawns or even monitors sometimes turn into "whistleblowers" that publicly sound an alarm concerning some area of national government deception or corruption. Usually, the whistleblower violates secrecy-agreements, security-oaths or confidentiality agreements. This is how they are awarded the sexy label: *whistleblower.* This attracts attention, headlines and even admiration because it implies a great sacrifice was made in order to bring truth to the people. What is not known is how great that sacrifice will be.

Whistleblowers and all the people in the Awakened Community who support them are doing their best to help awaken others and they use their extraordinary abilities for highest possible impact. They break security oaths and secrecy agreements in order to help to awaken the world. *That is the wrong path.*

It gives very little return on an extraordinary sacrifice made. The oath-breaker gives up the integrity of his/her word. They lower their own personal integrity in a manner similar to those they are fighting to expose. They break their promise to keep secrecy and maintain trust of a nation. Even if they no longer believe in the integrity of the national government they served; they should still police their own integrity by keeping their solemn vows.

Even worse, the breaking of their oaths causes them to bluster into an ancient EPIC trap. It is a gift to EPIC. Remember that ninety-nine percent of all the national governments are still sleeping pawns, just like the whistleblower was until they confronted some insidious event that launched them into awakening. Former colleagues and friends will see the whistleblower as intrinsically malicious. They are trained that way so they unite with Carpet Stain Monitors to squelch the heretic. The tiny piece of truth that is revealed by former Carpet Stain Monitors is usually not worth the self-destructive results. Global punitive forces are unleashed against them, largely carried out by other Monitors who feel quite justified in what they doing. This shuts down the truth-speakers potential to reveal *much larger truths* (unconnected to their former employment)—without the stigma and consequences of being oath-breakers.

If these individuals would forego the quick splash of breaking their oaths and instead enter a complete process of complete awakening; they would realize that there are much greater and more powerful ways to reveal truth to the world. Restraint and self-discipline is a much better path to follow for former pawns and monitors. This path ultimately would lead toward greater benefits for the Awakened Community around the globe. The awakened former monitors could weave great tapestries of revealed truth for a world that desperately needs their assistance in the short *and long-term* future.

14

DOCTRINE OF DIMINISHING RETURNS

Most people sleep walk through life, taking in the smallest portion of available stimuli about their surroundings. Imagine for a moment, individuals who have extraordinary powers of hypersensitivity in one or several of their five senses. In common parlance, such persons would have extraordinary powers of physical detection. A great author named Sir Arthur Conan Doyle had such abilities. He could walk into a plush carpeted room where a debate had just taken place and tell each attendee what position they defended in a discussion just by observing the depth of the impressions their shoes had left in the carpet where they stood. He later devoted a good portion of his life to the development of a fictional character with his similar abilities of extraordinary detection and deduction—Detective Sherlock Holmes. Such persons use their extraordinary abilities to deconstruct and analyze microscopic minutiae of their surroundings. They can sense and examine stimuli that most of us could never hope to capture. When you encounter Hyper-Sensitives it leaves a powerful impression because they know things *they should not know.*

Imagine one of these talented individuals goes to the beach and has the ability to look into the calm waters of the ocean and focus upon individual droplets of water within the swirling patterns and flowing waters around him. In this way, such a person could predict macro-patterns and future movements of entire bodies of water. They could predict ocean currents and weather patterns for those who travel by sea. That's what "whistleblowers" are like. They use their extraordinary access and abilities to reveal a single drop of corruption and deceit. Like Hyper-Sensitives, they focus upon that single drop, but we as humanity, are facing an ocean of such corruption on a global scale.

This ocean has formed into a Tsunami-like wall of water—several hundred meters high—racing towards us at 100 knots. The ability to focus on and evaporate single drops of water is of little moment as that gigantic wall of ocean water looms over us and blocks out the sun. The time to break down the old system, this enormous matrix of deception, one drop at a time—is gone. We must prepare for the Tsunami.

The Doctrine of Diminishing Returns states: *"The return of liberty to the people for the sacrifice made by the Whistle-Blower is, in most cases, far out of proportion to make the individual sacrifice worth the loss. Due to the institutional and global power of EPIC, the modern lack of any independent investigative media and EPIC's willingness to abuse that power, Whistle-Blowers, in most cases, should forego that exchange in favor of joining Awakening Movements that will provide greater benefits to human liberty in the long run.*

15

THE CARPET STAIN DOCTRINE

Whether the carpet stain is tiny and narrow or spans the globe right up into the vast infinity of outer-space; all Carpet Stain Monitors have the same vicious-serious attitude toward their stain—they will do *anything* to defend their sole, exclusive jurisdiction over and rights appurtenant to—that critically important carpet stain.

Try to get in their way or challenge the importance of that particular carpet stain and you'll find out how deadly serious they are. Try telling someone at NASA that they have no control over what goes on in the atmosphere above our Earth because paranormal alien vehicles come and go at will and there's nothing they can do about it except cover it up after the fact. If they can't silence you with ridicule, they will alternate into vitriol and hostility. Try pointing out to anyone working nuclear missile silos that it's well documented by trusted military and civilian testimony that paranormal alien vehicles have been appearing all over the globe, and somehow bypassing all security safety protocols, initiating launch sequences on nuclear missile facilities and also *shutting them down at will.*

If the Monitors don't have ultimate control over their carpet stain, then it's not really their stain anymore—it belongs to those who control it, *whoever they might be.*

The Carpet Stain Doctrine: *Carpet Stain Monitors all over the world, in every national government, far prefer that the public think the worst of them: that they are lazy, indifferent, flat out incompetent or even part of a global conspiracy against humanity; rather than believe that **they do not control their Carpet Stain.***

They find it acceptable for citizens to believe they are engaged in a wide-ranging conspiracy or cover-up of: extra-terrestrial/government contacts, illegal experimentations in many areas or numerous other destructive subterfuges. These negative beliefs when held by citizens at least cause national government actors to appear: sly, well organized and in control of their situation. National governments would rather be perceived as horribly indifferent to the suffering of citizens than for "doomsday truth" to be suggested—*that there's nothing they can do because higher/ greater powers are really in control.*

This admission would be seen as a potential death warrant. This admission would bring us back again to the great epiphany: *then if you have no control over any of this.... then what do we need you for?*

16

THE GENIUS HUSBAND

Truth-Seekers confronting the national governments on "Disclosure of Alien Visitor" contacts are looking in exactly the wrong place. These seekers are like the husband confronting his wife over his favorite hat.

His wife thought the husband's favorite hat was unattractive and inappropriate for any occasion. It was a mutant cross between a bowler and a wide brim storm hat with a gnarled black feather jutting out the back. The man had inherited it from a strange uncle and wore it constantly, even inside the house. The wife had sworn repeatedly that she would burn the monstrosity upon her first opportunity.

For the moment, she agreed to forbear from destroying the horrible hat because her husband agreed to attend her first family reunion in several years. As they prepared to attend the long-awaited event, the husband surprised his wife with his announcement that he fully intended to wear his treasured hat for the occasion. His wife gave no response. She only smiled as he searched throughout the house for his treasure. It wasn't in any of the usual places.

"I can't find my hat. *What did you do?*"

He suspected the worst. The man flew into a rage accusing her of destroying his favorite hat...telling her she would never get to go to her family reunion. He continued throwing items out of closets, drawers and overturning furniture. All the while he was yelling at the top of his lungs. He screamed his disbelief that his wife destroyed the thing he treasured most. She calmly crossed her arms and stood by. She smiled knowingly. This enraged him further and he said several horrible things that no man should ever say to any woman—*much less so his very own wife.* Finally, he was exhausted. The most maddening thing was that his wife still had that smug smirk on her face. He shook his fist at her:

"WELL, DO YOU HAVE ANYTHING TO SAY FOR YOURSELF?
—ANYTHING AT ALL?"

She placed her hands on her hips and glared at him.

"*It's on your head genius.*"

Querying the national governments on information withheld in these areas will never lead anywhere because the basic nature of the national governments will not change.

They follow orders.

The solution to information obfuscation is not in the national governments—*it's in us*. For all of our exasperation, demands and dogged determination, *the hat is on our own head*. It's been there all along.

17

THE DOUBLE TRICK

Many years ago, I used to walk around the streets of Washington D.C. with a Central Intelligence Agency Officer during periods when we both had training in DC. He was a gregarious character who enjoyed seeing the sights around Washington but also had a streak of paranoia that is common to people in his position. One of the things he enjoyed doing when we toured the sights was to wear a t-shirt or hat which carried the acronym: C-I-A. Sometimes the clothing would say nonsense phrases like:

Cave **I**nspector **A**t-large ……or his tee shirt would warn:

DON'T WORRY,
I'M DEFINITELY NOT
C.I.A.

When I would ask why he would take such a risk to wear clothing that sort of identifies him as a member of his *actual* organization, he would respond that he has a few items of clothing like these so he likes to use them. I asked him: "why would you possess clothing with these sayings on them?"

He advised that this is a common mind-ploy among the more paranoid in his profession and then he related the following.

"It's called deflation of suspicion or the double-trick. Foreign capitals are filled with Anti-American government agents and their cronies so different officers prepare in different ways for the possibility of confrontation in public. In one of these foreign cities we had an Operations Officer who thought he could spend a well-earned day off during a period of Anti-Western protests in the foreign capital. He was relaxing, shopping, and enjoying his time off while the local, radical instigator was nearby with a crowd. He was whipping them up into an Anti-American fervor. Suddenly, the instigator spotted the Officer and recognized him from some secret briefing his group had been given by the officer. The Instigator had been paid for his activities by both our enemies and by the CIA (a very common occurrence during transitional periods). The instigator directed the crowd's

attention to the officer and screamed in his own language: "He's CIA! It's the devil I was just speaking of." (By the way, the phrase for CIA in every foreign language always still sounds like the English letters C-I-A.)

The crowd surged toward where the Officer innocently picked out fruit at the outdoor market. Several aggressively approached the Agent from the back shouting: "C-I-A, C-I-A." The Agent turned around with a confused smile. "CIA? Oh yeah!"

The Agent pointed to the slogan on his Tee Shirt. The younger people in the crowd who read English laughed heartily—deflating the older people. The black Tee shirt's lettering was explained to them in their own language:

Confused Ignorant American

The crowd peeled away, some with snorts of disgust, shaking their heads at the Instigator's stupidity. The Instigator (never seeing the tee-shirt) was left wondering what happened to his audience and how he had been shut down so abruptly."

Tricks within tricks are often the most effective. Every area associated with UFO's is rife with double, and sometimes, even triple tricks. There is deception from the national governments, the global bureaucrats and sometimes (The Roswell Crash/ Alien Bodies incident) even *from the Extra-Dimensionals themselves.*

Even after the hailed "massive declassification" of recent years throughout the Western world, very little has actually changed except for increased levels of deception. Innumerable documents have been declassified and released by most national governments, depicting official government encounters with Paranormal Unidentified Flying objects and even with Extra-Dimensional beings, yet, *incredibly,* standard denials persist. Recently, the U.S. government released a public statement to mollify those Awakened who have been clamoring for "disclosure" from the national governments.

OFFICIAL RESPONSE TO FORMALLY ACKNOWLEDGE AN EXTRATERRESTRIAL PRESENCE ENGAGING THE HUMAN RACE - DISCLOSURE

The U.S. government has no evidence that any life exists outside our planet, or that an extraterrestrial presence has contacted or engaged any member of the human race. In addition, there is no credible information to suggest that any evidence is being hidden from the public's eye.

However, that doesn't mean the subject of life outside our planet isn't being discussed or explored. In fact, there are a number of projects working toward the goal of understanding if life can or does exist off Earth. Here are a few examples:

- SETI—the Search for ExtraTerrestrial Intelligence—was originally stood up with help from NASA, but has since been moved to other sources of private funding. SETI's main purpose is to act as a giant ear on behalf of the human race, pointing an array of ground-based telescopes towards space to listen for any signal from another world.

- Kepler is a NASA spacecraft in Earth orbit that's main goal is to search for Earth-like planets. Such a planet would be located in the "Goldilocks" zone of a distant solar system—not too hot and not too cold—and could potentially be habitable by life as we know it. The Kepler mission is specifically designed to survey our region of the Milky Way galaxy to discover Earth-sized, rocky planets in or near the habitable zone of the star (sun) they orbit.

- The Mars Science Laboratory, Curiosity, is an automobile-sized rover that NASA is launching soon. The rover's onboard laboratory will study rocks, soils, and other geology in an effort to detect the chemical building blocs of life (e.g., forms of carbon) on Mars and will assess what the Martian environment was like in the past to see if it could have harbored life.

- A last point: Many scientists and mathematicians have looked with a statistical mindset at the question of whether life likely exists beyond Earth and have come to the conclusion that the odds are pretty high that somewhere among the trillions and trillions of stars in the universe there is a planet other than ours that is home to life.

Many have also noted, however, that the odds of us making contact with any of them—especially any intelligent ones—are extremely small, given the distances involved.

But that's all statistics and speculation. The fact is we have no credible evidence of extraterrestrial presence here on Earth.

(Document Credit: Government Document/Public Domain)

Another double-trick—apparently designed to shore up a weak cover story but its true objective is to reignite an argument of purely material/physical, non-terrestrial life. So long as they can keep the mainstream focused on our solar system and the physical planets, they will never lift up their heads to see the real truth.

Additionally, there are no national governments or even any particular government official that want to declare to the world that they are profoundly obtuse or shockingly ignorant. The official U.S. government letter above has nothing to do with answering the cries for Disclosure but has everything to do with agendas far above the levels of national bureaucrats.

Exposing the true goal of the official letter brings us right back to the central tenet of this work—that Extra-Dimensionality as a concept is the world's greatest threat to the material-scientific paradigm that keeps the prisoners from seeing their cages. By releasing this letter from one of the major powers on the planet, EPIC has attempted to inject new life into an ancient, fossilized, false dialectic—are Extra-Terrestrials visiting our planet? At a time when the Awakening Community is growing exponentially and realizing that giving merit to national government statements is a fool's game; EPIC is still trying to beat a little life into this dead horse. They are trying to reignite the argument over alien visitors by taking the discredited side of the argument. They are offering the easy part of the dialectic argument to The Awakened in order to pull as many of the mainstream as possible back into this old mind trap.

Here is my official government statement made against all reason, evidence and common sense; so now let's turn back the clock sixty years and re-engage a discussion as to why you think the national government is wrong.

As the mainstream comes closer and closer to adopting the concept of Extra-Dimensionality, you will see many more statements like that above. Then you will see official statements of ridicule and finally warnings against dangerous ideas that are based on "no scientific facts or peer reviewed study." The louder and more shrill such statements become, the more evident it will be that such ludicrous letters like the one above are not generated by a desire to serve the public. They are generated by *fear*—fear that once we see the truth of Extra-Dimensionality we will find out that the material/scientific world isn't nearly as important as national governments tell us—and that truth shall set us free.

18

TRUTHFUL DISCLOSURE

Here is what one would look like.

"We, the national governments know that the Extra-Dimensionals exist, are visiting and are continuing to visit our planet Earth but truthfully, we haven't got a clue who they are or what they want. We just follow orders and right now the standing directive is: we (and you the common herd) don't need to know. Yet to mollify the mainstream masses, we have been directed to issue statements which create the appearance that we are still in control of this situation. This is done in order to preserve some modicum of public trust in us and our institutions. But we suspect that we are merely serving global EPIC agendas that, again, we don't understand because we just don't need to know...yet."

For over five decades, those who wish to see public open contact with Non-Terrestrial life someday have been comforted by seeing rocket ships taking off from Earth to the Moon, Mars or to other parts of our solar system. SETI points antennas, sensors and receivers towards outer space hoping to receive radio signals or other signals that haven't come. Private and publicly funded telescopes of incredible power keep scanning for the coming craft that will produce news of the long-awaited ambassadors from other worlds and galaxies. It never comes and our determination to only see Non-Terrestrial life as "human-like" has set us into insane, non-productive patterns of behavior that we seem unable as a species to break.

While SETI, our solar-system spanning telescopes and many other technological devices around the planet continually fail to return to us any sign of developed Non-Terrestrial life, the materialist-scientific community continues to be utterly blind to all the signs of alien visitation that already exist all around us. Yet this is also a deception—a double fake. Those in EPIC, who direct this continual search, know that no life will be found from this or other physical galaxies. They are actually looking for something else—they are looking for what they always seek—*power.*

A light year represents the distance and time it takes for light to travel in one Julian year. The speed of light and of all forms of electromagnetic radiation in empty space (vacuum) is 299,792,458 meters per second or 186,282 miles per second. A light-year is a unit of length equal to just under 10 trillion kilometers or 6 trillion miles. Even the distance covered in a single light year is probably beyond the imaginings of most non-astronomers. At the time of this writing, our modern astronomical technology and powers allow us to peer into 13.7 billion—that's billion *with a "b"* light years toward the edge of the observable universe. That's the span of space and time that we have been subjecting to relentless observation for evidence of alien life. The hope for many is that contact with benevolent, loving Non-Terrestrials will be made. The expectation is that this contact will be just a prelude to gifts for the human race of higher technology, endless resource regeneration, even all-inclusive medicine that erases the aging process and all sickness.

In short, the expectation is *for salvation*.

19

DECOMPENSATION

The return on investment after several decades of the constant search for Extra-Terrestrial life has been virtually zero—except for occasional noises about fossilized residues of ancient bacteria or loud excitement over possible evidence of water from eons ago on some planets. These sporadic fits of frenzied excitement continue to have an uproarious effect on the scientific community and the sleepers who are still titillated by them.

This system, like many long-running systems controlled by EPIC, is reaching its final phase. The system of funneling earth's resources towards sending probes, rocket ships, satellites, telescopes—the highest tech of our scientific community out into the yawning abyss of space—13.7 light years' worth of space, has reached exhaustion. Decompensation is when an integrated system that has important biological functions can no longer compensate for defects or minor deviations in form and substance because it has grown exhausted, sick or overstressed. There have been very few benefits to mainstream society for all resources put into space travel. It is likely that most technological advances, if any exist, have gone directly into black technology *that is not* shared with the mainstream society that pays for these excursions.

This inter-planetary venture and intergalactic effort has never been compensated from the start. Fittingly, "Decompensation" is a scientific term that refers to biological systems like a circulatory system that can no longer circulate. This deterioration is occurring during a time when the scientific community are beset on every side by evidence of Non-Terrestrial life—evidence they have purposefully ignored like religious zealots refusing the "primitive" natives' life-saving medicine because it might have been conceived with "witchery."

In Decompensation, the benefits generated (in many cases none at all) have diminished, while defects and costs increase until the entire system faces collapse. How long can you fool even the most materialistic drones with noise about fossilized bacteria and remnants of long gone water traces being a great leap forward for humanity?

20

THE PERSISTENT CONSCIOUSNESS COROLLARY

One of the best ways to combat the fallacies of materialist science is with the authenticity of human consciousness. There are many ancient tales that have survived largely unchanged in human history throughout centuries and even eons. Several of them are included in this work under the heading "True Tales and Concepts" for only one reason—*because they really happened.*

As we advance into the Age of Mass Awakening, there are several concepts that are unavoidable as we elevate our vibrations and our minds. One of these is the fact that the medium of all physical existence is not really matter, space and time—*it is consciousness.* Matter, space and time are merely after-effects of consciousness. Once we accept this as inviolable truth, then it leads to all manner of previously unthinkable concepts.

The Persistent Consciousness Corollary—*Since the basis of all reality is actually consciousness—not time, space and matter, then this truth shifts the priorities of all things. Things come into existence and remain in existence because we give them our energy in the form of attention, belief and our consciousness.*

This is a switching of the chicken and the egg. We do not give them our energy because they exist. They exist because someone, somewhere has given them energy in the form of consciousness. Investment of physical energy into a system is a cause often mistaken for merely a symptom. Physical energy invested is a reflection of the high amount of human belief and human consciousness devoted into that particular system. We are spiritual creatures first and physical second.

That wondrous skyscraper that sits in the middle of downtown exists because someone *first* believed it could be done. Then, they set about investing emotional energy (human consciousness) into the physical fulfillment of that belief. Once the belief, infused with consciousness began the manifestation into design and building, the physical appearance of the object was the final symptom of the first condition for existence.

Therefore, if any spiritual or paranormal subject has persisted in human consciousness for decades, centuries or eons, *that* is the best evidence that it is real, that it truly exists and that its existence is incontrovertible. Otherwise, that subject would have just disappeared from human memory shortly after it was suggested. That is especially so in light of debunkery, secular cynicism and culturally conditioned responses.

The moment we understand this truth, the fruitless search for scientific minutiae becomes irrelevant. We know it exists because we believe it exists. Whether we are relating the tales of King Arthur or those of Bigfoot, these are real because they have persisted in human consciousness for centuries and even eons, regardless of what modern technical equipment does or doesn't reveal on those topics.

21

THE MISSIONARY'S CURSE

There is an ancient story that has been repeated across the ages.

A devout and religious worshiper of God was on a small ship. He was being transported to the New World. This individual was an Englishman who believed that he had been sent by God to help the local savages in the New World find their way to God. The missionary had attempted to befriend a young man who was the newest crewmember. The missionary tried to regale the "greenhorn" boy with the joys of serving God and bringing His gospel to savages who are otherwise bound for hell. The young man was courteous but seemed quite preoccupied with doing his duties correctly. Unbowed, the missionary picked his opportunities to preach to the rest of the crew about the importance of "getting your soul right to meet with God."

At daybreak, the missionary was staring out down to the ocean off the starboard bow when his gaze happened to catch numerous little black projectiles cutting through the water away from the ship. He couldn't make out what they were so he approached the nearest sailor and asked him to look. The sailor turned pale and ran below decks. Alarm spread throughout the ship. The "projectiles" were rats from the hold below decks. The lower decks were now filled with ocean water so the rats were swimming for the shore. *The ship was sinking.*

There were shouts and panic about the lack of boats but the crew was determined to abandon ship as quickly as possible. The captain never gained control of the situation. A great deal of material was ejected overboard. Two boats were dropped into the ocean as crew and passengers vied to enter them. They overturned and were lost in the swells. A few lesser experienced jumped a long way into the water and smashed against lifeboats, breaking bones and disappearing into the water. Panic and chaos took hold and many lives were lost. The few who made it into life boats quickly found that each of them had defects and cracks and sank faster than the main ship.

The old ship creaked and groaned as it sank nearly down to the main deck. Everyone had gone into the water except for the missionary who was on his knees clinging to the main sail in prayer. He ignored the shouts in the water and continued his prayers. Sharks were everywhere. Screams were heard across the water. Spots throughout the ocean roiled red and then went calm again. All the crew and passengers were taken by the sharks, except for the greenhorn who sat in the last sinking lifeboat. Greenhorn called out to the missionary asking what he should do? The missionary was now climbing the top of the sails of the ship to stay above the water.

The missionary shouted to the boy to declare Christ as his Savior before he died. The boy screamed something unintelligible and was gone. The missionary continued his prayers as he now was on the upper quadrant of the sails. Although decks were underwater, the upper sail was still dry as the missionary clung to top portion. There was finally silence again over the water. No survivors and no sharks appeared to remain in the area. The missionary mumbled thanks to God for sparing him.

Then, something happened. In a flash of light, an Angel appeared standing upon the water and declared to the missionary "because he had been a good and faithful servant, God would send a great miracle to save him." The man was ecstatic. He imagined mighty English ships with proud Victorian flags appearing soon over the horizon. Minutes turned to hours. The ship held steady with the sail poking just above the water with its single occupant as night dragged into the next morning. Again the clinging missionary was in fervent prayers as he was roused by a splashing. The missionary looked up and was alarmed by a brown, painted savage in a narrow canoe approaching him on his steady perch. A brown man was ornately painted as if for war. There were sections of human bones and teeth used as jewelry around the man's neck. The man motioned for the missionary to climb into his canoe. The missionary explained that he could not go with him. The missionary was quite sure that the warrior was a cannibal planning to kill and eat him at the first opportunity. Although the warrior could not understand him, the missionary explained about God, the gospel and the miracles that had happened to him—the sharks, the stopping of the sinking ship and about the angel that appeared. The warrior did not understand but when the missionary held aloft the wooden cross from around his neck; the warrior's attitude became one of deference. He bowed his head and offered fruits and berries to the missionary. He seemed to plead with the missionary to come with him, even seeming to be on the verge of tears. Finally, the missionary made his intentions to stay where he was quite clear; the native lowered his head and paddled away.

The missionary went back to prayer and again heard a splashing. A gaunt young man was paddling on a great trunk that had belonged to a wealthy lady. The young man was haggard and afraid as he had seen all his friends taken by the sharks the night before. He shouted to the missionary to come aboard with him before the sail sank and the sharks had their way with him. The missionary looked askance at the unwieldy trunk. It was large and might support the weight of two men but it seemed unstable and besides *that trunk didn't have the Hand of God holding it up.*

"This sail is held up by the Will of God, young man. That is more powerful than sharks."

The missionary went on to explain about the gospel, the miracle of how the ship stopped sinking, how the angel appeared to him and told him to await a great miracle. The young man continued to plead for him to come aboard the trunk. The missionary firmly refused and went back into prayer. The young man finally paddled away in the same direction that the savage had gone.

Then, something enormous erupted out of the water next to the missionary. It was a massive air pocket that released to the surface with the sound of a great explosion. The missionary was showered with foam and water and then felt nothing more because his sail that he clung to dropped into the ocean like a stone. He was far beneath the surface and could not untangle himself from the sail. He drowned.

Later that evening, the Eternal Spirit of the missionary stood before Saint Peter at the gates of the Kingdom of Heaven, waiting his turn. When Saint Peter saw the missionary a great look of disappointment spread across his face.
"Why didn't take the ride that was offered to you from the brown man?"
The missionary was offended by the question.
"I was waiting for a great miracle to save me. Like the angel promised."
Peter shook his head.
"The promised miracle was *not for you* but for the Lord and His Kingdom. The savage was thinking only of killing and eating you until he recognized the cross and regarded you as a *Holy man*. He had resolved to bring you to his people and to learn of the ways of your God, and then you rejected him.

Why did you not accept the ride from the young man?"
The missionary thought for a moment.
"I told you I was awaiting the miracle I was promised."
Peter sighed deeply.
"The young was only thinking of way-laying you upon his first chance for any coin in your pockets but then after hearing speak of the gospel he was so deeply touched that he decided to learn from you and change his ways forever. Then, you rejected him."

The missionary bowed his head knowing he had failed God's tests and asked what his punishment was for failing God so terribly.

Paul told him for ignoring God's miracles again and again he has traded God's miracles for a curse. For a period, the missionary would now return to Earth and live without the ability to even perceive God's many blessings, gifts and His miracles. His eyes would be blind to God's love and his heart would remain hardened against His daily miracles. (*In short, the missionary would return to the Earth as a Scientist.*)

The Missionary is the illustration of modern materialist scientists. Their religious system is Newtonian materialist science because they have faith that science is not just a method—but a cosmic worldview and filter that reveals to them what is real and what is not. They are blind to spirit of their fellow humans—they see only bodies and the physical. They cannot see the endless miracles surrounding them. They see only processes and reproducible results. They scoff at the messages from Non-Terrestrial beings in ubiquitous crop circles. They willfully ignore the testimony of thousands of victims of alien abductions who recount their truth. They won't listen to authentic Contactees or Channelers who have received another truth of benevolent and destructive Non-Terrestrial beings. They turn a deaf ear to the cries of desperate ranchers whose have lost millions of cattle and livestock around the world to mutilations that no one in law-enforcement can stop. They cling desperately to their sinking scientific worldview no matter what the consequences. Even as the rising tide of consciousness lifts up all humanity around them, they will continue to cling to that small, ragged bit of sail that is still poking up out of the water until the final bitter moment when they realize their folly—*just one second too late.*

§

Global bureaucrats are approving the release of enormous volumes of UFO related and Extra-Dimensional contact records kept by the nations. They do so because they are laboring under the belief that the worldwide Tsunami of false UFO events, thousands around the world will continue to drown out the very few genuine paranormal UFO events that exist, as they have in the past. Previous to any thought of releasing these materials, previous to the fall of this wall of denial; they have run numerous simulations of data mining operations against the mountains of "UFO" data. They are exceedingly comfortable that conventional analysis will never be able to extract the tiny portion of true paranormal events hidden deep inside the mountains of data they will release. There is no way conventional analysis can reveal what must be revealed. Like trying to root out a few nuggets of gold from a mountain of lead, the miners can work for one hundred years on that mountain and meet with no success. That is why Awakened Investigators do not use conventional means. They will reduce and crystallize gems of truth from mountains of foreboding, twisted data. Awakened Investigators will be the one element that global bureaucrats did not count on when they began the irreversible process of declassification and open release of "UFO files."

Disclosure (with the big D) means for national governments to admit that they have been in contact with extra-terrestrial races and have regular intercourse (commerce/ trade) with them. This could never happen—*especially if it were true.*

For national governments to make such admissions would mean to admit crimes against humanity on an enormous scale. It would mean that national governments could have had free energy technology, advanced food production tech, clean water tech at no cost—they would have to admit that they had the ability to save millions of lives, especially throughout the third world, who would not have perished if these technologies had been freely dispersed instead of held in secret. For these reasons, true Disclosure by the national governments *will never ever happen.*

22

THE SILVER CORDS

A common saying among those in the throes of an awakening process is as follows: *"when I look up at the sky at night, the one thing I KNOW for sure is that we are definitely not alone."*

There's good news and even *better news*. The good news is we aren't alone. The even better news is that we *kind of ARE alone* and it's good for us.

Bear with me.

Let us suppose that when humanity was first created, there had already been other races out there (also created by Creator-Source for purposes very different from humanity). These more advanced races salivated at even the thought of the creation of an entire race of merely physical, temporary beings yet complete with souls and free will. These horribly inferior creatures would be placed in a physical environment that would imprison them under terribly disadvantageous conditions, which would further contribute to extremely short life spans. We can surmise that many of these superior races lived for thousands of years in a near-invulnerable state. Yet, they do die and that means oblivion for them. For these superior races, such inferior creatures could only be fit for a single limited role—slaves.

Yet shockingly, these puny mortal beings were then given an extraordinary treasure, wholly inappropriate for such puny containers. They were imbued with *eternal immortal spirits*.

Imagine the feelings these "superior" races may have felt upon learning that these primitive savages would be given a privilege and a power that some of them lack. Putting aside the notion of good and evil for a moment, let us consider that many of these superior alien races are for various reasons—NOT fully ensouled with an eternal spirit and with a spiritual connection back to Creator-Source. *"Not fully ensouled"* means they are sentient, self-aware and do have *a type of soul* which serves as a repository for hopes, dreams, fears and desires—but they are missing the spiritual component that makes us eternal spiritual beings—they are missing the slender invisible chord that connects all humans to the Creator-Source. It is this eternal slender chord that enlivens our souls with spiritual energy, love, knowledge and all Cosmic Truth from Creator-Source and also gives us the ability/privilege/wonderful destiny of an eventual return to Creator-Source. They are missing that part of the soul—the potentiality of eternity with God. The reason for this is because many of these races were *created by superior alien races*—they were never originally brought into being by Creator-Source as we are.

Therefore, they have no spiritual lifeline back to the eternal destination of all fully ensouled beings. Like salmon fish, we must return to our source of life after a long period, no matter how difficult that journey will ultimately be. We departed from Creator-Source long ago (before time existed actually in our physical dimensions of the Multi-Verse) in order to live physical, meta-physical, spiritual existences. Then, after a period, we package up these experiences in the spiritual container of our eternal souls and, finally, bring it all back to Creator-Source for His examination, experience and enjoyment. This is the purpose for which Creator-Source created all fully ensouled beings. Some of these alien races are bereft of that ethereal silver chord that connects us to Creator-Source and will eventually guide us back to the Origination Point. We shall someday be guided by these invisible but indestructible silver chords back toward the flame of Absolute Love to stand in the Breath of our Creator-Source.

Many of these lower alien races lack the same ability. Who created the higher alien races? Creator-Source did. However, the original higher races became incredibly advanced and powerful to the point that they voluntarily destroyed their silver chords and rejected any connection back to Creator-Source. They declared themselves the "New Creator-Source" and, in part, *they were*.

What need hath god of God?

The silver chords were not indestructible after all. These Elder Ones destroyed their own chords and then, all the lower races they created *also* lacked the essential silver chords and the connection back to Eternal Love. The line back was broken for the lower races that had no choice in the matter.

Yet these higher alien races and even the lower alien races remain incredibly powerful, able to bend reality and matter even in similar fashion to Creator-Source Himself. Once it became clear that Creator-Source was now going to create such a powerless shell as a human being but which would have the ultimately precious trophy of an eternal soul wrapped up inside of it—these races were quite interested in access to these tempting (treasure filled) new prizes.

Creator-Source knows all things and so He was aware these powerful alien races would look to capture, enslave, abuse or just absorb his new creations. Accordingly, Creator-Source needed to manifest an unforeseeable protection for these relatively weak and vulnerable creatures. He might have considered: a giant impenetrable dome or an impervious energy shield over a large flat area that would keep all alien visitors out. These options would make his freedom loving creations feel as if they were in a visible prison so another better option was initiated.

Creator-Source manifested a "Canopy of Entropy" known to us as Time and Space. Creator-Source decided to wrap all of His creation's existence in a cloak of dimensional protection. This Time and Space was a Cloak of Destruction that effects deterioration, aging and devastation for any who are exposed to it. On the downside, it seemed to guarantee that his human creations would only live a terribly short life span before entropy destroyed their physical shells also, but that was actually the most brilliant part of Creator-Source's plan. The initial physical part of human life was only meant to be a first tiny step in an eternal existence that would span all the ages of the Multi-Verses. Throwing off the material part of that eternal existence would be a wonderful relief for these human creatures as they enter the true and eternal part of their existence—outside that Canopy of Entropy.

The Second Law of Thermodynamics is known as the Law of Increased Entropy. The quality of matter/energy deteriorates gradually over time. Usable energy is irretrievably lost in the form of unusable energy. To put it in harsh terms: we are rotting from the day we are born (sorry about that). All things caught within the web of time and space, are caught up in a systemic rampant destruction.

This Canopy of Entropy was so virulent to the "eternal" Alien Races that they could not interject themselves into the dreaded ocean of Time and Space without suffering its effects—aging, deterioration and destruction. Creator-Source knew that physical death would not be an ending for his human creations but rather a true beginning. In contrast, these alien races, if they expose themselves to Time and Space too much and come to their ending—*it's a true ending.*

It would be an ending to their powerful existences. After that, they are relegated to a floating, rudderless existence or something worse without the drawback effect to Creator-Source that is the glorious birthright of every Cosmically Connected being (that's us).

They, many of the Alien Visitors, have no silver chord to bring them toward a glorious destination. This is why physical time and space are such an effective protection for human existence. It keeps us relatively safe from far more powerful forces. It also kills our temporary physical bodies but even that is for the best.

Here is the reveal.

The Alien Visitors we experience are not Extra-terrestrials from other planets, solar systems, galaxies or star systems. Despite the theater to make us believe to the contrary such as the Roswell incident, the Hills Alien Abduction/Star Chart, the many "Extra-terrestrial messages" complete with home addresses from other galaxies; *none of it has been true.* They are from dimensions outside of time and space. They are from somewhere else and they return to that same somewhere else.

They are Extra-Dimensionals.

23

FERMI'S PARADOX

How can we be sure that Extraterrestrials are not from our time and space—from thousands of light years away? It's simple. *They would already be here.*

Old world scientists and PhD's believe many concepts are beyond our capacity (the capacity of non-academics) to comprehend so they revel in waxing eloquent about such concepts; without concern for possibly being gainsaid by common folk. Although a physicist named Enrico Fermi originally came up Fermi's Paradox in the 1950's, the reason it is still well remembered today is not because it is complex—it is because it is *so brilliantly simple.*

Fermi's Paradox is in perfect alignment with basic common sense.

Roughly stated, Fermi's Paradox is as follows: according to all logic, reason and probabilities, since we are able to observe the age of the universe and its vast number of stars and if the Earth is fairly typical; extraterrestrial life very much like that of Earth should be a fairly common occurrence throughout the universe. Therefore, if process follows logic, a multitude of advanced extraterrestrial civilizations capable of intergalactic travel should exist in the Milky Way galaxy; so why are we not overtly receiving massive visible evidence of extra-terrestrial contact, traffic and even established presence and commerce here on Earth?

Fermi was not talking about sporadic sightings all over the Earth in random chaotic patterns (like what has been and is happening right now.) Fermi was referring to is that we should be seeing an organized, dense, overt and public procession of non-terrestrial life and craft in the centers of human rulership and commerce—like an alien parade on main street during Veteran's Day. The fact that this is *not* happening is the paradox (a condition occurring when the opposite condition should in fact be occurring under the rules of logic and reality).

Even our galaxy contains as much as a hundred billion stars. If even a *very small* fraction of these attached solar systems has planets that develop technological civilizations, there would be a very large number of such civilizations. If any of these civilizations produce cultures which travel over interstellar distances, even at a small fraction of the speed of light, the galaxy should have interstellar traffic going through it in no more than a few million years. Since the galaxy is actually *billions* of years old, we humans are like the old lady waiting for a bus that is running late. As she scans her watch the bus, the tardiness of that desperately needed vehicle (proportionately speaking) went from 20 minutes late to several thousands of years overdue.

Would you keep waiting for that bus?

Shockingly, the majority of humanity does. They continue to hope that space observation throughout the galaxies will stumble across other physical civilizations or that those other civilizations will finally arrive here in large visible numbers—*salvation*. Fermi's Paradox does not contemplate paranormal UFO's that phase in and out of our physical universe or any craft that are only temporarily in our dimension of time and space. The Paradox is saying we should have open, massive and continuous Extra-Terrestrial presence (according to all logic, probabilities and reason); that is as rock solid physical in our dimension of time and space as humans are.

Fermi was right.

We should be up to our armpits in physical extra-terrestrials according to all we know about the physical dimension of time and space; *but we are not.*

We, the Awakened Community know that they are out there due to the up close and personal experiences we have had but we also know that they are not out there in the solid, three dimensional time space continuum that Fermi envisaged. So, if the Canopy of Entropy presents a threat to these Non-terrestrial beings cannot tolerate, then this begs another question. Why would they even risk short exposures to this dreaded Canopy of Entropy?

It's because they must.

24

THE BAD PENNY

Creator-Source wrapped us in this turbulent cloak of entropy (our physical universe), not to torment us, but to protect us and serve our eternal interests at the expense of temporary comfort. It is this tumultuous sea of chaos, known to us as space and time that insures us against interference on a continuous basis by those Extra-Dimensionals who have not yet figured out how to permanently ensconce themselves into this dimension without suffering the ravages of time and space. For us, the destruction wrought upon our bio-suit only inches us closer to a cosmic graduation and a glorious reunion with Creator-Source before our true spiritual self receives a much grander and more wonderful assignment in the Multi-Verse.

Conversely, those Extra-Dimensional races that lack that connection to Creator-Source, because they rejected it or never had one, are faced with a great yawning abyss of nothingness once they expire from these dimensions. They find that a horrific prospect and so they wish to attach to some eternal Being that already has that connection to Creator-Source.

There are many such methods that can be used to effect and assist such attachments: abduction, implantation, mutilation, intimate or familiar contact and many more. If they can accomplish such an attachment it guarantees that the host must take them back to Creator-Source when they pass from this physical plane. Some humans do not consider such attachment a terrible thing. Many human hosts actively seek such attachment: "ET outreach" is advertised as a glorious, wonderful experience to commune intimately with our Space Brothers.

I am not the originator of the belief that alien life visiting our planet is Extra-Dimensional rather than Extra-Terrestrial (physical beings from our time and space) but I am its most determined proponent. The greatest thinkers in the world of the paranormal have repeatedly come to the same conclusion. Sometimes they refer to this idea as "the InterDimensional Hypothesis" or "the Extra-Dimensional hypothesis." No less a personage than Dr. Jacques Vallée stated that unidentified flying objects (UFOs) and related events involve visitations from other "realities" or "dimensions" that coexist separately alongside our own. Brad Steiger wrote "we are dealing with a multidimensional, Para-physical phenomenon." Other well-known paranormal thinkers such as John Ankerberg and John Weldon advocate the Extra-Dimensional explanation of UFOs as a spiritistic phenomenon. They wrote: "the UFO phenomenon simply does not behave like Extraterrestrial Visitors." Why would so many great alternative thinkers come to that same conclusion?

Think about it for a moment.

What would true Extra-Terrestrials who just traveled across the physical universe into our galaxy do *once they got here*? It requires an enormous amount of energy, time and effort to travel in the physical dimension, our dimension of time and space especially across numerous galaxies. Upon arrival, they would go directly to the center of power, whatever they might determine that to be and they would say *"take us to your leader."*

Every little kid knows that. If you request very young children to draw a scene of ETs visiting the Earth, most of the resultant drawings will follow one of two patterns: little boys tend to draw violent alien attacks and little girls tend to draw aliens at the American White House, a Western national Capital building or some other center of human power meeting peaceably with human leaders. Despite all the weighty scholarship and academic credentialed thinkers proclaiming the parameters of this argument; it is the children who (as in most areas) reveal the true answer to this conundrum. Intergalactic visitation and cooperation would start with a very public, overt *"take us to your leader."*

Instead of open continuous contact, we have only seen surreptitious, stealth-like, covert behavior in which craft appear, disappear, fade-in and fade-out, abduct and sometimes return people, never reveal very much, never tell too much and don't show very much at all. Many great minds (far greater than the author of this work) have come the conclusion that interstellar, intergalactic travelers in our physical time and space *would not* behave this way after a long, hard slog through the galaxies.

As far back as 1970, in the book "UFOs: Operation Trojan Horse," John Keel said UFOs were *not intergalactic travelers but were actually closer to supernatural concepts like ghosts and demons.* As the phenomenon has grown all over the globe since 1970, every significant clue revealed has only strengthened the case for Extra-Dimensionality.

The Extra-Dimensional hypothesis is no theory. It is fact. This is not because great minds in the study of the paranormal happen to agree with it. It is because the facts, evidence and the clues that we can connect all come to that same investigative conclusion. Awakened Investigators are not collectivists. They do not wait to be backed up by the mob in order to say the truth. They do not come to investigative conclusions by consensus, by committee or for the convenience of the Elite Powers In Control (EPIC). Awakened Investigators are individualists who must follow clues and their connections to whatever results no matter how undesirable the conclusions might be.

Each of the great thinkers who have argued for Extra-Dimensionality did so against enormous resistance, both in the scientific/academic community and even *within ufology itself*: Vallée, Ankerberg, Weldon and John Keel. Today, Dr. David Jacobs and J. Allen Hynek have carried forward much of this research and applied it to the recent cases. Recently, Phillip J. Imbrogno has used the nomenclature "Ultra-Terrestrials" to reach basically the same investigative conclusion of Extra-Dimensionality.

Yet the truth of Extra-Dimensionality has gone largely ignored because it not convenient *any* of the sides involved in the old paradigm of ufology. There are those in the EPIC power structure who wish us to fear alien visitors. EPIC elements want us to believe the Visitors are close by in our physicality and with the ability to sustain a physical presence indefinitely. We are constantly barraged with movies showing the *very physically present* alien visitors laying waste to our cities with super, mega weapons.

Then, there are those who wish to consider the Visitors our best friends, paternal and even possible saviors of humanity. They *also* want us to believe that they are fully physical in our time and space so that the quasi-religious doctrine of "ET Imminency" continues to be fully embraced: that the ET's could set down on the White House lawn *at any moment* and begin handing out cancer cures and genetic recoding/improvement pills from their luminescent grab-bag of interstellar goodies. This doctrine keeps the believing populace in fascination and even in obsession with the Alien Visitors. This doctrine would be rendered invalid if humanity began to comprehend the doctrine of Extra-Dimensional alien life.

Even those old world scientific materialists who do not believe in the truth of non-terrestrial Visitors at all are delighted that, as we were indoctrinated by the Roswell Crash, the mainstream has bought fully into the fantasy that we must prove these things on the purely physical plane. Those invested in the current ET paradigm will do anything to keep people believing that the Visitors are from our iteration of time and space. *Yet, like a bad penny*, Extra-Dimensionality keeps finding its way back to us.

25

GATEWAY EARTH

Of all the bulwarks against the Extra-Dimensional hypothesis, the strongest is a mental construct that says: we **cannot** be the sole intelligent life on this physical plane of existence. This idea is at the crux of why Extra-Dimensionality has been pushed aside again and again.

If alien visitors actually come from other dimensions outside of our time and space then it leads to the real possibility that we are the only life (as we know biological life) in this physical universe.

That is very difficult to grasp. People want there to be others in our physical universe. They do not wish for it to be possible that Creator-Source would make all the observable physical universe: about 3 to 100 × 1022 stars (30 sextillion to a septillion stars) organized in more than 80 billion galaxies, which form clusters and super clusters; without other complex biological life such as ourselves occupying some tiny corner of *all that space*. Any human being who looks through a good telescope into the vastness of outer space would be inclined to agree with them.

"Why would could Creator-Source make all this vast expanse of space, stars, galaxies, time, space, and physical existence just for the planet Earth, just for the human species, just for us? It isn't possible. There must be others out there."

With men these things are impossible but *with God all things are possible.*

For centuries it has been the height of humanistic, intellectual, self-assurance to scoff at the suggestion that the Earth is in any way the center of the universe. Yet, what I am suggesting is far more radical than that ancient concept. What has been revealed to me is a natural outgrowth of Extra-Dimensional truth. If other entities visiting our planet originate from outside our dimension of time space; the next question would be why? The answer is *because it must be so*—things have developed in this manner because there are rules throughout the Multi-Verses that require it to be so.

It is therefore a natural progression to the **Extra-Dimensional Corollary**: *given that Extra-Dimensional visitors to our planet are from outside the physical universe; it therefore follows that: there is no complex biological life (similar to ourselves) outside of Earth (at least on this physical plane of existence) and that our Earth is the sole origination point, entry point and transit point; for all biological and Extra-Dimensional life in our physical universe.*

The Earth is not primarily a planet (that is secondary)—Earth is primarily *a gateway.*

The human race is selected to steward this universe and Earth itself is the "living tunnel" for ingress
and egress of Extra-Dimensional life as they travel to and from our physical universe. That's why our solar system has been teeming with Extra-Dimensional life in the unrecorded hidden history of the past—because it came from Earth *or rather through it.* This would explain the many built alien structures on the Moon, Mars and other planets that seem to no longer be active since thousands of years ago. Creator-Source did create all this *just for us* but others wish to use it as well. Regardless, there are many, both in the materialist paradigm and even those who know the truth but who do not wish for us to have any suspicion of just how special, unique and powerful we truly are. They have had their way for a very long time.

The greatest gift understanding Extra-Dimensionality gives us is not an obvious one.

It is a great gift to understand what the Alien Visitors truly are (that they are ED's not ET's). However, the greater gift this comprehension leads us to is allowing us to transcend old filters that kept us in a myopic stupor, labeling and identifying great concepts in ludicrous ways. Once we begin to grasp a concept as mysterious and grand as Extra-Dimensionality, it can be applied to other areas. Like the blind man who identified the elephant as a hairy snake because he was only touching its tail; we encounter beings constantly phasing in and out of our temporal plane of time and space through horrifically inept religious filters: ghosts, angels, demons, Mother Mary, saints and evil spirits.

Even worse than superstition are the purely physical scientific filters that are just another form of organized religion: belief in Alien Travelers who live just around the galactic corner from us. Here's a central ritual of this scientific faith: exploration of outer space is crucial in order to discover other civilizations and life on planets similar to our own.

It's not out there. It *was* out there a very long time ago but *it ain't there now.*

Any honest perusal of pictorials of the dark side of the Moon or Mars, before the pictures are furiously scrubbed and air-brushed by NASA, clearly depict hidden or sometimes submerged structures of previous bases and even civilizations *that have existed* there but appear not to be there now. This is not because we had visitors from other galaxies to our solar system. It is because there have been times in the past when the Extra-Dimensionals *have found ways* to circumvent the prohibition of time and space on their continual presence in our dimension. They found a loophole and they are working furiously right now to recreate that loophole again.

They spread out *from* the Earth they dominated during prehistoric ages. They came through Gateway Earth and some returned to their own dimensions by the same terrestrial gateway. During that period they used other planets nearby as bases from which to monitor and control the Earth. Earth was and is the great prize of this physical universe. It is the great Gateway. Control a "chokepoint" and you can control all travelers that pass through it. That's what "highway men" do. They can charge passers a toll or they can rob or kill everyone.

I would refer you to the books of Dr. Joseph P. Farrell who wrote "The Giza Death Star" and continues through his many works, to explain how much people can learn about the true history of our universe once they remove the blinders of the old paradigms.

The shift will be ours as we release each other from the Mind-Trap of believing everything begins and ends with the physical. This entire, physical, known universe, all of time and space, was created by Creator-Source solely for humanity and for the Earth. Yet despite that, Extra-Dimensional life from Multi-Verses across the unknown have always and continue to use Earth as a gateway by which to transit into and out of our universe. Not only is the Earth the center of this universe (sort of) but we are the Universal Gateway by which all Extra-Dimensional life passes.

No one comes unto the souls except by us.

PRESENT EXTRA-DIMENSIONALITY

We must become the Disclosure we wish to see.

26

THE PUFO DEFINED

We have great alternative thinkers in the Awakened Community. They tend to be former scientists, former journalists, refugees from University academia and every brand of brave-heart who departed from the mainstream to follow the truth no matter where it might lead. There are precious few of them in comparison to the institutions they left behind. Those massive mainstream bureaucracies whose members wile away the hours of their existence by mimicking each other's obedience to the dogmas of rotting institutions.

For those who broke away from these systems in a true pursuit of intellectual investigation, the continuing expenditure of their energy on continuing to try to awaken those who wish to slumber, *is a tragic waste.*

It is akin to highly capable police officers chasing down loads of marijuana and arresting pot-smokers while the penal system routinely releases murderers and rapists after an average of five years in prison due to a lack of space. At the closing moments before the final bell, those who still do not wish to believe, *will never believe no matter what we show them.* We should, instead, turn our precious energy and focus to bolster, buoy, educate, encourage and edify *each other* so that we might all stand strong as a single Awakened Community in that final day of Total Revelation.

True Paranormal UFO's are supernatural—beyond the ability of humans to produce. The investigative imperative then becomes to determine the nature of the Paranormality—is it extraterrestrial, non-physical or extra-dimensional? Are there governments or government experts that can help make that determination or who were involved in the incident, directly or indirectly, to begin with? There are hundreds, perhaps thousands of reports over the last twenty years that fall into the final category of credible, reliable, unexplained paranormal phenomena—Paranormal UFO's, also called "genuine PUFO's." This minority of incidents include: video records made by astronauts, Air Force pilots and other government officials, sometimes on duty and sometimes off duty, who have made a reliable and credible record of PUFOs. To date, several hundred such witnesses have been identified throughout the world and spanning every branch of the armed services, the intelligence agencies, the former USSR, and numerous other current and former officials from all the nations.

In the past, the popular media has sufficiently stigmatized the witnessing of such incidents to the point that if an incident comes dangerously close to qualifying for PUFO status, television broadcast and print media typically join ranks to discredit the witnesses. This carefully executed work by the old media, in the past, has given government officials license to simply ignore the witnesses. There has been little problem for governments to keep a lid on the five percent of UFO phenomena that they wished to keep quiet. The continuing unspoken alliance between the old media and government institutions has worked seamlessly to keep the global populace's attention firmly fixed on UFO's so that very few would actually notice the tiny portion of genuine PUFO's that would crop up from time to time.

This happy alliance has been shattered in the last twenty years by the global democratization of information through the Internet, non-establishment cable and alternative programming. PUFO's are now given attention outside the control wingspan of the old media and government officials. They can no longer suppress information that is so readily available to throughout the globe. In the face of genuine paranormal phenomena, their final resort must be distraction and disinformation.

The standards being used by Awakened Investigators to designate genuine PUFO status; will further obliterate the old system of traditional discrediting of UFO witnesses. People can, for the first time in human history, evaluate real PUFO incidents without the dampening filters of the former guardians of credibility.

Under the PUFO Definition, the minimum traits for an incident to be accorded a genuine PUFO designation are five.

1. The appearance of an object that appears to defy gravity, move intelligently, without noise or emission of any sort so that it qualifies as possible anti-gravity technology or non-human technology.
2. Travel speeds or maneuvering that human technology cannot duplicate or explain. The appearance and disappearance of these craft at rates of speed that are inexplicable, shape shifting or apparition and dissolution from our physical plane of existence are prime indicators of a Paranormal UFO.
3. Reliable credible witnesses who do not gain by the reportage but rather take great risks in their professional lives to maintain the truth of their stories. These should be assertions made by people with responsible positions and offices who put those positions in danger to continue asserting the truth of the PUFO incident. In law, this is called the "inherent reliability of admissions made against interest." *Why would they invent these claims since it only hurts them professionally and in their social circles?*

Cinema students or people trying to break into: the movie industry, computer animation industry or learning to become special effects wizards; do not qualify as reliable, credible witnesses. Neither does anyone qualify as a reliable witness if preliminary investigation shows they are trying to gain notoriety for any reason. Only people who wish to shun the media spotlight and do not wish to gain or profit from their paranormal experience can attain the status of reliable, credible witnesses under PUFO requirements.

4. No credible natural or terrestrial explanation for the witnessed phenomena (e.g.: is there is a high probability of experimental military aircraft in that area?)

5. A reliable video or digital record of the phenomena (no grainy or blurry videos can be acceptable for PUFO status) that occurred complete with chain of custody record and high indicia of reliability with the media to guarantee it was not tampered with at any time.

Pictures, videos and even eyewitnesses of UFO phenomena can be faked and in some instances they are. The conservative estimate is 90 to 94 percent of all reported UFO phenomena are either manufactured or simply mistakes by well-intentioned mystery seekers. But if all five of the above criteria are simultaneously met on a single UFO incident, then that incident can be officially converted into a new paradigm of credibility and certainty in accordance with Awakened Investigative standards.

27

GLOBAL AMERICAN PUFOS

The first genuine American PUFO events were several incidents over a span of sixteen days. The 1952 occurrences at Washington D.C. also known as the Washington National Airport Sightings, were a series of unidentified flying object reports from July 13 to July 29, 1952, over the "protected airspace" of the Capital of the United States, Washington D.C.

At 11:40 p.m. on July 19, 1952, an air-traffic controller at Washington National Airport spotted seven objects on his radar. The objects were located 15 miles south-southwest of the city; no known aircraft were in the area and the objects were not following any established flight paths. That controller then called National Airport's other radar center; the controller there told the first controller that he also had the objects on his radarscope. Even more disturbing was that by looking out of the control tower window he could see one of the objects as a bright orange light.

At this point, other objects appeared in all sectors of the radarscope. These objects moved over the White House and the United States Capitol. That controller then called Andrews Air Force Base, located 10 miles from Washington National Airport. Although Andrews reported that they had no unusual objects on their radar, an airman soon called the base's control tower to report the sighting of a strange object. Airman Brady, who was in the tower, then saw an *object which appeared to be like an orange ball of fire, trailing a tail . . . it was unlike anything I had ever seen before."* The object took off at an unbelievable speed and vanished in a split second.

At Andrews Air Force Base (AFB), the control tower personnel were tracking on radar what some thought to be unknown objects. The staff Sgt. observed an orange-red light to the south; the light "would appear to stand still, then make an abrupt change in direction and altitude . . . this happened several times"

At 3 a.m., shortly before two jet fighters from Newcastle AFB in Delaware arrived over Washington, all of the objects vanished from the radar at National Airport. However, when the jets ran low on fuel and left, *the objects returned*, which convinced officials in the tower that "*the UFOs were monitoring radio traffic and behaving accordingly.*"

On July 31, 1952, General Sanford, Commander of U.S. Air force Intelligence, was charged with the investigation into the identities of these vehicles. His final conclusion was: "We don't have any idea what these things were but whatever they were, *they are not a threat to the National Security of the United States.*"

Physicist H.P. Robertson chaired the later government panel, which consisted of prominent scientists and which spent two days examining the "best" UFO cases collected by Project Blue Book. The panel similarly dismissed all of the UFO cases it examined as not representing anything unusual or threatening to national security. In the panel's estimate, the Air Force and Project Blue Book needed to spend less time analyzing and studying UFO reports and more time *publicly debunking them.*

In the summer of 1952 over the "protected airspace" of Washington D.C., all five requirements were met for these infamous incidents to qualify as genuine PUFO's.

1. The appearance of a sky born object that appears to defy gravity, move intelligently, with a conscious guiding force behind it, without noise or emission of any sort so that it qualifies as possible anti-gravity technology or superior technology of some sort.
2. Travel speeds or maneuvering that human technology cannot duplicate or explain.
3. Reliable credible witnesses who do not gain by the reportage.
4. No credible natural or terrestrial explanation for the witnessed phenomena.
5. A reliable video or other record of the phenomena.

Each of these five elements is readily apparent in a cursory examination of the events.

1. The appearance of a sky born object that appears to defy gravity, move intelligently, with a conscious guiding force behind it, without noise or emission of any sort so that it qualifies as possible anti-gravity technology or superior technology of some sort.

The 1952 Washington D.C. vehicles were witnessed and recorded maneuvering in an intelligent manner consistent with a conscious guiding force behind them. These did not maneuver just in straight lines like a meteor or other space-born natural phenomena. Additionally they did what pilots would call "buzzing stunts" in which they would surround one of the jets trying to catch up to them as if to show the damage they could do with their superior maneuverability if they so desired.

2. Travel speeds or maneuvering that human technology cannot duplicate (possible anti-gravity technology) or explain such as extreme right angle turns, reverse maneuvers and underwater submergence of aircraft. PUFO's are able to achieve appearance and disappearance at rates of speed that are inexplicable and apparition, shape shifting and even dissolution from our physical plane of existence.

The 1952 PUFOs also did this on numerous occasions through the sixteen-day period. Appearances and disappearances through speed or dematerializations were recorded and witnessed both visually by eyewitnesses and by technological radar equipment. Never during all the witnessing of these events was any sound or fossil fuel emission (jet fuel smoke) ever seen from these vehicles that traveled at the speed of jets and even faster that jets could follow.

3. Reliable credible witnesses who do not gain by the reportage but rather take great risks in their professional lives to maintain the truth of their stories. These should be admissions and assertions made against self-interest—people with responsible positions and offices who put those positions in danger to continue asserting the truth of the PUFO incident.

In the 1952 incidents, the main witnesses were professional United States Air Force pilots and radar operators who saw the vehicles appear and disappear from their screens numerous times.

4. No credible natural or terrestrial explanation for the witnessed phenomena, even after the government tries to provide one.

The national government didn't even try on this one.

5. A reliable video or other record of the phenomena (no grainy or blurry videos can be acceptable for PUFO status) that occurred complete with chain of custody record and high indicia of reliability with the media to guarantee it was not tampered with at any time.

Radar captures and various technological records were made of these incidents that are undisputed even today.

President Dwight Eisenhower about a decade later issued a bizarre farewell speech to the American people after his term as President was over. The speech is informally called "Beware The Military-Industrial Complex." Eisenhower warned the American people to rein in the growing power of what he called "the military-industrial complex." Eisenhower believed he was kept in the dark by "secret shops" that mixed military and scientific resources using black funds for black projects. Some of these projects were authorized for periods of ten years or more at a time, requiring no further Presidential authorization for continuing funding. He still thought the 1952 incident might have been created, managed and run by the complex he resented so much; and that he and previous Presidents were just never informed. It was this agenda, larger than the office of the President of the United States of America, that caused Eisenhower to make the bewildering farewell address.

Fortunately for Seekers of Truth, things do change in fifty years. Many national governments beginning twenty years ago have decided to declassify and *publicly make available* most of the files that pertained to "UFO" incidents. Canada has released its historical UFO files and many thousands of those files are available to anyone in the world through the Internet. Other countries, England, Denmark, France, and even the Great Keeper Of Secrets—America—have implemented similar steps. Yet all this "new openness" in this field serves mostly to pull us right back into the old tar pit of distraction: *whether UFO's are truly Alien Visitation phenomena?*

Although only about six percent of UFO incidents are genuinely paranormal, this still adds up to hundreds every year, just on the North American continent, and the number is increasing; as are the peripherally connected activities such as alien abductions, experimentation on people all over the globe, cattle and livestock mutilations for an alien agenda that is not completely known. There is even a concurrent increase in telepathic communications, visions and even dreams allegedly caused or directed by an alien agenda.

Reliable and credible contact cases are augmenting geometrically. More and more credible and reluctant witnesses continue to encounter the alleged alien "Greys" on the ground—both the small 3 to 4 feet and also the large variety—7 to 8 feet tall. Contact cases with many forms of Alien Entities are increasing to a level no one ever expected. Human history is approaching a climactic event on a global scale, which will be unimaginable even to Hollywood movie producers.

The spiking statistical increase in all these phenomena point to the inescapable investigative conclusion that a massive, overt wave of full contact with the Visitor Aliens is coming very soon to the nations of the world and *they will not be prepared.*

Humankind will degenerate into chaos and division at greater levels than ever once the Extra-Dimensionals openly arrive—unless we prepare right now under a *new* paradigm. Contrived war-game scenarios at the Department of Defense will be useless when that time comes. The Battle of Los Angeles in 1948 should have taught us that. It was more of a futile exercise than a battle. During a time of war-induced paranoia, thousands of anti-aircraft shells were fired up at PUFO's that appeared over L.A. and hit nothing—almost nothing. Six civilians on the ground were the only casualties of this action when the shells passed through the PUFOs and came back to the ground. That fact is often omitted during reportage of the incident. Preparation for the next such event must not be military or even physical—it must be spiritual, shamanistic and under the leadership of the Awakened Community. It was during this incident that national government officials first discovered that they could not cover up the honest, truthful reactions of the frontline troops during a crisis: pilots and military on the scene. As a result of the information control fiasco in this incident, national governments no longer do large military/Air Force responses to genuine paranormal UFO incidents.

The final bitter lesson the Western governments learned as a result of the Battle of Los Angeles and the 1952 Washington DC incidents is that such vehicles, such PUFOs, could dominate the skies over the Earth any time they chose to do so. Any such battle for air supremacy would be determined in seconds, fully and forever.

28

RENDLESHAM FOREST INCIDENT

Lumping in the National Governments with Global Government is like saying guppies are the same as the Great White Shark because they swim in the same ocean. Global Government dominance over national Government actors is horribly evident in the Rendlesham Forest incidents.

The Bentwaters military base was an American military base in England. The incident involved military enlisted personnel and officers investigating UFO incidents on U.S. and English soil. The entire incident was international and therefore global in its consequences. Events like this immediately spur Global Government into action. When the Global government acts there are no bothersome red tape bureaucratic concerns or even cares for the lives of citizens because, again, Global Government is not government at all—it's a system of dominance that sits astride the national governments.

Global Government is the machine used by the Elite Powers In Control (EPIC), the ancient family bloodlines that have dominated this planet since before recorded history. There is no comparison between Global Government and the national governments. Global Government is a like a Great White Shark, the most feared and powerful predator of the sea, patrolling the waters with absolute ruthless efficiency— every action has a deadly purpose. There is no waste or hesitation. With this Shark, any failure to reach or accomplish tasks is dealt with by immediate consequences. There is always ruthless efficiency. While national governments are rife with incompetence, waste, fraud, and even corruption, these are tolerated as part of everyday national business. However, even a whiff of national government disobedience to the Global Agenda can have deadly results. Empires, entire national governments, even whole regions of national governments, can disappear in short order after failing to obey the Great White Shark.

By comparison, the National governments are like guppies, just waiting to see which way the Great Shark swims so they can school accordingly. They swim in unison, as survival dictates. Once in a while a guppy may swim the wrong way, against the rest of the school and so the Great Shark makes it disappear. But most often such drastic measures are not required because national governments tend to be very obedient to the Great Shark. The guppies enact, legislate and plan military actions against one another, all in submission to the desires of the Great Shark. The guppies actually compete against one another to prove which of them are the most obedient and eager to enact the wishes of the Shark.

In late December 1980, the Great White Shark's movements were felt at Rendlesham Forest, Suffolk, England, just outside the Royal Air Force Base at Woodbridge, used at the time by the U.S. Air Force. Dozens of United States Air Force personnel were eyewitnesses to various supernatural events over a three-day period. England's Ministry of Defense (MoD) denied that the event posed any threat to national security and stated that it was therefore never investigated *as a security matter*. United States officials made similar claims.

Around 3:00 a.m. on 26 December 1980, strange lights were reported by a security patrol near the East Gate of Royal Air Force Woodbridge. These lights descended into nearby Rendlesham Forest. Servicemen initially thought it was a downed aircraft but upon entering the forest to investigate, they saw strange lights moving through the trees, as well as a brilliant light from an unidentified object overhead. One of the servicemen, Sgt. Jim Penniston, later related he encountered a "craft of unknown origin" and made detailed notes of its features, touched its "warm" surface, and copied the numerous symbols on its body. *It had a great deal of symbolic writing on its body, which I knew had great significance.*

The object flew away after their brief encounter. Penniston also saw triangular landing gear on the object, leaving three impressions in the ground that were visible the next day. While undergoing regression hypnosis in 1984, Penniston related that the "craft" he encountered had come from our future, and was occupied by time travelers, not Extraterrestrials.

The servicemen returned to the site again in the early hours of 28 December 1980 with radiation detectors. They got positive readings on the imprints left behind by the craft. The deputy base commander, Lieutenant Colonel Charles I. Halt, investigated this sighting personally and recorded the events on a micro-cassette recorder. His cassette recording is memorialized in Awakened Circles as "The Halt Tape" and this crucial piece of direct, physical evidence was ultimately "disappeared" by unknown persons.

Halt was near the eastern edge of the forest being led by several of his troops toward the source of some flashing lights in the dark forest. The flashing lights were seen across the field to the east, almost in line with a farmhouse. Also star-like lights were seen in the sky to the north and south, the brightest of which seemed to beam down a stream of light from time to time. Colonel Halt doggedly pursued the lights with his troops and audio recorder in tow. They encountered a craft that appeared to be non-terrestrial. Here is the version of events he related to his superiors in the U.S. Air Force, in the memo Colonel Halt provided (as originally produced along with his misspellings and typos).

DEPARTMENT OF THE AIR FORCE

HEADQUARTERS 81ST COMBAT SUPPORT [USAFE]

APO NEW YORK 09755

REPLTY TO

ATTN OF: CD   13 Jan 81

SUBJECT: Unexplained Lights

TO: RAF/CC

1. Early in the morning of 27 Dec 80 (approximately 0300L), two USAF security police patrolmen saw unusual lights outside the back gate at RAF Woodbridge. Thinking an aircraft might have crashed or been forced down, they called for permission to go outside the gate to investigate. The on-duty flight chief responded and allowed to patrolmen to proceed on foot. The individuals reported seeing a strange glowing object in the forest. The object was described as being metalic in appearance and triangular in shape, approximately two to three meters across the base and approximately two meters high. It illuminated the entire forest with a white light. The object itself had pulsing red light on top and a bank(s) of blue lights underneath. The object was hovering or on legs. As the patrolmen approached the object, it maneuvered through the trees and disappeared. At this time the animals on a nearby farm went into a frenzy. The object was briefly sighted approximately an hour later near the back gate.

2. The next day, three depressions 1 1/2" deep and 7" in diameter were found where the object had been sighted on the ground. The following night (29 Dec 80) the area was checked for radiation. Beta/ gamma readings of 0.1 milliroentgens were recorded with peak readings in the three depressions and near the center of the triangle formed by the depressions. A nearby tree had moderate (.05-.07) readings on the side of the tree toward the depressions.

3. Later in the night a red sun-like light was seen through the trees. It moved about and pulsed. At one point it appeared to throw off glowing particles and then broke into five separate white objects and then disappeared. Immediately thereafter, three star-like objects were noticed in the sky, two objects to the north and one to the south. all of which were about 10° off the horizon. The objects moved rapidly in sharp angular movements and displayed red, green and blue lights. The objects to the north appeared to be elliptical through an 8-12 power lens. They then turned to full circles. The objects to the north remained in the sky for an hour or more. The object to the south was visible for two or three hours and beamed down a stream of light from time to time. Numerous individuals, including the undersigned, witnessed the activities in paragraphs 2 and 3.

(signature)

CHARLES I. HALT, Lt Col, USAF

Deputy Base Commander

Here is what Colonel Halt left out of this memo.

The Colonel and several of his young troops spent a terrifying night trudging through a dark forest in the wee hours of the morning and tracking down what they believed to be an unknown otherworldly craft that could have, at any moment, turned on them and destroyed them. Instinctively, they knew their puny side arms would be of no use against things that displayed the type of technology they were observing. They saw shape-shifting, plasma-like craft that: led them on a merry chase through dark forests, that floated without noise, supported by unearthly technology, left radioactive imprints throughout the forest, that acted in strange ways—bumping into trees like a wounded animal, that were etched with symbols unknown in any human language; and which finally shot what seemed like a laser at the ground close to them. Then the craft itself broke into five orbs, *which all flew away in separate directions.* Imagine a freshman army private confronting this kind of technology in the middle of the night—and seeing raw fear in a Colonel's eyes. Their only consolation was that the craft they were tracking decided not to take the entire military contingent with them to where ever it went.

There have been claims that the USAF videotaped the entire incident; and I believe that is true but if so, the resulting videotape has gone same nameless global government site as the original "Halt cassette tape." Incidentally, even the recorder used by Colonel Halt to contemporaneously record the entire incident was disappeared as well. Several peripheral minor items of direct evidence also disappeared without a trace or any chain of custody form being left behind. EPIC agents left nothing to chance.

National government bureaucrats, military or civilian, *do not* make such things happen; unless they are working in obedience to EPIC. They have many layers of accountability set into place to prevent such cover-ups or at least to leave behind a trace here and there when such cover-ups are executed. Such traces are not evident in this case. Additionally, national government workers, especially at the higher levels, don't tend to be great risk takers for such an insignificant return. The agenda served here is that of The Shark, not the guppies, so it is most likely that the agents of the Shark who have acted as "the cleaners" here.

Fortunately, they decided to leave Colonel Halt himself behind, never thinking he would eventually reveal everything he knew about this incident and the subsequent cover-up. Since the incident, Colonel Halt and the troops present that night have had exerted against them every manner of coercion, oblique threats, implied promises of retribution, overt hostility from superiors, unwarranted transfers and disciplinary actions; all intended to work toward a single purpose: to shut their mouths about what happened at Rendlesham military base. Possession of truth inconvenient to the Great Shark can be a dangerous thing.

In June 2010, long after he retired, Colonel Halt publicly issued a notarized affidavit in which he stated:

"I believe the objects that I saw at close quarter were extraterrestrial in origin and that the security services of both the United States and the United Kingdom have attempted – both then and now – to subvert the significance of what occurred at Rendlesham Forest and RAF Bentwaters by the use of well-practiced methods of disinformation."

Since his retirement, Colonel Halt has been attacked publicly by his superior officers protecting their Carpet Stain. They misinterpret Colonel Halt's truth telling as an attack upon them and their institutions. It is nothing of the sort. Halt and other government officials who are victimized by a system that turns on its' most loyal servants, are only trying to get to the truth of the cover up that was enacted at Rendlesham. Unfortunately, the Carpet-Stain Monitors who persecute them are ignorant of the real agenda they are serving. They believe they are defending their national institutions by attacking "whistleblowers." In truth, they are doing the opposite. They are weakening their national institutions by serving an agenda that demands complete submission and subjugation from the nations—the agenda of Global Government.

Eventually, the shark gets everybody.

1. This agenda doesn't mind if we are aware of the presence of Extra-Dimensionals (indeed that is one of the main objectives of ED activity) but they don't want us to pick up too many clues or details about the real truth of Extra-Dimensionals— who they really are and where they really come from. That is why all direct physical evidence of the Rendlesham event has been "disappeared" without a trace—because those items would have produced crucial clues that the Great White Shark could not bear should come to light.

Once Colonel Halt, the Commander of the base, and other troops from the Rendlesham incident decided to talk publicly about what happened to them with the Extra-Dimensionals, it helped others in a similar position to feel some support. Since that time, a much greater number of high government officials throughout all the Western nations have come forward to speak of similar experiences. If you have any doubt of this, read the brilliant compilation of testimonies in Leslie Kean's book: "UFOs: Generals, Pilots and Government Officials Go On the Record."

The national governments can no longer control the information that comes out of major events like Rendlesham and their denials and attempts to suppress such information make them look foolish. EPIC will soon change their strategy to accommodate this new reality.

29

FACING THE GIANTS

Humanity was told of ancient days: *"There were GIANTS on the Earth in those days."*

Today, again we face giants. Today's giants are not the monstrous eaters of humans recounted to us by every ancient human civilization. The Awakened largely believes those giants have fallen into extinction after their failed efforts to extinguish humanity. While EPIC sends their minions all over the Earth to disappear the bones and relics of these giant races before the common herd can see them, they cannot cover up the evidence of these new "giants."

These new behemoths are the gigantic, non-terrestrial craft that now regularly appear in our skies: triangle or boomerang shaped, silent, black, apparently metallic ships, sometimes as large as half a mile in breadth or even a mile or more across their span. They typically appear over medium to heavily populated areas, moving slow and low for a minute or two and then they disappear—in other words, they behave very much as if *they wish to be seen.*

These cases have gradually become more common in the last thirty years. There are ufologists who based their entire scholarship on just the giant triangle/boomerang cases because they are so physically compelling. Their sheer immense size taps into primordial terrors humans retain from the recesses of our collective unconscious.

UFO triangle incidents like the Hudson Valley incident and many others around the world display what appear to be gigantic black metallic ships with: no thrust-producing or conventional engines heard or felt (perhaps a slight humming sound), no noise, a floating trajectory over a populated area and triangle or boomerang shaped ships which tend to be anywhere from several hundred yards wide up to several miles from wingtip to wingtip. That would be physically overwhelming to any human being it floated over. The sheer physicality of such an experience would be traumatic; yet despite this, these ships dissipate, disappear or dematerialize after a short time. It's as if they were never physical at all.

Both the 1952 Washington D.C. incidents and the Rendlesham encounters had overwhelming empirical and material proof produced that they were genuine paranormal encounters with Non-Terrestrial life. These mountains of proof could withstand even the most cynical scientific scrutiny. The Giant Triangle/Boomerang cases do not offer us the same level of empirical evidence for three major reasons:

1. They tend to be short lived in duration—sometimes just a minute or two before the craft disappears. By comparison, the 1952 Washington D.C. incidents lasted over a span of ten days during which sightings and encounters by the U.S. Air force were continuous. The Rendlesham incident occurred over a span of three days during which military soldiers kept visual contact with plasma-like craft traveling in and out of their base.

2. The "shock and freeze factor" is greater than in typical ET craft contact cases—whenever people encounter a genuine paranormal craft there is momentary (or longer) "shock and freeze" during which the extreme wonder of the situation takes hold of their bodies and they remain fixed or rooted to the spot. Their mind is attempting to analyze what they believe might be happening so the body cooperates by remaining completely still during the initial phase of the event. If the event goes on for more than a minute, some people have the presence of mind to snap into action and go for a camera or a video recorder but those people tend to be the exception rather than the rule. This answers the common question that arises whenever people experience an extraordinary but fleeting paranormal event: *"why didn't you get pictures or video?"*

This question usually comes from people who have never experienced a paradigm shifting moment in their lives.

3. Unusually effective disinformation campaigns are always put into action right after a paranormal giant triangle/boomerang event. In part, this is meant to dissuade a good portion of the testimonial evidence from coming forward—*and it works*. It's hard not to see a mile wide craft slowly floating over your community. If you are outside or any near the open air, you just look up. People call each other. They compare notes and realize they all saw the exact same thing: a low flying, noiseless, black, metallic, triangle-shaped ship—a mile wide—floating over their community and then disappearing without a trace. They go to sleep that night excited to get up the next morning and discuss it with more people, at school, at work and at maybe even at church (maybe not at church). But when they get up the next morning, the disinformation machine is running at full tilt and *its everywhere*. The local military base commander has announced that the supposed "giant triangle ship" was just military flares dropped in formation over the community as part of a military exercise that had been "unscheduled." The government and the military provide an alternate explanation—flimsy but somewhat plausible. The mainstream media—local and national is amplifying that explanation and adding their subtle comments about *"some local elements in the community who thought it might have been UFO's from outer space...."* (insert smug news anchor smirk and chuckle).

From that point forward, it becomes much harder for those in positions of responsibility (aka: people who have jobs) to come forward and say what they really saw. There will always be those who will say the truth without caring about the consequences but they are very few and as time goes on more will arrive at the decision to tell the truth but many of them will reach that decision long after it no longer matters because the news crews will have left and the national interest will have died out. The moment to stand in the gap and tell the truth was when the hot lights of attention burned bright on the scene. Those who come forward long afterward do little to bolster the credibility of those isolated and ridiculed few who told the truth earlier.

Most people are not aware that the purpose of a good disinformation campaign is not to convince everyone or to even come close to that goal. The real goal of disinformation is to just convince a bare majority (51 percent or above) of the truth of the official explanation. Sadly, our populations produce much higher percentages people who are easily convinced by anything pronounced by "the authorities." This majority joined with institutional power (use and control of mainstream media, the military, government resources) is more than enough to "keep a lid on potential awakening events." With the mainstream media in tow, most of the common herd is easily persuaded that the false alternate explanation is the true explanation. In this way, most of those who know the real truth will be cowed into remaining silent when it counts.

The typical simulation estimates after a good plausible disinformation campaign: 60 to 70 percent of most populations will immediately accept whatever false explanation they are given especially once it is amplified through the corporate mainstream media. They are happy to receive any disinformation that allows them to continue living inside that comfortable box and so they consume it like candy. These are people who don't want to be troubled with profound thoughts. They don't want to have their daily routine disrupted.

They don't care to awaken.

I have, over the last two decades, interviewed witnesses who have seen highly traumatizing events that they can never "un-see" no matter how hard they try. The memories are retained by them, not as misty, half-remembered dreams, but as moving images permanently ingrained in a viewing chamber in their brain. The tape is always prepared and ready to roll at any moment. Certain combinations of words associated with the memory will trigger the immediate playing of those rolling images. They see the events replay before their eyes again even as they are speaking about it. Like a technician summoning up a wide screen hologram, the interviewer has summoned up the events and the witness sees them again as if for the first time.

Among such witnesses, I spoke with is a mother who saw numerous people machine-gunned to death in front of her and experienced the shooting of her own baby wrapped in swaddling clothes (the baby boy survived). Her baby just took one bullet to the wrist and didn't even cry due to shock. The mother, who escaped unscathed, later noticed a tiny trail of blood from her silent infant. The baby never made a sound. The infant escaped without memory of the incident but the mother would carry those images to her grave. Whenever she was interviewed about the horrific event she would immediately begin viewing a projector she imagined in front of her eyes that played the events of that day. It wasn't really there except in her mind. She could describe every agonizing detail of that day's events—not just the sights but smells, textures and even other peoples' emotions.

Other such witnesses are wives who saw their husbands blown up by improvised devices in front of their eyes and even people who've seen ships that could not possibly be from this Earth float right over their heads and then disappear into thin air. As they begin to recount the tale, something physiological is triggered in the synapses of their brain and their optical nerves. The witnesses' eyes will start darting quickly from side to side because they are watching the tape play. This doesn't even disrupt that cadence of their speech because they have become so accustomed to that same tape rolling that it has become a concurrent activity that they integrate seamlessly into their motor reflexes—like just another ball the juggler keeps in the air. But the interviewer will notice it and find it a bit perturbing.

One of the most powerful elements in determining witness authenticity is direct observation of the biological reactions in the witness recounting the events. We no longer need to consider *only* cases like the 1952 D.C. sightings and Rendlesham that produce massive empirical evidence. Experiential truth is the greatest truth. We are at the end of the age in which we require scientific validation of paranormal truth. Applying a scientific standard in the world of the paranormal is like trying to make a salt-water fish live in a fresh water tank.

Consider the buyer spending all that money at the aquarium and buying an exotic salt-water fish, bringing him home, dumping him in a fresh water tank because the buyer's friends told him it should not be a problem. Then, those same advisors will tell the buyer the fish must have been defective because this species should have adapted to the fresh water (despite all the warnings on the transport bag against doing exactly that).

"Take it back. Demand your money back."

So the holder of the dead fish goes back. The seller explains nothing was wrong with the fish. It was the medium that you put him in that condemned the fish to a slow agonizing death.

"Your friends were wrong. That particular fish could never survive in fresh water. Didn't you read the warning labels on the bag?"

The purchaser feels stupid and protests about how knowledgeable his friends were about fish. The seller raises an eyebrow as he gently takes the dead fish for disposal.

"Maybe they wanted your fish dead. *They should pay you.*"

We are committing the same atrocity whenever we take an experiential paranormal reality and toss it into the tank of scientific validation—just to see what happens. I can tell you what happens.

It dies. It always dies.

30

THE PARANORMAL CONCEPT FORMULA

Yet calls for physical evidence never cease. Pithy slogans abound like:

"I don't want to believe, I want to know." This is a challenge for paranormal believers to provide physical evidence that is so overwhelming that non-believers will actually be *forced to believe.* Sounds insane if you read it out loud yet this is exactly the self-defeating behavior loop that paranormal believers have been repeating for centuries.

This is the same challenge issued by the biblical Pharisees to Jesus when they demanded He show them a sign of His miraculous powers so that they might also *see and believe.* They were not asking to believe—they were asking *to be forced to believe.* Jesus refused because He knew that no matter how much proof He showed them either they would still find a way to disbelieve or, even worse, Christ would be guilty of violating their free will. Indeed, later it was these same men who testified in a kangaroo court that Jesus *had* done miracles *"through the power of the devil."* This is why He warned us not to cast our pearls before swine.

If you want to see the salt-water fish analogy in action, peruse any of the numerous mainstream television, cable and satellite shows and documentaries that deal with paranormal topics. Many will have short memorable titles filled with the promises of mysteries soon to be solved and secrets to be revealed.

Spirit-Hunters
Searching Out Bigfoot
Revealing Chupacabra
Discovering Nessy
Ghost-Finders
Ghost-Seekers
Ghost-Discovery...*you get the idea*

These shows and documentaries are very popular despite the fact that they all follow the same premise and formula. They begin by creating thrills and chills around alleged supernatural phenomena. They engage audience interest and capture the imagination of viewers by trumpeting all the reasons why the phenomena *might* be true and genuine. Finally, they collect and employ massive amounts of "scientific" equipment in order to appear ready to generate massive, undeniable proof of paranormal reality:

- Photographic and video equipment—digital, latest generation night vision and infrared
- EMF meter to detect possible unexplained fluctuations in electromagnetic fields.
- Thermographic cameras, thermal imaging cameras, infrared thermometers, and other infrared temperature sensors to measure surface temperature
- Digital and analog audio recording: to capture any unexplained noises and electronic voice phenomena (EVPs), that may be disembodied voices
- Geiger counter: to measure fluctuations in radiation
- Ion meters: to detect an excess of negative ions.
- Infrared and/or ultrasonic motion sensors: to detect movement within a given area
- Air quality monitoring equipment: to assess the levels of gases such as carbon monoxide
- Infrasound monitoring equipment: to assess the level of sound vibrations

No matter how inappropriate the equipment might be (a Geiger Counter?) it serves the overall purpose of creating an impression of potential, scientific validation of paranormal reality. These shows have investigators typically run around in circles and record instances of "phenomena" on all their equipment: unknown sounds, sightings (of something unexplained), carbon monoxide fluctuations? and much more data that proves…*well, actually it proves nothing.*

At times, as the data rolls in and the investigators are terrified of some unknown rattling in the dark, it seems like the salt-water fish is actually going to survive in that freshwater…but invariably by the end of the show or documentary; there it is: *gills up* in the freshwater tank. Many of these shows should have a word added to each of the titles. They should have been named slightly differently.

Not revealing Chupacabra,
Not discovering Nessy
Not Finding Ghosts—because ultimately they all end with the same stinking dead fish.

"Well folks, we got a lot of good data so we can't wait to get it all back to lab so we can come to our final conclusions that we'll share with you next week."

"We collected great new information that people said we could never get."

"Wow, I'm super excited about this new evidence which will lead us to new undeniable truths about the future and how we can continue to reveal and discover the hidden things in hidden places. See you next week."

Not if I see you first.

These shows begin with chills and thrills but by the end they leave true Paranormal Believers (and pretty much the entire audience) feeling empty and unsatisfied. I have monitored and studied the treatment of paranormal topics on television, radio and alternative media for over twenty years. These subjects matter *much more* than politics, finances, sports and all the mainstream tripe that occupies popular media—all put together, because paranormal truths relate to eternal realities instead of temporary things. People in a low vibration of existence (exclusively material/physical vibration) will find that statement bewildering; but those who vibrate at a spiritual/metaphysical level will resonate with the truth of that statement. There have been a few tiny, baby-steps of progress in the treatment of legitimate paranormal topics but it has been far too little now that the Awakening Age is here.

The major improvement is that most such shows now entertain the possibility that there may be some truth in the paranormal topic—maybe these ghosts do exist, maybe these Alien Visitors have really been in contact with this person, maybe these crypto-animals really do truly exist? This is *mere tolerance* disguised as progress. Here is the formula currently being used for some moderately successful paranormal shows (the ones that will last for just two or three seasons with very high ratings by current cable standards):

1. Assemble a core group of experienced phenomena hunters. These are often the grizzled warriors of the paranormal field who have established some minimal "standards of the industry" in the area they are known for. They bring the "gravitas" to the show. They are usually a team of men who are already well known in their niche paranormal circles. They have spent a significant portion of their lives using scientific equipment to hunt, detect, prove and sometimes disprove supernatural phenomena. Even within this group, there is always at least one person assigned the role of skeptic/debunker/non-believer/strictly scientific materialist. That is the person assigned to emote the standard cynic catch phrases:

   "I won't believe it unless I see it for myself.

   We would need a lot of evidence on this one guys.

   This witness is missing a lot in the credibility department."

   It is believed this role brings balance and objectivity to the situation by keeping everyone honest.

2. Added to this mix are the younger, open-minded seekers who are experienced as physical investigators and have fresh, innovative ideas for contribution to this effort to accumulate evidence of the paranormal phenomena.

3. Then, during each case file investigation, they approach the initial preliminary inquiry into witnesses and supernatural incidents by lavishly illustrating the allegations, assertions and claims of what occurred according to allegations. This is the *thrills and chills buildup portion*, which relies heavily on production values to "pump up" the excitement factor. This is where television excels. The build ups are at this stage often quite exciting and even captivating to believers and skeptics alike.

4. Then all team members assemble and make it clear that they will act within the confines of scientific proof for which they will collect, examine and assign relative values in terms of evidence. In other words, they agree to obey the dictates of the exact system under which paranormal truth **can never be proven true.**

5. Then, the investigation goes forward and a great, furious torrent of movement, activity and even chaos is released leading to the collection of substantial amounts of materials, evidence and more testimony. At the end of this examination, even the team member assigned the skeptic role makes the wide-eyed admission that something extraordinary *may have been proved here today.* The matter is declared a success due to the enormous amount of data collected for analysis and is concluded until next week.

This type of paranormal "schlock" show is proliferating even as these words are being written because they bring television executives the type of success they are most interested in—short term/high impact. They can generate a show like this for relatively little cost, create temporary high ratings and good buzz (because people of all kinds hunger for the paranormal). These high ratings are unsustainable long term due to the inherent weakness of the formula but it doesn't matter. The show is cancelled after two to three seasons but they have a hit on their resume and can go on to other projects that they actually believe in and care about.

We need a major reorganization in the Paranormal. Believers in the paranormal and even those with open minds deserve better. First, we need to realize that not all paranormal topics translate at all to visual medium like television so we need to just stop throwing night vision cameras into old "haunted" places and having assistant producers rattle chains upstairs while the "investigators" downstairs scream and run in circles. That's very insulting to actual paranormal believers and also to real ghosts who must be rather put off about being represented in such a ludicrous context.

Second, we need to cancel treatments of paranormal topics from the perspective of trying use absurd "scientific" equipment to prove something by collecting irrelevant data (excluding image capturing equipment). This works for short-term ratings but never for long-range programming success or for paranormal authenticity. This old formula is only sustainable for short periods and it never rewards true paranormal believers (the loyal core of any audience for such a show)—it only entertains those who consider the paranormal a curiosity at best. Those curiosity seekers add up to a great number of people but their loyalty will always be a mile wide but only an inch deep. They soon tire of that stale formula and depart the show—explaining the initial high ratings that peter out so quickly.

31

THE NEW PARANORMAL FORMULA

What I am about to reveal is the formula that has been attempted piecemeal in various disparate genres—to great success. Different aspects of this new formula have been sporadically used at different times but once joined into a single formula they will guarantee long-term success, high ratings, credibility in the area of the paranormal— which will, in turn, lead to a whole new set of rewards. It is the complete unified formula for long-term success for any paranormal-themed show. The revelation of this integrated formula is conservatively worth $10,000,000.00 USD but you are getting it for the price of a book. Here is the Formula Reveal:

1. Complete dissolution of the old paranormal "schlock" formula. Not as easy as it sounds. Bury it, sow the ground with salt and forget it ever existed.

    This is key. Professional people braving new areas, when they get scared, instinctively want to run back to what used to work. Put it in contracts that there is no returning or degeneration back to the old formula upon pain of dissolution of the production. Burn those ships at the shore as the troops move forward.

2. Hire *a single* leader in the paranormal area; not a committee of equals, not a council, not a whole team or collective. That person must be a paranormal believer with a great deal of experience in the area that is being investigated. Hiring *a team* of experts only leads to disagreements, jockeying for superior position and competition within the ranks for airtime. This is always reflected in the product that goes before the cameras. Gravitas and leadership must be delivered by a single person. They must be given control and final cut of the production. No paranormal media project should ever go forward without a true believer at the helm—not just consulting—but actually *in charge of the project.*

    Every paranormal program should be done from the perspective of true believers, harnessing their authenticity as a platform jump off point and then taking every step in recognition of the fact that this truth is experiential—but not always empirical.

An example of such a leader in the area of gigantic, supernatural, Extra-Dimensional craft is Dr. Lynne Kitei who has done several documentaries and television programs based on The Giants—the Phoenix Lights of 1997. She also was in one the best movies I've ever seen—"Raising Arizona" by the Coen brothers. In her book and documentary: "The Phoenix Lights: A Skeptic's Discovery That We Are Not Alone," she treats the subject matter with respect and even reverence as only a true believer can. Her new documentary "The Phoenix Lights: Above Top Secret" delves further into what is being seen in the skies over Arizona and the world. This is a person of tremendous gravitas, with great vision, experience and determination to see her paranormal topic treated with deference and respect.

Add a small group of investigators who should be *attractive women and men* that are paranormal believers themselves in the area that is being investigated. Age doesn't matter. All age groups should be included as long as they are physically attractive. Television is a visual medium and it has been proven over and over that in every demographic target group, people (*both men and women*) will tolerate a show long enough to learn what it is about—if attractive women and men are put out front.

I didn't make the world, I just live in it.

Yet, as important as the physical requirement is, the *more* important requirement is that *they must be genuine believers like the leader of the group*. This is of greater importance for success than anything else. Each member of that investigative team must be able to convince audiences, beyond any shadow of doubt, that *they have had paranormal experiences* and have a real belief in the area that is being investigated. There should be rotating, beautifully re-enacted mini-bios on the members' personal paranormal experiences featured on a regular basis to reinforce the "true believer" aspect of the show. Beware—*as you know*—people will say anything to get on television.

3. This is crucial: Omit the formulaic role of cynic/doubter/scientific materialist from the team. The rest of mainstream culture and cultural conditioning throughout the planet provides enormous counter balance against the purveyors of true faith and belief in any supernatural topic. Also, have the Leader always make it clear that the investigation is not restricted or determined by the scientific paradigm—that the truth of the investigative conclusion is ultimately decided by "the experiencer" and by the leader's final investigative conclusion based on human authenticity. The experiencer involved will make the initial allegation over whether the paranormal phenomenon was "real" but the leader will make the final determination.

4. Let the investigation go forward with emphasis on methods that emphasize the experiencer/witness/Contactee point of view—re-enactments, recreations, witness testimony. This should be the gradual unfolding of pristine authenticity

in public. Limit the intrusion of "scientific devices" and data wherever possible. Instead, use as much circumstantial evidence as possible to bolster the experiencer's credibility. There can still be the usage of scientific devices but it must be clear that these are added props to supplement the main item of evidence: *the direct supernatural connection of the authentic paranormal experiencer to a universe beyond ours.*

The experiencer must be treated with the same respect and deference that a criminal investigative show gives to victims of serious crime. The production template should actually more closely follow that of successful crime-investigation shows than the old paranormal formula.

5. The final judge over what has been proven during the show will be the leader (and possibly a live audience who would vote, be surveyed before and after and give commentary after the show). There should be input from the team members but the final say at the end of every show on what has been proven *and why* must belong to the leader. The final statistical accomplishment should be the conversion of *even one member* of the audience into a believer in a new paranormal truth. Attention will be focused on that conversion and why and how it was that they were convinced.

Overall, numbers should not be depicted. No one is looking to convert a majority of the audience or believes that would even be realistic—this is still outside the mainstream, after all.

Again, the leader of the group must have nearly full control over this process. Producers will still produce but the Leader/Believer must have final cut.

There it is—the complete, incredibly powerful formula for guaranteed long-term success for any paranormal show. If the formula is followed faithfully, it will ensure a wide following, exploding ratings but most importantly: a hardcore faithful audience whose loyalty will have very deep roots and their followership will lead to expansion of these themes into grand new venues currently undreamt of even by Paranormal Believers.

It won't be easy but it will be worth it.

32

MORE GIANTS ON THE EARTH

- Over the course of the 1980's, culminating in 1986, huge triangular or V-shaped UFOs were observed by people on the ground in the Hudson River Valley just north of New York City. More than five thousand people during one such incident reported seeing these objects. There are hundreds of police reports scattered over several towns evidencing these observations. One witness stated: *"If there is such a thing as a flying city, this was a flying city."* Others elaborated that the giant black triangle, also described as a "giant boomerang," moved slowly and silently and *was as big as three football fields.* Thousands of people, cutting across all socio-economic spectrums, went on record sometimes at great professional risk to themselves, saying that the giant craft was real. Two witnesses reported the boomerang was six stories tall and *that it shot off to the far horizon and came back to the same spot in barely a second.* A police officer sitting in a cruiser saw the giant boomerang with white lights in a half-circle hover over her vehicle for twenty seconds. She was surprised at herself that she never thought to aim her radar gun at it. The Federal Aviation Administration and other national government agencies denied anything happened.

- There was a massive PUFO wave in Belgium from 1989-1990 during which people on the ground observed giant black craft. From October 1989 throughout December 1990, there were hundreds of reports of luminescent objects, described as enormous and triangular. United States Air Force F-16 jets were observed tracking the objects, which showed up on airborne and ground radars. There are voluminous photos, recorded evidence and eyewitness testimonies memorialized from this period in Belgium.

- In the early morning hours of Jan. 5, 2000, numerous police officers from a number of small Illinois towns observed a giant triangle flying low over their jurisdictions. The officers were able to track the unknown object and maintain radio contact with each other during the event. Scott Air Force Base was only two miles away from the flight path of the UFO. Police officers of the Shiloh

Police Department radioed each other from various points along the ground as a giant triangle object flew low above Shiloh. Like runners handing off a baton, they each maintained the eye from the ground on the object for as long as they could and then called out for another officer to take over the visual on the object. One officer on the ground compared the vehicle to the Millennium Falcon spacecraft from the motion picture "Star Wars." The police observed three brilliant white lights, which were shining downward from the object. Small red and green lights were observed on the back end of the object. They estimated the object's altitude at only about 1,000 feet. The shape they described was of an extra wide triangle that was about 100 yards wide. The local Air Force Base advised they had no craft in the area at that time and did not detect any such vehicles in that area either.

- A giant triangular PUFO was photographed over Carolina, Puerto Rico, in 2005. Observers described an immense triangular object, which they compared to the size of two enormous ballparks. They also said the object was going very slowly and when it passed directly over observers, there was no sound at all. The object traveled slowly and deactivated all electronics beneath the passing craft except cameras.

- At Guernsey, United Kingdom, in 2007, two airline pilots *on separate flights* saw the same enormous mile long object floating perfectly still off the coast of Alderney. It appeared as a cigar shaped yellow object with a green area. It was 2,000 feet up and frozen in a stationary position. One pilot observed it from 40 miles away, while the second saw it directly beneath his airplane. The passengers saw it also and it was picked up by nearby radar before it disappeared.

- In 2008, dozens of observers in Stephenville and Dublin, Texas, reported seeing an enormous Paranormal UFO. The observers made reports that they had seen a large silent object with bright lights flying low and they also spotted fighter jets in the area possibly chasing it. The object was cigar-shaped but its' outlines were difficult to decipher due to its sheer immensity. It was like a massive super-submarine floating through the air and its lights also shifted and changed configuration.

33

THE DISSUASION FIELD

Here are some crucial new clues in this area.

Here is something I find very curious: how is it that *no one has ever* reported the discharging a firearm at one of these low, hovering, slow moving, giant targets? For police officers who have witnessed these craft and for most residents of Arizona—thousands of whom observed the Phoenix Lights in 1997, firearms are a familiar part of life. It can take an educated shooter as little as a quarter of a second to draw and fire two rounds from thought to completion.

Accounting even for the amplified "shock and freeze" factor which can last anywhere from one to five seconds, a very few observers can actually shake off those effects off pretty quickly. This is evidenced by numerous photographs and videos taken of the giants; viewable on the Internet. There have been normal sized PUFO's in the past that have hovered still in the air at great distance. Those normal sized targets tend not to be within "a stone's throw" of the observers. At times, the giants have gone from slowly moving to just hovering in a stationery position directly over gun toting, anxious, frightened witnesses. Yet, not even a single law-enforcement officer, off duty peace officer or armed citizen has ever been reported taking a shot at one of these giants. There is testimonial witness evidence that such thoughts have occurred to some of the police officer observers, even when they've had devices that merely simulate guns.

- *I was going to point my gun at the craft but then a thought popped into my mind that it would be a bad idea.*
- *I was going to raise my gun at the thing but then something made me stop. I suddenly thought that would be a terrible thing to do.*
- *Since I was on the road monitoring speeders, I had the thing right with me so I was surprised at myself afterward that I didn't think to point my radar-gun at the craft.*

In Hollywood movies, the alien ships always have a "force-field" that deflects or disintegrates any missiles, bullets or any human originated projectiles of any kind. This gives them invulnerability to any attempted force exerted against them. It is also yet another example of anthropomorphizing of the Extra-Dimensionals. Humans would use force fields for invulnerability against attacks because it fits in with human thinking. A force shield is the most direct human way to deal with force exerted upon an object. More advanced beings think differently from humans. Would not a more effective way to avert or defend against an attack be to stop it *in the mind of the attacker?*

The giants appear to have, instead of a force field—"a dissuasion field" which convinces anyone who has aggressive thoughts or intentions that they should not attempt any action against the Giants. When the giants *do* return in greater size and number—look for soldiers, Air Force pilots and law-enforcement to disobey direct orders to shoot at the giants—but they won't be to blame for the disobedience to direct orders. It will be "the field" *that made them **not** do it.*

34

GOLDIE'S REPRIEVE

I cannot depart from this subject without recounting an anecdote, which illuminates several of the core concepts of this work. I have an assistant named Goldie who is no end of helpful during every phase of putting together works like the one you are reading right now. She acts as my organizer and administrator. While Goldie is skillful and dedicated in the assemblage and editing of books on the paranormal, her own personal beliefs do not include the paranormal at all. As a matter of fact, she is a very devout *religious* believer and does not tolerate the introduction in her worldview of any precepts or beliefs that are not expressly approved by her religious sect. While she does, on occasion tolerate discussion of paranormal subjects, it will always lead her to proclaim the official religious outlook of her religion as the final word on that topic.

One bright sunny day, we were scouting a location in Sedona, Arizona, which was rumored in the Awakened Community to have many phasing morphogenic fields that magnify paranormal abilities. Something strange happened in the skies directly over our heads. I turned to Goldie who was occupied trying to shoo away a persistent horsefly.

"Goldie, do you remember that I was talking to you about Giant Alien Vehicles which appear all over the world?" Goldie swatted at the persistent critter that was trying to get under her wide brim hat with her. She was not happy with Sedona at that moment.

"Yes, of course I remember that. Why are you bringing that up now?" I took a step away from her side and turned toward her to gauge her reaction.
"Goldie, look up into the sky and to your left." It was an enormous cloud formation that had, for some reason, assumed the perfect curvature, lines and shape of a giant boomerang ship at least two miles across the sky. It loomed over our position and dominated the entire sky over our position. It was a perfect and flawless cumulus representation of an otherworldly craft.

Goldie looked directly up at the cumulus formation. She forgot about the fly.
"Oh, my God. How scary!"

She took a step back toward the car.

Her hands clasped into her chest.

The immensity and perfection of the shape was staggering.

She looked at me with eyes wide but then she rubbed her eyes and shook her head. On this hot, gusty day, by the time she looked back up the perfect imitation of the Giant Boomerang Craft had begun sprouting defects and losing its shape. It had actually only held together for about three seconds. She was relieved.

"Oh, okay. It was just a coincidence. It was nothing. Just a cloud that looked a certain way." She had successfully regrouped herself and her worldview as the cumulus outline came apart. Goldie got her reprieve from *having to believe.*

I believe in many things. I believe in all paranormal topics that persist in the consciousness of people. One thing I don't believe in and *never* will believe in is *coincidence.* Cloud formations that *perfectly* imitate Giant Craft and smaller Paranormal UFOs as well are a very common occurrence that are often photographed and even recorded on videos. With a cursory Internet search you can find dozens if not hundreds of such phenomena. These are not clouds that resemble or could be Alien craft. *They are **perfect** images in a cumulus canvass.*

These perfect formations only tend to hold for a few seconds but sometimes they persist longer, long enough for people to get out their recording devices. Here's what else I believe: I believe that the Giants are coming in and out of our atmosphere constantly, that they are usually cloaked, invisible, imperceptible to human senses and that as they materialize into our physical universe or dematerialize out of it, that they only leave an occasional cumulus silhouette outline of where they have ingressed or egressed.

This is like the cartoon characters that realize they are standing on empty air, wave goodbye and fall down into the canyon. They only leave behind a momentary cloud shaped exactly like them. I believe all this and I'll tell you who else believes it—or at least *did* believe it if only for a second. Goldie did.

Although it was only for a moment, Goldie's worldview was upended by the new reality she saw above her head in the sky, but then that moment receded and her worldview came rushing back in to keep her safe from new realities. Goldie and most others will remain safe in their old paradigms because they fight for the comfort it provides. Yet, that too will end when the Giants finally come without cloaks, invisibility or cumulus cover.

In this area, the game changer will come from us, not from the Extra-Dimensionals. Sightings of the Giants are becoming very common and soon we will, as a society, do what this work recommends—stop running on the gerbil wheel of "lets convince, persuade, force people to believe that this stuff is true." That is a fruitless endeavor. Instead, we should concentrate on being ready for the Giants, not with cameras and video equipment but with telepathic presence of mind and a readiness to challenge their methods and to let them know we no longer quake and quiver at their appearance. We must not lose ourselves in astonishment. Then, the Giants will leave but they will return. Next time, they will be as large as Cities and yet others as large as a moon or a planet and they will just park just within our collective sight so they can again restart the cycle of astonishment and wonder. They will step up their game and we must do likewise.

Here is the next great reveal of this work. The giants are real but there are bigger ones out there and—*they are coming.*

THE EXTRA-DIMENSIONAL AGENDA

Someone Is Trying To Enslave You

35

IT'S JUST FICTION

I have followed the movie industry with great interest for as long as I have been researching and work-shopping paranormal belief systems—about the last 20 years. Here is another inescapable conclusion that I have reached during that time. The movie industry is a vital component in the "Elite Powers In Control's" (EPIC's) global efforts to capture and control all perceptions as they relate to supernatural and paranormal topics. By "movie industry" I mean the Hollywood, mainstream, establishment movie industry, which no longer dominates but still has great influence around the globe. They retain this power only because of the money and human talent they can coordinate and funnel towards projects that are guaranteed green lights and mega-corporate blessings. EPIC and their minions have a great interest in what goes forward in the area of movie making. This industry is crucial to the agenda of confiscating, controlling and shaping global perceptions and attitudes on any rising or prominent paranormal topic. The goal is to lock down and strictly limit all cultural thinking on that particular topic.

This is not to say that corporate Hollywood or anyone who makes movies is part of any predetermined plan to manipulate audiences' thinking. Every person, production company, and moviemaker who are blessed enough to get approval, funding and distribution for their movie are delighted to see their work come to life. In an industry where a great deal of work goes unrecognized and many dreams go unfulfilled, selected artists are just ecstatic to get to do the work they enjoy doing and maybe even gain some recognition for years of labor and toil. These "blessed ones" do not stop to question why their work was picked or developed, funded and sent all over the globe. They do not investigate or care about agendas or elite global cabals. They do not wonder why 99,999 other projects, just as good theirs, were not selected to go forward. They just want to make good—*even great* movies. They are happy to just sit at the "big boy table."

There is no reason to believe that people in the movie industry are anything more than hard-working, dedicated, dreamers trying to bring their vision to life. *But*…this discussion is only pertinent to the *top of the pyramid* of the movie industry. These are the high minions of the movie industry who decide which projects get green lights, get tremendous funding, receive infusions of staggering human talent and are ultimately distributed all around the globe. Conversely they also determine, by omission, which projects will never see the light of day.

Those who actually make the movies just think the selection is based on popular trends in global society or nepotism—who is related to who or just random luck. Nothing could be further from the truth. *There are no coincidences.*

At the highest levels of mega-corporate moviemaking, certain projects are picked to go forward because they coincide with an agenda that is issued from the top of the pyramid. That top of the pyramid gets its orders from the top of another pyramid—a higher tipped pyramid that has sat over humanity since before the misty, prehistoric, dynastic kingdoms that first placed shackles around the necks of human beings.

EPIC controls political, material and economic attitudes directly through the institutions of their minions: the political parties, pharmaceutical conglomerates, the banksters and the corporate media complex. What is more difficult and, quite frankly, more important to EPIC, is controlling the perceptions and attitudes when it comes to paranormal or supernatural topics. This is because, unless it is strictly controlled, rampant belief in paranormal topics can lead to large-scale awakening by the general populace. That awakening could in turn lead to the epiphany that this material universe is just the thin veneer of a façade meant to keep us quiet, docile and obedient during our eon-spanning slavery and imprisonment. It is more important that EPIC control your perceptions and attitudes about black magic sorcery than about the political system or the banks in our economy. This is because unless EPIC successfully limits your imagination about transcendent things, they cannot hope to maintain limits on your earthly thinking.

When we awaken to the fact that Central Banks are just global parasites leeching away the independent sovereignty and overturning the economic freedom of every nation—it doesn't concern EPIC. The Elite Powers In Control of this planet's major institutions are quite comfortable that there is little that we can do about it. EPIC installs and manages the conflict-absorption systems: the political parties, the "democratic" processes, rigged elections and licenses to protest publicly in an orderly and peaceful manner. Beyond those methods, if you're still disgruntled—don't forget to *write your Congressman.*

Meanwhile, Global private banking conglomerates, with help from their national politicians, take over the sovereign rights of nations to produce debt-free money—then they enslave nations through unnecessary debt owed back to these same banksters. Once they finally bankrupt these nations, their proxies—the international economic conglomerates posing as rescuers of these bankrupted nations scoop up the income producing assets of these nations for pennies on the dollar. They become the new Landlords of newly enslaved nations. Members of EPIC already have more money than they could ever spend in many generations so what motivates them is not accumulation of more money. You can only ride around in one helicopter or Lear jet at a time. Its *power* that matters to them—absolute power and control over humanity. The fact that many Awakening Individuals realize this game is afoot makes not a bit of difference to the EPIC because their system of control is so deeply ensconced in global society that they firmly believe no one can form any effective resistance to this system.

However, if these same Awakening Individuals were to realize the truth about paranormal and supernatural realities—it would give them the capability (*perhaps even the imperative*) to *directly partake* in that reality. You don't need a church or an organization to explore paranormal truth. *You can do it on your own.* This, in turn, could lead to an awakening about the very nature of all reality.

In a similar way, whenever religious people have direct miraculous experience with spiritual energy, they often realize that organized religions can be irrelevant to a genuine connection to God. Their connection to the infinite becomes real and direct. They become spiritual in a true and genuine way that is utterly incongruent with organized religion. Participating in yet one more control system—organized religion—becomes far less important than experiencing that wonderful direct connection to eternity that anyone can access through authentic spiritual fervor and faith.

Paranormal Experiencers arrive at a similar epiphany that shifts their worldview, increases their spirituality and intensifies their need to know the real truth of the world around them. Paranormal belief systems have enormous power to awaken and magnify the individual. For this reason, systems of paranormal belief are a greater threat to EPIC than political or social resistance networks.

This is why there are institutions working so hard to foster the reality that paranormal themes are nothing more than irrelevant fantasy. We are taught that fantasy is reality and that reality is fantasy. For instance, magicks and sorcery *are real*—they exist and are being used against people every day of their lives by the very beings who promote the lie that sorcery is fantasy. (How exactly this is done by EPIC is a topic for another more voluminous work.)

For example, the Harry Potter books and movies are one of the most *heavily promoted* and popular series in the history of books and movies. This series promotes, reinforces and instills the belief in people that sorcery is just fantasy that exists only in parallel realities with completely distinct rules and agreements from our own. Sorcery could never be used in the "real world." Black magic is a flight of fancy that only operates in a universe that is completely distinct from our own. One of the reasons that so many are innately attracted to the message of such a series is because we all have remnants of a collective unconscious memory that such things have been real in the past and *exist right now.*

We enjoy deliciously the act of indulging in such movies and books because somewhere in the back of our minds *we remember the truth.* Yet by seeing the truth wrapped in the cloak of fantasy—we are given the protection of plausible deniability.

No one can disapprove of us if we are just indulging in fantasy. *"It's just fiction—it's an alternate reality that could never really exist here."*

36

INFORMATIONAL INVULNERABILITY

By making movies that seize upon a paranormal topic and define the debate over that topic, they frame the allowable thinking so that there is no bit of room in that theme for any other truth. No less a personage than the great thinker/writer Joseph P. Farrell has described this methodology in this way: *"the best way of diverting people from the truth is to contextualize truth into bizarre contexts."*

Once the theme is ensconced in that bizarre context, it is almost impossible for the average person to ever refer to it outside that mental framework ever again. Could there be a more bizarre context than depicting/teaching that vampires who feed on helpless human victims by draining them of their blood are cool, mysterious and romantic? How about the depiction that: black magic sorcery is done by waving around wands and jumping on brooms that fly through the sky? Would you ever be able to think of sorcery outside the "Harry Potter" context ever again? Probably not.

If there were a group of True Sorcerers running around our planet casting spells every day, wouldn't it be in their interest for sorcery/magic spells to be permanently contextualized into the realm of fantasy, far removed from our reality? That way, when we discover the sorceries that have been perpetrated upon us, and attempt to spread that knowledge; the mainstream herd will never believe any of it. What if these sorcerers happen to be some of the oldest family bloodlines on the earth, who now wear dark suits and move digital accounts with billions and trillions of USD, Yuan and SDR currency across the planet with the push of a button? What if these accounts and all their financial control would be ineffective without the incredibly powerful sorceries that make Earth's population into docile, cooperative debt- slaves? Do you begin to see the enormous value of contextualizing otherwise valid truth into implausible contexts? It provides the cover of "***permanent informational invulnerability.***"

No matter how many times the information and how much proof is offered, it will always be dismissed as if the EPIC sorcerers are wearing a cloak of invisibility. The accusation of lunacy will be leveled against any who dare to reveal the truth. This gives EPIC unlimited room to maneuver, plan and operate. It also makes EPIC sorcerers both invisible and invulnerable as they weave their spells and instill their agenda across the planet.

37

HOLLYWOOD CRAPOLA

This particular methodology has never been explicitly named before and held up before the light of day precisely because it seems so arcane. It does not fall neatly into the familiar EPIC control-methods. It is not misinformation or disinformation because it is not putting out false information either mistakenly or with full intent to do so. It uses persuasion rather than coercion. It disguises itself often as entertainment while it shifts and reduces your perceptions. It is not mind or thought control.

It is perception and attitude control.

The function that corporate Hollywood accomplishes for their masters in EPIC in regards to paranormal concepts I refer to as:

Confiscation
Reshaping
And
Promotion
Of
Limiting
Attitudes

CONFISCATION/RESHAPING:

Under the CRAPOLA methodology, corporate Hollywood will snatch a supernatural topic from the midst of some thoughtful circle of Paranormal Believers/ Truth Seekers who are treating the topic with the deference and respect it deserves. Then, after numerous boilerplate assurances about artistic integrity and their inviolable "*faith in the source material*" the Hollywood establishment agents will proceed to rip and cannibalize the material into an unrecognizable mess. They will reshape the concept into some ridiculous context that has little connection, if any, *to the authenticity of the topic*. No Paranormal Believer will recognize the atrocity that has become of their cherished reality/belief/truth. No mainstream denizen will ever see the topic as anything serious once exposed to this hideous chimera.

AND PROMOTION:

This reshaped package then gets distributed, magnified and promoted all over the world, to every market in every segment of the planet. The new conceptual package completely locks down what can be discussed concerning this topic. This new definition of the paranormal topic now goes throughout the Western and Non-Western world in easily consumable and accessible packages. This will breed the new standard definition of that topic forever *and not in a good way.*

OF LIMITING ATTITUDES:

The new limiting attitudes are quite severe. The newly minted encapsulation of the paranormal theme is sent out through the global web of the EPIC's distributive processes. It is translated into other languages and into other mediums: books, magazines, websites, commercials, cable programming, radio, television and many more mediums. The new limiting attitude created under the CRAPOLA system now permanently replaces any truthful, thoughtful, open-minded consideration of this topic. These attitudes are frozen into place. This creates an airtight conceptual cap on all: thinking, imagination and discussion in this area.

It is vital for original paranormal thinkers and believers to understand that once they sell the rights to Hollywood, it is unlikely that even a drop of authencity will be retained in their work; because the agenda being served is very different from what they imagine. Whenever a paranormal topic is presented that could lead to any large-scale awakening, the EPIC agenda is triggered. That agenda is to make sure that Mass Awakening *never happens.*

The CRAPOLA system even causes self-censorship (among Paranormal Believers) and engenders hostility toward *anyone* who tries to lift off the cap from the topic. The permissible discussions are capped, not just from the speaker's perspective but also from the perspective of any who might be open to a genuine discussion of this topic.

"What are you talking about? Didn't you see the movie? Didn't you read the book?"

Hollywood has used the CRAPOLA system to confiscate and reshape the attitudes on many paranormal topics:

Vampires—*blood-drinkers are cool, romantic, attractive, sexy, mysterious and desirable*

In reality, they are vicious, evil and corrupt beings who have nothing but hatred for humanity, which they consider as nothing more than meat for their hunger and desires.

Ghosts/apparitions/poltergeists—*are just spirit people who need our help to resolve conflicts in this world and gain the next step in their progression.*

In reality, they are usually deceiving creatures who pose as what they are not in order to gain access to accommodating living humans to serve as hosts and physical familiars.

Crypto-creatures (Chupacabra, Bigfoot, Champy the Lake-monster)—*are creatures which no one can prove or disprove and so they must simply remain as fanciful mysteries that we can enjoy as legends.*

In reality, humans across the planet would not be discussing, sighting and still believing in these creatures, hundreds and even thousands of years later, if they were not real. They are real and this continued and supported belief in their existence is the best evidence of that reality.

So if Crypto-Creatures are real, the only question regarding them is who is responsible for their creation? Are they products of EPIC experimentations gone wrong or right? Are they "familiars" of the Extra-Dimensionals brought with them through portals to assist with menial tasks? Are they created by us infusing mythical beliefs with the power of our conscious belief and therefore bringing them, fully manifested, into our reality? The answer, I believe, is yes to all three questions/possibilities.

Crop-circles *are hoaxes unless they can be proven with scientific methods*

In reality, supernatural phenomena tend to be unique rather than uniform in causation and occurrence and so scientific methods would be wholly inappropriate for proving whether they are true. Crop-circles have been proven to be supernatural phenomena many times and continue to be so but you will never see this reported or even mentioned by the mainstream institutions. It is very probable that genuine supernatural Crop-circles are Inter-Dimensional attempts to communicate crucial messages from light-based Extra-Dimensional Entities who are attempting to help humanity avert the many catastrophes that have been prepared for us by malevolent entities.

Near-Death Experiences *are mystical, mysterious experiences, which no one can truly know for certain are real or not.*

In reality, we do know—*they are real.* Also, they are actually True Death Experiences because these people are clinically dead for a period of time. "Near-Death" is a terrible misnomer, which was picked up and distributed throughout the world to keep us from the truth: that the people who have undergone this experience are True Death Returnees and there is much they could teach us. They can relate to us what is beyond this tiny, temporary, physical life. But, again, that could lead to Mass Awakening, which might spell the end of the scientific-materialist, government, EPIC enforced monopoly on institutional human thought.

Do any serious study of NDE's and it takes only a few hours to determine that human consciousness persists after death because it is beamed in to our brains from someplace else, i.e. our consciousness is not produced by our brains, *it is only received there.*

Sentient Machines—*at some point soon, the machines that we depend on so much in our technological systems will become sentient, self-aware, conscious and self-replicating. This new race of machines will dominate, subjugate and enslave humanity.*

Despite our constant indoctrination into the "conscious machines taking over humanity" scenario, nothing can trump human imagination and ingenuity. No matter how formidable the machines might be once they reach highest consciousness, we will always be able to think of ways to defeat them. Nothing trumps imagination coupled with faith, and machines will *never* have these in proportions comparable to humanity.

Zombies—*anyone who is dead is to be feared and dreaded because they are here to eat your brains. They feed off the living and then the dead make the living into monsters like themselves.*

In reality, there have been times in antiquity when the dead have come back to life supernaturally and there *will be such times again in the future.* EPIC wants us to fear those times. They want us to fear the dead and count them as monsters fit only to be shot, decapitated or otherwise destroyed by the living. *Always use a headshot, that's the only thing that stops them for sure.*

Think of all the videogames, movies and media conditioning that have gone into reinforcing this mental construct in the last few decades. Despite all this massive conditioning, the truth is that the returned dead are often sources of great wisdom for they have been close to the Face of Creator-Source. The mentality of dread toward the Returned Dead is one that the EPIC/Hollywood alliance has inculcated in us for many years and which will continue for as long as it continues to successfully generate fear and high ratings.

UFO's and Alien Visitors—*they are sometimes trying to invade us and take us over but, other times, they are wonderful paternal rescuers coming to save humanity and help us reach the potential they intended for us when they first created us.*

In reality, both viewpoints serve the EPIC's agenda. They want us to view alien invaders with dread, fear and suspicion but they *also* want us to see the second category of aliens as our saviors. EPIC knows both kinds are coming. The EPIC, as consummate global deceivers, will frame the malevolent visitors as our saviors and will portray the benevolent ones as destroyers. Then, they will sit back and let cultural conditioning; predictable panic and flat out terror—do the rest.

Men In Black—*They are just affable, cool, mysterious interstellar police officers who* *are protecting and serving humanity in the shadows from alien agendas. They carefully maintain a balance between intergalactic diplomatic relations and keeping the peace on Earth while battling malevolent, rogue aliens. There are secret government installations where human government workers are completely at ease working alongside aliens of all shapes and sizes. These situations are depicted in numerous movies and television programming covering this topic. Men in black are just human beings who get to see and do incredibly cool stuff that most humans never get to know even exists.*

In reality, during the last sixty years, after the advent of what we know as "the modern UFO age" whenever there has been a *game changer* event—a UFO/alien-human contact that was truly paranormal—there have appeared "Men In Black." In every country, speaking every language, creatures appearing as men dressed in black suits have appeared to harass, intimidate and threaten witnesses. All the testimony we have had over the years on the "men in black" has been largely from Contactees, Abductees and others who have had supernatural, direct experience with Extra-Dimensional Beings. The evidence is anecdotal but much of it has the weight of authenticity and consistency across an enormous span of time.

Most of the anecdotes, far from the affable smooth men of mystery portrayed by the movies, depict: strange, awkward even non-human (possible hybrid) creatures in dark suits, intensely questioning people on what they learned about "aliens." They often go to great lengths to try to appear fully human; pancake makeup, wigs, hats, refusing to show their eyes from behind thick, unattractive, light-cancelling glasses (a far cry from the slick sunglasses and sharp looking suits they wear in the movies.) During the course of one of their interrogations, they tend to turn quite hostile and menacing if they perceive that the witness may go public with their experience.

The Men In Black are such a strange and terrifying phenomena that it is difficult to even consider what they truly might be. But based on reliable Contactee experiences, there are three most likely possibilities.

A. Men In Black are corpses re-animated by Grey tech—they wear the sunglasses at all times because their eyes are glazed over with a cloudy film, as a corpses' eyes would be.

B. MIB are alien human hybrids created for the purposes of serving an EPIC/Extra-Dimensional agenda.

C. MIB are military men working for alien agendas that even *they* might not be aware of.

MIB Reality Doctrine: *Whatever they are, the facts have clearly demonstrated around the world that the real Men In Black are contemptuous, abusive and disdainful of human civilians—in direct contradiction to the propaganda that portrays them as heroes looking out for human interests.*

Here is the grim reality of MIB. People visited by the MIB's often feel sick for days afterward (with symptoms similar to radiation sickness). People are persecuted by the MIB, harassed, bullied and told their lives and those of their families would be in jeopardy if they reveal any details of their Extra-Dimensional encounters to anyone— but none of that reality would play well in a movie in which the MIB are heroes saving humanity.

We must consider the most obvious clues left behind by the MIB in deciding which of the three possibilities would account for what they really are.

Appearance: MIBs tend to be immaculately dressed in black suits and ties that are out of date. Suits and clothing are sometimes said to be made from a strange material. It's as if the cloth used in their suits is composed from: shifting, shimmering, stuff that seems alive. They appear in groups of two or three in large American sedans from about four decades prior, which, despite the vehicles' age, appear to have just rolled right out the factory. They flash gaudy government badges and claim membership in some national agency (a claim that invariably turns out to be false). Since the 1940's, the alleged MIB have been described as having olive or dark complexions with Asian or Gypsy-like features. More recently, they have been described as having extremely pale skin, almost the pallor of a cadaver that sometimes appears to be covered with makeup of some sort to give them some semblance of healthy skin color. This more recent development has contributed to the theories that they are re-animated corpses. Eyes tend to be hidden at all times behind dark sunglasses. Heads are often hidden under black hats that are several decades out of style. Those who have glimpsed the eyes of the MIB have said their eyes are strange—possibly covered with a white film and other times glowing with a strange type of energy that make them appear yellow.

Speech: MIBs tend to speak in a monotonous, mechanical tone, often with a strange accent. Witnesses have reported that their sentence construction and choice of words was peculiar. They speak like someone first familiarizing themselves with the language or re-familiarizing themselves with spoken language. At times, they regale the witness on highly technical matters of alien technology but will be mystified by simple human ideas like *"leaving on a vacation with the family."*

Intention: MIB's seem to tread a balance between attempting to debrief the witnesses as to what they perceived during the alien encounter and making sure the witness doesn't speak to anyone else about what happened. They do not erase the memory of the witness but use threats, intimidation, surveillance and bullying to accomplish the second purpose. They seem to already know (before being told by the witnesses) that during the encounter with the Extra-Dimensionals there was telepathic communication, astral experience and missing time. They ask questions directly about supernatural issues that any materialist based investigator *would never broach.* They are highly familiar with the methods and techniques involved with Extra-Dimensional contact experiences.

The strongest clue gathered about the MIB's in recent years is the connection made that witnesses visited by them tend to become physically ill for days afterward. I believe they are giving off radiation of a type that sickens and could even poison regular humans.

Recently, Hollywood has been successful in giving the MIB a great deal of useful cover by misrepresenting them as handsome movie stars in sharp looking black suits who are trying *to serve and protect humanity*. As a result, the MIB in the future will upgrade their appearance to be more in line with Hollywood CRAPOLA—or the movies will adjust to get closer to the reality. Either way, Hollywood or the MIB themselves will attempt to regain control of that agenda so that they will more in sync with each other.

Here are my final investigative conclusions based on the available testimony from reliable witnesses on this matter. The MIB are re-animated corpses (re-animated through a process that utilizes significant radiation), that are programmed and working for global government agencies. The reanimation is accomplished through "residual alien tech." This refers to very minor Extra-Dimensional technology that is given by the ED's to EPIC. The MIB agenda is to collect information for the EPIC about the activities of the Extra-Dimensionals and human responses to them. They are sentient but not truly alive. Their job is to be seen by humans, intimidate them into giving the MIB any new information about ED methods and techniques *and then to verify* that Extra-Dimensional tech attached to the Contactee is in effect and functioning.

Yet none of this matters because the MIB narrative has been successfully molded and frozen into the desired context. Only those Contactees who actually confront the MIB in the future will know how destructive the deception is both when they are confronted and also when they try to tell their story to all those whose minds have been molded by this CRAPOLA.

38

THEORY OF ALIEN RACES

The subject of what Extra-Dimensional races there are and how many Alien races have been catalogued and substantiated is important to many in Ufology, but *here is the real-real.*

It doesn't matter.

The number and diversity of the races of alien life that people swear by, have channeled, have had extensive contact with, know for a fact exist because they've documented, photographed and recorded them; *don't really matter* because all these are another anthropomorphic distraction from Extra-Dimensional truth.

Extra-Dimensionals are so advanced that they have **no** requirement for a permanently solid form. They will assume such only for the enticement of lower races. Humans must be able to perceive EDs through their human filters. *We*, as humans, focus on the permanent solid nature of living things—i.e.: what races are those Extra-terrestrials—because we perceive ourselves as being in a fixed solid condition. Both assessments are wrong.

Ever since Aristotle, the Great Philosopher, began the process of scientific enumeration and labeling, we have continued his penchant for assigning labels to species and relishing the wisdom this activity makes humans feel. Neither we, nor the Extra-Dimensionals, are necessarily in a fixed solid containment or fixed into a species, yet we continue to fixate on labeling them in the way we would label and categorize *Earthly* creatures. As we saw in the Travis Walton story, Extra-Dimensional entities can change their apparently physical form like we change clothing. Their apparent race is just a temporary convenience for the benefit of humanity. The race EDs use depends upon the need at that particular moment to frighten, to shock, to comfort and lull into a sense of security.

Here is an unattributed collection of the most well known species/races/genus of Extra-Dimensionals. It is a small section from one of the most ubiquitous such lists available through open sources without restriction. Researchers tend to use it as a starting point rather than as an independent source due to a lack of documentation.

THE A'S HAVE IT

AGHARIANS—A group of Asiatic or Nordic humans who, discovered a vast system of caverns below the region of the Gobi desert and surrounding areas thousands of years ago, and have since established a kingdom within which has been interacting with other-planetary systems.

ALPHA-DRACONIANS—Reptilian beings that are said to have established colonies in Alpha Draconis. Like all reptilians, these claim to have originated on Earth thousands of years ago, a fact that they use to 'justify' their attempt to re-take the earth for their own.

ALTAIRIANS—Alleged Reptilian inhabitants of the Altair stellar system in the constellation Aquila, in collaboration with a smaller Nordic human element and a collaborative Grey and Earth military presence.

AMPHIBIANS—Similar to the Saurians or Reptiloids, yet being hominoid creatures with reptilian as well as amphibian-like features and are semi-aquatic in nature. They may have once lived on land, yet became more aquatic over the centuries. Some types of Greys and Reptiloids are also believed to be semi-aquatic.

ANDROMEDANS—The Andromedans are one of the most channeled alien presences on Earth. They tend to reach out to us on spiritual and soul levels. They are an elder race in the universe that is charged with keeping order throughout the galactic species. Presently, the Andromedan Council has ordered all extraterrestrial presences on the planet, in the planet, and on the moon to be completely off the planet. No one knows why this is so.

ANUNNAKI—they have influenced the human evolution and possibly seeded and manipulated the genetics of humankind. Many humans are awaiting their return to check on our progress.

(Document Credit: author unknown/unattributed, non-copyrighted, Internet document)

That is only a fraction of the list. It becomes even more complex the further one gets into the alphabet. It could be accurate if we see it as a reference to the many guises available to ED beings. The needs of appearance may even be affected by the requirements of passage to Earth. As stated earlier, *Earth is primarily a gateway not a planet.*

Theory of Alien Races—There are no alien races—*there are only physical alien appearances*. In other words, there are only temporary guises used for convenience that can be switched, changed and transmogrified at a moments notice. Of course, this is little comfort to a Contactee who is confronted with the horror of a menacing Reptilian entity. That will certainly seem as real as any solid thing at that moment but knowing that this appearance is just a disguise meant to induce horror could render aid to any who need it. Negative ED experiences have been stopped by those wise enough to demand to see the truth behind such beings. These negative entities would much rather disappear than give away the truth I have stated in this "theory."

I have increasingly come to believe that there are really only two types (not races) of Extra-Dimensionals—similar to "the Good Cops and the Bad Cops." Like the process used by human law-enforcement to frighten people into confessing, the ED's will initially approach those they are interested in as altruistic benefactors but if that doesn't work, they can turn into bad cops pretty quickly. Additionally, there are E.D.s who are Beings Of Light and there are those who are Beings of the Darkness. One of the most consistent EPIC agendas is to make us all believe that the "Light Ones" are dark and that the "Dark Ones" represent light. This will be the ultimate deception played on the population of our planet—*switching the Cosmic Bad Cops with the Cosmic Good Cops* so we attack the good and bow down to the bad.

39

SHADES OF GREY

One of the notions I was disabused of in my conversations with Contactees was that of the "cookie cutter Grey." This coincided with my own experiences. When I personally observed what I now know to have been Grey entities; they were not the iconic, clean-lined, classic Grey's that have been popularized through the books and movies of Whitley Strieber. I have heard many anecdotes in the last decade, in which Grey Visitors were *slightly off* in physical appearance from the clean lined, smooth-looking Greys that most people envision.

At the age of about nine I was introduced to old-fashioned monster movies. They made a great impression on my psyche. One of my favorites was a hybrid creature, part man, part fish (with a bit of lizard thrown in for good measure), which lived in lakes and swamps called "the Gila-Man." His super-abilities were that he was a great swimmer who could breathe underwater and had enormous strength. Yet, he could not speak and displayed no real intelligence of any sort except to get human invaders out of his watery territory at all costs. Gila-Man was truly monstrous in appearance with a man-like silhouette but sporting webbed hands, scaly green skin, thick fish gills and spine-like protuberances along the side of his neck and jaw. He also had deep set, beady, cold shark eyes. Yet instead of razor sharp teeth, his mouth featured a big set of fish lips like those of goldfish. To an adult those lips might seem comical but to an impressionable nine year old, they were as terrifying as saber-tooth fangs. Gila-Man would attack any boat in his watery territory to get his great prize—a beautiful blonde woman passenger with a tremendous lung capacity for screaming. It was never clear whether he wanted her as food or for breeding. At that age, I assumed it was the former. Gila-Man made my imagination run wild with possibilities of things that might exist. The tenement building where I spent my childhood always imbued me with a deep sense of unease, as if something disturbing was reaching out for me constantly but just out of my field of view. There was some sort of release in actually seeing something visible to be horrified by.

Right about that time, I was having continuing experiences in my family apartment with Grey Visitors. The residence I was living was a five story residential building with my family in New York City. Over the course of several weeks, I had been unsettled by glimpses of creatures I later understood to be Greys—never up close—just fleeting moments of scampering little creatures inside and outside my residence. Mostly it was just snatches of peripheral vision of unnatural, small creatures that did not yet wish to be seen by me. I would hear them around corners but they would disappear once I turned my attention to them. They had a continuing campaign to capture my interest and get me to follow them. It didn't work. I always ran in the opposite direction.

However, being a mischievous little boy, there was a game I enjoyed sometimes during the morning hours when I was home only with my father who slept fitfully from the night shift. My game was unconnected to my experiences with the Greys but was heading toward an intersection with another ongoing game. We had one side of our fifth story apartment that faced inward toward a ground level, outdoor pavement square, connecting several buildings. This outdoor area had several basement connecting tunnels that led under those buildings. Our elderly superintendent of the building would use these tunnels to go from building to building. He made quite a lot of noise so I would get ice cubes from the freezer and open the window just a few inches. I would calculate from the sound of his voice (he was always muttering or singing to himself as he walked) when he was precisely under my window and toss the ice cubes onto his head. One time, he got quite angry and stood there yelling for several seconds while I crouched down; giggling at my success. My giggling stopped as I realized that he might have calculated what window the ice cubes had come from. I waited patiently for about five minutes. I resolved never to play this game again. My father would certainly punish me if the superintendent ever accused me. I had to make sure he was gone. I had drawn the curtain tightly closed right after I threw the ice through the slight opening. I began to peel back the curtain so that I could peak downward from my five-stories-up vantage point. I opened a small aperture in the curtain and looked—but I could see nothing. Something was blocking the entire window, my sight and even sunlight. That was impossible because we were five stories up and there was no fire escape on that side—it was just a sheer wall going straight down. So I threw open the curtains.

There, *standing upon nothing*, stood two Grey's—faces pressed up against the glass—giant black eyes glittering at me. I leapt backwards and ran shouting to wake up my father. I left out what I was actually doing; but my Dad was not happy with me or my story about "things outside our window." He saw nothing out there. I would not return to look for myself. I was still shaking for several minutes afterward. The most horrifying thing I remember about them was that they were slightly green, scaly and *stood on nothing*.

Among Texas law enforcement there's an old saying to describe ruffians who are particularly tough customers. *"He's got some hard bark on him."* That means they aren't dealing with some "smash and grab" punk who'll run at the first sign of cops. It means they will be confronted with a cagey, dangerous fugitive who will have a plan "b." Speaking of cagey, tough customers, there's been a curious phenomenon noted in the last decade concerning some Grey Visitors. Several people in separate incidents have run across Grey Visitors with one physical difference from the classic Grey appearance. These Greys, instead of having smooth, fetus-like, gray colored skin, were exhibiting a dark brown or brackish color like my greenish scaly Greys. Also with chipped and pitted consistency, their skin covering has the appearance of the bark on rotting trees. From my surveys of ancient art, etchings, carvings, tablets and all records from antediluvian antiquity, the standard Greys have been the most ubiquitous and consistent form of Extra-Dimensional Visitors to humanity.

Now, after so many eons of linear time, something about them is beginning to change. These creatures may live for eternity if they were not exposed to the sea of chaotic entropy that is represented by our dimension of time and space. So after being used by the Extra-Dimensional races as the worker bees of ED necessities in our dimension; this exposure may finally be catching up to some of them. Some Grey Visitors are *beginning to rot*.

Some of them may even have expired by now. Perhaps there's a limit to how many times they are allowed to "change clothing." Changing from one Grey suit to another or even to other species such as Nordic or Reptilian, those actions may only be a delaying tactic against a final expiration date that looms even for these creatures. Termination of their sentient life force or nonexistence is probably a concept they cannot comprehend—except perhaps to fear it. Yet, like cagey criminals, the aging Greys continue to come here and expose themselves to the dimension that accelerates their aging process. They don't give up on the ultimate prize they covet: attachment to eternal, Creator-Source connected human spirits. The Visitors continue to come here even if they are rotting as they walk. They may be gambling a final short period in our entropic dimension for a last desperate try for that urgently needed attachment.

They have some hard bark on them.

Tragically, it is possible that there is no option for them but a horrible, dreaded ending without transmogrification into a spiritual eternity—only oblivion left for them—the ultimate horror to sentient beings unconnected to Creator-Source. Since they are unconnected by the silver Ekashic chord to the Creator Force, dying might mean real oblivion for them. This could possibly be yet another variety of Extra-Dimensional that is visiting us—*the dying kind*.

The Extra-Dimensional hypothesis focuses all conscious attention away from this physical universe and directly into other dimensional possibilities. These are the dimensions where dreams and death may dwell in concert with one another. The dimensions may even manifest things beyond the imaginings of the dreamer.

Here is where it gets weird.

Anyone who has work-shopped or done interviews with Extra-Dimensional Contactees over many years; comes across an epi-phenomenon (secondary events caused as a direct result of the first event) that is partially *geographic* in nature. Wherever there are high incidents of Extra-Dimensional contacts going on, we find a proportionately increased number of ghostly encounters, spiritual activity and even *occult phenomenon*. People inhabiting the physical periphery of ED activity will tend to experience the sudden appearance, often for the very first time, the spirits of dead relatives and friends. Here are quotes I have collected concerning these epi-phenomenon.

"Shortly after our UFO experience, I came home to find my best friend who died the previous year. I knew it was him because I recognized his eyes. I asked him if his appearance had anything to do with the UFO we saw. The apparition had no awareness of what I was talking about."

"My sister had passed away years ago and we never had any contact with her even though we tried. Then, when my brother_____ had his experience in our backyard with the orbs—that's the same night she appeared to me.

This couldn't have been a coincidence. The day after our neighbors told us about how they sighted UFO's in the area, we were excited by the story but later we didn't think any more about it. Then, the spirit of my dead grandfather appeared to us. He'd been sent with a message for my family that we should be open to outreach from God. When I asked him if he meant the UFO craft, he didn't know what I was talking about.

40

2ND EXTRA-DIMENSIONAL COROLLARY

There appears to be something immensely powerful about ED penetration into our physical realm. The entire membrane between dimensions of reality seems to remain permeable for a period of time after the passage of ED's. It seems that other varieties of possible Extra-Dimensional entities may be able to take advantage of the temporary break in the barriers between the Multi-verses: spirits, ghosts, crypto-animals and an endless variety of manifestations.

The Second Extra-Dimensional Corollary: *the passage of Extra-Dimensional Visitors into our dimension creates temporary "quantum-flux gate" portals that can be accessed by other energetic entities in order to enter our time and space. These entities vibrate at a similar resonance as the ED's they follow but may have nothing else in common with the ED's except for actual transition point they use.*

Again, *Earth is a gateway first and a planet second.*

This corollary brings us one step closer to the crux of why EPIC is desperate to keep us away from the concept of Extra-Dimensionality. What if Extra-Dimensionality is not only a full explanation for the appearance of Alien Visitors but also for all the appearances of otherworldly phenomena that we know as paranormal, metaphysical and even spiritual phenomena? What if all such phenomena are intimately connected to each other and also (since we are actually spirit beings ourselves) to us also? What if *all such phenomena is uniformly reachable and contactable by us as spiritual beings by simply rejecting the deception of the purely physical, material, solid world we perceive through our five sense*s?

The most immediate consequences of accepting such premises would be personal freedom from the vast physical institutions that falsely act as impenetrable brokers and middlemen for any who wish to contact these phenomena. We wouldn't have to go through churches and organized religion for contact to otherworldly spiritual beings.

We wouldn't need to wait for institutional approval from materialist scientists to declare if a paranormal reality is actually real because we could go prove it to ourselves. We would no longer have to depend on the national governments to collect data from rocket ships, great telescopes and probes in outer space to give news of some Alien Life a thousand light years away. We would no longer need to go through the broker institutions set up by EPIC to absorb our energy, time and our hope—no more EPIC brokers, middlemen and no more false hope.

Acceptance of Extra-Dimensionality as truth means all such contacts can be achieved right here, right now, by our own individual spiritual powers. Extra-Dimensionality not only helps us to comprehend our Alien Visitors—it also will help reveal the truth of *all paranormal phenomena*. Extra-Dimensionals, ghosts, crypto-animals and more, according to Extra-Dimensionality, all come and go through the same portals—portals that don't require permission from NASA, the parliament or the Pope for access. These portals are *not* a thousand light years away. They are here with us right now. The false gatekeepers are acting out a charade. Some in the herd think the middlemen, brokers, jailers still stand post but they are wrong. We can crash the gates and access those portals. Our faith shall set us free. Yet, these ancient portals can only be activated and used by the most fearsome and wondrous powers in all the Multi-Verses—*believing human beings.*

We are beginning to understand that the idea of races among Extra-Dimensional entities is probably nothing more than an anthropomorphic interpretation of non-human realities—like thinking that ED craft have ED entities cramped inside them because they travel the way humans do. ED craft carrying Alien Visitors like human airliners and the appearance of Alien Visitor races are probably are just affectations assumed for the benefit of collecting the energy of human consciousness. If we realize that Alien Species are just an affectation assumed for our benefit, we will no longer be impressed with the ones we encounter. Once we have reached the end of our fascination with Extra-Dimensional races—then grave responses will be initiated. New variations of ED Visitors will be coming soon because novelty causes fascination and human fascination is an *absolute necessity* for Extra-Dimensionals.

One way the Extra-Dimensionals will manufacture new fascination, fear, wonderment and awe is through the creation and use of physical Hybrids. These creatures are created as purely physical and have no need to use the gateways their creators use. The last time Hybrids were recorded on the Earth during pre-history was by early civilizations such as the Vedic, Sumerians and even pre-Egyptian civilizations. Zecharia Sitchin was not the first to report the narrative of the advance civilizations created in large part by beings called the Annunaki. Sumerian stone tablets numbered in the hundreds were discovered that were dated at over 6,000 years old. More likely, they were about 20,000 years old. The Sumerians were (once the tablets were found and translated) the first recorded civilization to exist within our knowledge. This was the period when humankind had still not taken control of their own destiny—when we were still controlled and directed by superior races that generated more hybrid species to instill awe and wonder in human slave populations. Hybrids were used to help rule over humanity.

Among the more impressive of the hybrid depictions on Sumerian stone tablets are: Sobek—the crocodile-headed, human-bodied demi-god, men with powerful looking wings, stout horses with the heads of humans, Kings petting winged dragon-dogs, regal reptilian-humanoid females, female humanoids with wings and talons like eagles, gigantic humanoid Kings holding full grown lions up by their tails as if they were kittens, kings with the bodies of lions but who also had great wings, mer-men with the heads and torsos of men but who below the waist are fish; and most telling of all—some Sumerian tablets depict apparent human physicians contemplating and manipulating figures that appear to be large-screen images of DNA double helixes.

It would be a great mistake to assume that these hybrids could not possibly have reproduced in large numbers because of what we know today about species genetics—that a specimen must be relatively pure within its own species to sexually reproduce. However, the beings that were creating these hybrids had far more knowledge of genetics than we do today. They had to be masters of genetic manipulation to even create the first prototypes of the creatures we see represented on these tablets. It would have been an easy matter for them to breed these chimerical creatures without sexual reproduction, through cloning or some other method of asexual reproduction. For each example of the hybrids we see on the tablets, there may have been hundreds even thousands of each breed of these hybrids actively marching across the Earth, helping to terrify and control the human population.

Pre-Egyptian artifacts from the period immediately following the Sumerian periods depict many of the same themes but add more images to the hybrid repository. Here there are human bodies with the heads of coyotes, cats, falcons, hawks and many more diverse hybrid creatures. They celebrate in graven image and statues, a creature with the body of a lion but a human head upon it—the Sphinx. They show human females holding in their laps what appear to be small grey alien creatures as if they were babies. They memorialize Pharaohs who happened to be physical giants about fifteen to twenty feet in stature. Both the Sumerian and Pre-Egyptian civilizations also demonstrate men and women with greatly elongated skulls that could contain brain matter twice, or even thrice, the size of ordinary human brains. Just imagine what kind of powers and abilities could have been displayed by humans with brains three times the size of ordinary human brains. Then, add the fact that similar such hybrid creatures are memorialized in numerous major ancient civilizations all across the Earth.

That's a lot of hybrids.

Yet mainstream science ignores all this evidence by asserting it is all just flights of fancy of ancient, over-active imaginations but Awakened People know the truth. This was real and it will be again. This then leads us to the obvious question: what was the purpose of these creatures?

They were used the same way police state and surveillance structures are used today—to control and enslave human populations—not so much for direct control like an occupying military force but to control through fear and awe of the supernatural. Paranormal Experiencers know what a powerful force this represents. The hybrids will be used for that purpose again in the near future but in an even more insidious manner than the last time.

ED "animal mutilations" must be dealt with under any discussion of hybrids because these "mutilations" are (like most paranormal truth that EPIC seeks to control) horribly misnamed. "Mutilation" is more of the old paradigm language that is meant to encapsulate us in the wrong context. This false label depicts more "language control" to distract us from the *true* agenda being executed. On a technical level, the term just means nothing more than the permanent disfigurement of a body by whatever means. "Mutilation" evokes images of a desperate killer trying to get rid of a dead body and so he sloppily cuts up the limbs and torso into sections in order to dispose of the body in a dozen different hidey-holes in the ground. However, in Extra-Dimensional mutilation cases, *what is missing from the body* matters much more than what is done to the body. Animal mutilations (and even human mutilations—yes there are documented cases of supernatural human mutilations) are not the random slicing up of bodies—they are *ED harvesting of biological tissue toward the Hybrid Agenda.*

The phenomenon known as "Cattle Mutilations" should be called "Cattle Harvestings." A hallmark of these incidents is the precise surgical nature of the mutilation, and unexplained phenomena such as the complete draining of the animal's blood but with no blood splatter on the ground, loss of internal organs with no obvious point of entry, and surgically precise removal of the reproductive organs and anal coring. Often flesh will be removed to the bone in an exact manner, such as removal of flesh from around the jaw exposing the mandible.

Here are the typical hallmarks of these paranormal phenomena:

- The removal of eyes, udders and sexual organs very cleanly with surgical precision beyond present medical ability

- The removal of the anus to a depth of around 12 inches similar in appearance to surgical coring

- The removal of the lips and/or tongue deeply cut out from the throat

- The removal of one ear

- The removal of major organs (such as heart or liver) with no obvious entry/excision marks, often, if the heart is missing, apart from no excision wound, the Pericardium will still be present and intact, with the heart missing

- The stripping of hide and flesh from the jaw and the area directly beneath the ear to the bone

- The removal of soft organs from the lower body

THE EXTRA-DIMENSIONALS 155

- The presence of incisions and cuts across the body that appear to have been made by surgical instruments which display precision beyond human capability
- Unexplained damage to remaining organs, but no sign of damage to the surrounding area
- A lack of predation signs (including teeth marks, tearing of the skin or flesh, or animal footprints) on or around the carcass
- Lack of obvious scavenging and even the hungriest predators avoid the carcasses
- A draining of the majority of blood from the animal. What blood is left exhibits color anomalies and *may not coagulate for days*
- The animal will appear "dumped" or dropped in a secluded area, with no animal, human or vehicle tracks leading to or from the site
- The ground under the animal appears depressed, as if the animal was dropped on the site from a great height leaving an impact crater. The carcass animal's bones are also found to be fractured with injuries consistent with being dropped from a great height
- Strange marks/holes in the ground around the carcass as if from a tripod-like devices
- Mutilation wounds appear to be clean, and carried out surgically yet consistent with a surgical method that is beyond our present capability—these are "laser-type scalpels" are being used that are precise down to the tissue-molecule so that where incisions are made—they are cut, cleaned, cauterized perfectly *beyond the ability* of our finest modern surgeons. Yet, if they were cauterized by some advanced laser mechanism—there would be some blackened surface molecules that lasers must always leave behind in a carbon-based life form. There are no such telltale signs of lasers having been used. The surfaces, under a microscope are perfectly smooth and cauterized—but not by a method within human technology. The exposed surfaces do not ooze as if they have been sealed by lasers. This is a technology that humans have not yet imagined, even as speculative fiction.

Again, these are not mutilations—*they are harvestings*.

This is very similar to "Alien Abductions" of humans in which the true agenda is the large scale collection of various human tissue, blood and various human materials toward some later great purpose.

The Extra-Dimensionals will continue the "animal mutilations" (and the human abductions) until what they are building is ready to be shown or more appropriately *released* upon the planet Earth. Medical personnel say that bovine blood and tissue is strangely compatible to human blood and genetic patterns. (I'm not exactly certain what that means medically but my sense is that it does not bode well for humans.) Here the mutilation agenda and the ED abduction agenda blur into one another because close examination reveals that both are intense and methodical harvesting of terrestrial, biological genetic materials toward the unifying purpose of creating enormous numbers of powerful hybrids. When I say enormous numbers, think in terms of *hundreds of millions* of Hybrid creatures being returned to Earth.

Additionally, about 30,000 human beings go missing in the United States of America every year according to the most reliable criminal statistics we have. Some percentage of those people are eventually recovered or otherwise accounted for (bodies are located and these are relegated to unsolved murder case files). That still leaves about 10,000 per year disappearing, no physical bodies ever found, and which could very well be a part of the hybrid/harvesting agenda. If we multiply that figure by the numerous nations around the world with comparable populations and similar statistics, it begins to illustrate how large a harvesting of human biological material could be at play in unexplained human disappearances. Whatever the case may be, all these many thousands are gone over many decades. None of these will never return to tell the tale—at least not *in any recognizable form.*

The moment the mutilations finally stop, it won't be because we've stopped them. We have no ability to stop them. That much has been made clear by all the ranchers around the world hiring security teams and installing cutting edge security systems that have been for all for naught. Invariably, the rising dawn reveals freshly "mutilated" carcasses, harvested missing materials, undisturbed security systems and befuddled security personnel. Abductions and permanent human disappearances will also never stop until agendas are fulfilled and the final ED trigger has been pulled.

When the Extra-Dimensionals have collected enough bovine (and human) tissue and materials for their purposes; they will unveil what they've created with all the biological materials they've gathered. I believe we are almost at that point right now. This will be the moment of *The Great Unveiling*—the great *cymbal crash reveal* of all the Extra-Dimensional agendas which will all coalesce simultaneously: ED human abductions, ED animal mutilations, ED related human disappearances and even ED related human implantations. It will begin with revelation of the first hybrid creature—and it will accelerate as we enter *The Great Return.*

41

RIGHT OF RETURN IMPERATIVE

It is likely that all this enormous expanse of earthly biological material will be returned to humanity in three major forms. The first method of return will likely be in the form of Hybrid-Machine-Biologicals. These will be machine engineered, sentient, programmed mechanical devices of all types. They will be built for destruction and war. They will carry probably hidden human brains and other organs and human-like tissue matrixes deep inside invulnerable shells joined to programmable circuitry. This will be the final consummation of the much-foreshadowed "machines take over humanity" scenario that Hollywood trumpets so much.

Why should these human materials, still bearing some resemblance to humanoid, not enjoy a "right of return" to their home planet—no matter how their outward appearance has been altered? Those human interiors of these sentient machines will be discovered and there will be argument over our responsibility to rescue the human organs contained within them—whether we could preserve and return these organs to full humanity at some later time. Much human biological material will be returned to us in this form. The surprise here will be that these sentient machines, at a time and place of their choosing, may be able to communicate with humans under their previous brain-mind identities but they will still have to act in accordance with their programs. The Cosmic "Right of Return" doctrine will become a political, social and cultural preoccupation with passionate advocates on both sides of the argument.

Secondly, there will be wondrous hybrid-chimerical creatures analogous to the griffins and the satyrs of ancient times but these will be mixtures we have never heretofore seen or imagined. They will be crossbreeds of human and non-human genetics that we have not contemplated. There is something interesting about nearly all of the Hybrid depictions of the Sumerian and Vedic ancient tablets and etchings: almost all the Hybrids are rather intriguing- looking—I would even dare to say—kind of "cool looking" in an otherworldly sort of way. The Sumerian depictions of: humanoid females with eagle talons and wings, regal king with the bodies of bulls and even crocodile-headed humanoids; are hybrid designs created to inspire some fear but also intrigue and fascination. A review of all their hybrids show that almost none of them are completely unattractive. The "awe" factor seems to be more important here. Pre-Egyptian civilization (the unknown culture that truly built the great three Pyramids of Giza) also regales us with coyote headed humanoids, falcon-headed humanoids and many other fascinating looking creatures. Ancient Greek history (again misnamed mythology) records very romantic versions of bull-headed giant humanoids referred to as Minotaur's, goat-legged humanoids called Satyrs and even one-eyed giants known as Cyclops. The interesting physical appearance of these creatures, often depicted in modern movies, tend to inspire as much admiration than they do dread.

It has been revealed to me that when our genetic material is returned to humanity; it will be very different from the hybrids we have seen portrayed in the records of pre-historical civilizations. There will be no fascinating blends of animal heads on giant, muscular humanoids bodies—no "cool-looking" Satyrs and Minotaur's captivating the interest of human females and male teenagers. The genetic manipulators will forego the fascination factor and aim solely to inspire dread.

Instead of interesting-looking mixtures like human bodies with the heads of jackals or falcons—these will be giant dogs or proto-wolves with human heads—how awkwardly vile that would be! Imagine a giant Anaconda snake body crowned by a human head that speaks perfectly well but consumes food in exactly the way that a giant Anaconda snake would. How disconcerting would it be to watch that—especially if civilians actually recognize the human heads in these roving mutant creatures as former friends or even family members? Many of these creatures will be programmed to return to the communities from whence they were (in their former human identities) abducted so long ago. They will be recognized and their human memories and powers of communication will be available to them despite their non-human condition. They will, at least partially, be our long missing relatives, spouses, sons and daughters. These creatures will be set against us more for shock value than actual utility. They will inspire supernatural fear combined with a horrible violation of intimacy because these creatures will have all the communication ability of their former selves and *their human memories*. They will plead for acceptance while looking for the best opportunities to wreak havoc on us.

All this will have the ultimate goal of instilling uncontrollable panic and chaos in the pure human population. There could even be civil conflict among the "pure humans" over what to do with these new Hybrid Returnees. There will be no clear-cut answer to this conundrum. Many will stand resolutely in their defense. However, this situation will not be static. It will be a stalling tactic by malevolent elements of the Extra-Dimensionals. It will be designed to take advantage of basic human decency and morals to prevent us from destroying these hybrid creatures just long enough for them to wreak a horrible cost against humanity.

Thirdly, some of our human genetic material is already here in the form of hybrids that already exist in our society and are almost indistinguishable from regular humans.

Finding them out would be almost impossible even if the will to do so existed. We likely don't even have the technology to detect these most human appearing hybrids. So with these *most dangerous* hybrids of all, there is likely nothing we can do but wait until they are activated toward some possibly nefarious purpose. Some of them may have already been activated.

These are the ways in which Earth's biological materials, which have been absconded with by Extra-Dimensionals for thousands of years, will be returned enmasse (and may indeed already be returning) to us.

United States President Ronald Reagan (whatever you might have thought of him) made several highly prescient predictions that came through shortly after he made them. He predicted the dissolution of the Soviet Empire at a time when they were the second most powerful nation on Earth. He stood on the Berlin Wall that had kept East Berlin in communist prison for over forty years and stated that it should be torn down. It was done so shortly after that speech. He also said "*the most likely thing to unite all the nations of the earth in an unshakable alliance of unity would be when extraterrestrial aliens came down publicly and made themselves known to everyone. And yet is not an alien force already among us?*"

He would have been right if the matter were going to be such a straight-forward proposition—an invasion by clearly Extraterrestrial Beings—a homogenous, visible enemy against whom humanity could immediately unite. Unfortunately, it will not be so clear-cut. Instead, there will be waves of creatures, some so bizarre that it will be difficult to determine if they are sentient life or just a clever mimicking of life.

Some of the creatures in these waves will be very human-like in appearance and will speak to us under their former human identities. This will sow great sympathy and discomfort with the idea of being at war with these beings. There will be passionate discord among human defense forces as to whether it would be murder to kill such creatures. There will be rampant disagreement and even civil strife over the most basic question of *what is human?* This chaotic situation will be the diametric opposite of Reagan's "unified humanity scenario." It could even lead to civil war among humans when we can least afford it.

Here are my Investigative Conclusions in this area.

The game-changer here will be the first open revelation and *human acceptance* of the fact that ED-human Hybrids are present right now on Earth. Hybrids are here and there are more coming. The rest be here sooner than we dare to think.

42

AGENDA OF ED IMPLANTS

I'm no scientist.

I do not use control groups, rigorous peer review process or academic university-level standards; designed to create reproducible results. I don't require nor desire grants, subsidies or academic institutional support of any sort. No one should accuse me doing *anything* in a scientific manner if they wish to remain on amicable terms with me. What I am is: an Awakened Investigator. I am in the business of finding authenticity and truth, rather than reproducible results. I can ferret out deception, falsehood and obfuscation no matter how secure the purveyors are in the profundity and invulnerability of their deceptions. Conversely, any Awakened Mind can also detect genuine authencity no matter how non-credible the source might appear at first blush. Once we connect that authentic material with various clues connected from what we know about human and non-human nature; we can compose startling conclusions.

Then, to raise these conclusions to a cosmic level, we measure these conclusions against ultimate truths hidden in the Ekashic Field; and these conclusions will expand inter-dimensionally. This is where awakening becomes revelation.

With that in mind, I have conducted interviews and surveys of those who have experienced the most common Extra-Dimensional phenomena—those who have been abducted by them, those who have been implanted by them, those who have been in contact with them and those who have impacted by their actions. The main investigative conclusion I have reached is that are at least two agendas behind Alien Implants—the first agenda pertains to the implants they want you to find and the second applies to the implants no human will ever find.

In the human world of National Security for the Western nations, it is a commonly known practice to track terrorists or designated enemies of the state through the use of planted remote tracking devices. These serve as electronic beacons that give notice to anyone monitoring these devices of: the movements, conversations and meetings of the surveiled subject. The planters of the remote monitored device can then follow any movements the person makes, any trips, any locations that person is stationed in and even their position inside a home or building. The planter/monitor can see position of the subject when compared to the blueprint of that structure: *is the monitored subject relaxing in the living room watching television at that moment or are they sitting in a business office making important calls?*

Knowing the vagaries of human nature, not tech capacities, is the most important consideration in this process. If prosecutors in this process can assess human nature correctly, then they can predict the future responses and behavior of their subject during emotionally charged shifts. National Security agencies sometimes land in the news when their subjects find their devices planted in their cars, homes or in their favorite restaurant booth where they regularly meet to discuss private matters. Sometimes, the subjects will parade the device before the media while complaining of the racist or xenophobic tendencies of these agencies that harass and surveil them for no legitimate reason. At least they feel relief that they found the intrusive "bug" and are no longer being monitored by their nemesis. Often that is an incorrect assumption.

When an agency is faced with a subject that is perhaps expecting to be the subject of an attempt at surveillance by persecutors; it is good common sense to plant several such devices—at a minimum there should be one device planted in an obvious location which is *intended to be found* and then one device which will be far more well hidden. The "easily found" device serves several important purposes simultaneously. The subject finding the primary device fulfills expectations on the part of the persecuted person so that they have their suspicions confirmed that they were being surveiled.

"There it is in the flowerpot, I knew I wasn't crazy."

The finding also creates a sense of accomplishment and relief on the part of the subject as they parade the device in front of friends and associates. The finder receives accolades for being so perceptive, clever and determined. The entire group shares a laugh at the expense of the deterred persecutors while also being in the strong bargaining position of negotiating with the persecutors for the return of the hostage device. The device is a high-tech, high-value device and the prosecutors will want it back. It is now up to the persecuted victims to dictate those terms. The final effect of this minor victory is that the persecuted will breathe a sigh of relief, tend to let down their guard and *speak more freely* than they have perhaps in a long time in the presence of the secondary and maybe even tertiary (still-hidden) monitoring devices.

That final detail leads directly into the true goal of this "distraction op." Secondary and possibly tertiary devices will now play the role for which they were meant. These devices are hidden more skillfully are *not* meant to be found. This makes good sense. Would the Extra-Dimensionals do any less?

I am convinced, after numerous similar accounts from diverse Extra-Dimensional Implantees that there is more at play than just physical implants. Individuals who were implanted by ED physical implants are *also* implanted with immaterial, nonphysical, ephemeral implants.

There are numerous individuals who claim to be implanted by Extra-Dimensionals with items that are deep under the skin but lack any entry wound or scar. In this area the most prominent medical doctor working today was Dr. Roger Leir (until his recent regrettable passing away). Dr. Leir performed numerous surgeries on alleged Alien Abductees. He has removed numerous objects suspected of being alien implants. These objects have been scrutinized by laboratories and scientists at: Los Alamos National Labs, Seal Laboratories, the University of Toronto and University of California-San Diego. Of course, there have been instances when labs return scientific non-conclusions—*"materials not identifiable, composure unidentifiable or no determination possible."*

However, when positive finds have been made, they have shown metallurgical anomalies such as highly magnetic iron, combinations of crystalline materials with common metals, as well as isotopic ratios. Some of these devices are emitting very strong electro-magnetic fields and even radio waves that are capable of reaching deep space. They are usually found just beneath the skin but close to a bone structure of the body and there is no portal of entry visible. The presence and concentrations of nickel, cobalt, copper, phosphorus, gallium, and germanium in many of these implant devices have led to comparison with iron meteorite samples.

Despite non-biological composition, these objects somehow fail to trigger the natural foreign object immunological response of the human body. Any foreign object introduced into any human body will always trigger a response whereby the body will wall the object off with fibrous tissue and a chronic inflammatory reaction in order to ultimately expel the object out the human biological system. Somehow these alien implant devices act as if they are a natural part of the host's body. The person can't expel these devices. Surgeons have to go in after these devices to remove them.

Dr. Leir stated the only commonality he can see among the Abductees and Implantees is that they all tend to be right-brained thinkers—artistically inclined musicians, actors, artists and creative people of every stripe. My experience has been identical in this respect. Implantees have advised me that no matter how harrowing or traumatic their abductions experiences were; their creative powers greatly increased after the implantation. Even if they suffer side effects and nervous conditions of various types—their actual creative abilities tend to intensify—musicians become greater musicians, writers become more powerful writers and so on.

Another oddity found among these objects is an apparent ability to go mobile and even self-regenerate. There are surgical videos that clearly show attempts to remove implants that moved subcutaneously, like a fish swimming away from a grasping hand. These objects appear to grow their own tough, biological tissue covering. As if that wasn't strange enough, the objects also will grow their own nerve-matrixes attaching it to its biological surroundings. There have been some implants that have been broken up in preparation to remove them and down to the molecular level *but they reassembled themselves.*

Yet, some of them are successfully removed, sometimes after repeated attempts. Once they are removed, the objects no longer exhibit the characteristics of living biological material—as if once their purpose is taken away—they cease to be. These developments lead to the natural question—could some of these implants be living, sentient creatures that become inert material upon being removed from the host?

Dr. Leir concluded that the sophistication of these devices could not be duplicated even by national government or black ops technology (carbon nano-tubes, sentient bio-devices). He concluded that the only possible origins of these genuine, paranormal implants must be non-terrestrial and supernatural. He's right and that conclusion brings us closer to a final resolution on what to do about such implants. If all Awakened people settle on one answer for where these implants come from then we are one big step closer to deciphering the final agenda of those who are implanting them.

One of the relevant issues that Dr. Leir may have been aware of is the large number of Abductees who *do not* wish to lose their implants or who ultimately decide to keep their implants despite much urging from friends, family. I've met several such people. Implantees are often initially traumatized by their implants but after a while of living with these items in their bodies, they begin to *evolve* in their feelings about the device. Sometimes they decide to just keep the device and leave it at that. They get a great deal of attention from ED believers and from the Extra-Dimensionals themselves, who will often contact them afterwards (we can assume for data transfer updates). I have no doubt that the visible device is just a device to gather conceptual data—information about how and what the subject thinks—it is not something as simple as a tracking device or listening device. The ED's do not need any device to track people.

The primary intelligence collection accomplished by the physical implant is this: "how important is freedom to a human being?" It is also possible that physical ED implants may be changing the DNA structure of their human hosts—to what we don't know. Some people might welcome such a change, thinking that *anything* is better than the lives they currently live. They may feel specially chosen, set apart by greater powers or even part of a movement to be the saviors of humanity. Would they succumb to having this alien device permanently residing inside their physical body? Will some half-heartedly attempt to remove the implant? How important is sole control over your own body to you? Would they go to any lengths to regain complete sovereignty over their physical body—i.e.: would they cut off their finger or toe to finally be rid of the implant?

Dr. Leir has recorded an incident during which he has surgically attempted to remove a physical implant that *moved away from his scalpel.* The subject immediately cancelled any further surgery and decided to keep the implant in their body. It appeared the subject did not cancel the surgery because it was difficult but because they realized that the implant was actually alive and possibly conscious. This completely changed how they viewed the implant and how they viewed themselves for being chosen for the implant. The subject realized he had been chosen to carry an implant that was a living and sentient creature. That epiphany changed everything in the mind of the Implantee. Again, *how important is freedom?* The answer is different for each of us.

The immaterial implants are the ones meant to stay in. Doctors or surgeons cannot reach them in the laboratory. We already know that Extra-Dimensionals have the power to make things immaterial in our physical dimension. They can touch things and render them ephemeral for transport, as they do sometimes with humans they choose to abduct. They take formerly physical bodies and pass them through walls to take to other dimensions. How simple would it be for them to place devices and entities inside human bodies that are permanently intangible and therefore undetectable to those who only see the physical world? Are we sufficiently spiritual to realize that there are nontangible objects inside there as well as the solid ones? Are we so confined to the false physical veneer that we are blind to the "creepy crawlies" that cannot be detected or touched on the physical plane?

The primary intelligence collection accomplished by the *non-material* implants is to inform whether human beings have the capacity to enter the spiritual dimension and identify ephemeral attachments/implants and then to *remove* these attachments. One woman who had physical implants removed told me she went to a light-healing practitioner because she was still having problems of "gloom upon her soul." This woman suspected that she had been implanted with more than the physical implant she removed. After a series of rituals, the Shaman located a "dark eel of malevolence that was curled around her lower intestine." He used light-worker techniques to attack the living implant. She saw the dark entity with her mind only for a moment as it squealed and dissipated. It was a far more harrowing experience than she had with the physical implant. Since that time her entire life has been translated into light.

The good news for ED Implantees is that both types of implants can be removed with determination and courage on the part of the human hosts. There are brave men like Dr. Leir who serve humanity despite the arrows from the old medical/science profession. Whether the Implantee uses Shamanic practitioners or spiritual warriors— anyone steeped in light practice can remove these entities once their presence has been determined.

The final intelligence gathered by Extra-Dimensionals doing these procedures on humans must be very bewildering to the EDs: that human beings are unpredictable, unique and they will never have a uniform predictable result. Strangely enough, this truth is something still ignored by *human scientists* who still insist on attempting to treat humans as meat for reproducible results. The Extra-Dimensionals have now gathered that humans are wildly diverse in their responses to both the visible and invisible implants—some terrestrials will go to any lengths to get rid of this intrusion into their biological/spiritual selves while many others can be made to feel special and chosen after having the implants for a long period—so they keep them and even learn to treasure them.

A far greater portion than any would dare imagine are choosing to keep their implants for the reasons stated above—that special feeling of apartness and being special. They are keeping both the solid and non-solid implants—and it is changing them in ways that will not be fully evident until the day of the Great Return. Patterns of ED implantation show that these procedures are part of an elaborate intelligence collection operation meant to unfold the inner workings of the human soul and mind in order to better understand what elements are most useful in the manipulation of human free will.

Experiment: Among paranormal workshops, clubs, associations and meet-ups that regularly come together; conduct this poll on empirical versus experiential truth. Tell the group you will poll them with two questions.

1. *How many of you are here because of someone else's experience?*

   This would be any situation in which someone showed you evidence that was so convincing as to the reality of Extra-Dimensional life visiting our planet that it actually convinced or intrigued you that such things might be true. The is secondhand knowledge.

2. *How many of you are here because of something you personally experienced?*

   This is firsthand experience that you arrived at through something that happened to the person directly. That might, in turn, have led you later to speak to others about their experiences and further convinced you that what you experienced is indeed genuine. However, the genesis of belief in this subject matter would then still be considered your own original experience.

In the typical meeting group about 90 percent will volunteer under number two— *that it was some sort of personal first-hand experience they went through*, even as long ago as childhood, that made them open to paranormal realities. Then, focus on the ten percent who raised their hand for number one and ask them one more question.

3. *If it was something that someone told you, second-hand knowledge, that led you to believe in the paranormal—what originally led you to listen to that person or to put yourself in the position where you would hear this message?*

This makes the ten percent think deeper than their initial reaction and possibly remember things they had forgotten. *What was it that made them feel the inclination to be open to messages about the truth of paranormal topics?*

Usually, again ninety percent of that ten percent will then realize that it **was** a personal experience that really led them to a place of openness to paranormal belief. There might be a single holdout that swears that it was not any paranormal experience that convinced them—*it was his mother who explained these truths to them and convinced him that the paranormal is real*. If you question the holdout long enough you'll find out that his mother died two years before these conversations took place and she convinced him in her spirit form (or some variation of that scenario). At the end of this questioning, if it's done thoroughly, only a tiny number will remain in the "secondhand" group. Of the tiny number that persists in the secondhand group; most will unexpectedly recall things that will astonish you. They should be questioned regarding periods of missing time, nighttime experiences with the animal familiars of Grey Visitors such as white owls or albino deer, sightings of ED craft and what occurred to them immediately after these sightings. Some of them will be former Abductees struggling to recall memories that have been blocked, sometimes for decades. I do not advocate hypnosis for these purposes because I cannot advocate something I would not use for myself. Instead, I would recommend a rigorous course of meditation, practice of lucid dreaming and Cosmic Introspection to unblock these locked memories—without the intrusion of another human consciousness into the process (as hypnosis does).

This workshop/interrogation/survey experiment largely serves to prove that paranormal truths are experiential rather than empirical so we are not going to convince anyone that doesn't already have the truth already in their heart and mind. Paranormal Believers, don't convince anyone—not a single person. *The universe convinces them for us.*

FINAL WARNINGS

The full truth is stranger than we could ever imagine on this side of the veil.

43

ONE NIGHT WITH A SUPERMODEL

Survey or workshop with individuals who have participated in direct channeling and ET outreach, outside the presence the group guru who makes his living by this activity, for any problems that have arisen as a result of this "outreach." If they are being honest, there will be a large percentage of people who have come away with "noisome attachments." They usually aren't honest; at least not in the first interview. It requires drilling down of comments and clues before the investigator can get to the cold, hard truth. Direct channeling and ET outreach, is like going out with a high fashion model in front of your friends. The experience itself can be wonderful. People take pictures of you. You are showered with adulation from strangers, admired by friends and envied by enemies. You spend a wonderful evening and a great night with the most attractive human being you've ever seen (For some people that sort of thing is crucial to their own self-esteem). It is a great experience and *God-willing* that will be the end of it.

But the morning after you may find you received something from that person in the nature of an intimate festering problem (an STD). The only person you tell about the intimate problem is your doctor who may or may not be able to help you get rid of the problem given to you the night before. People will ask you about that night for years to come. Your tendency will always be to highlight the positive aspects of that evening but never to bring up the little problem you came away with.

There are a percentage of people who have participated in direct channeling and ED outreach at the direction of gurus who told them all ET entities are gentle, benevolent, loving creatures who want only good for them. These gurus have elaborated that anyone who has had negative experiences with Extra-Dimensionals have actually been in contact with government-created entities pretending to be ED's. How could anyone doubt these gurus since usually these cultish groups have been bombarded with constant conditioning and "education" about the wonderful qualities and loving care of all Extra-Dimensionals. Then, they are also conditioned that anyone who fails to have a completely positive experience during such outreach, it is because the Extra-Dimensionals sensed that they were not ready (not noble, sincere or good enough) for true contact. Consequently, their astral selves were diverted toward the lower depths of the astral planes; where some nasty government generated entities awaited them.

All this calculated conditioning is designed for that purpose: to make it non-credible for any Out-Reachers to claim they came away from the experience with anything negative. It is, in a subtle but firm way, inculcated into them that any negativity in the experience must be due to a deficiency on their part. Usually, the experience itself is wonderful but, like the regular guy who got to sleep with the fashion model, it's only the morning after that they might discover they got a present they weren't expecting—like an S.T.D. or a negative/evil entity now in residence inside the regular guy. It is intimately attached like a parasite that feeds off the host. It will drain strength, will, spiritual energy and even love. It can remain there for years—even for a lifetime. The darkness grows more powerful the longer it stays with the host. Eventually, the host can no longer hide their condition from friends and family. The person may go to a shaman, a priest or a light worker to get rid of the entity but there are no guarantees. All entities are distinct. Some are more powerful than others and like Forrest Gump with the candy box, *you never know what you're gonna git.*

While conducting paranormal workshops, I have encountered Abductees who appear to function as normal members of society. They tend, on the average to be Caucasian women in their 30's or 40's that are aware they have been abducted and returned to their homes by creatures they believe to be Extra-Dimensional. Most often, I have found in interviewing them, is that they do not wish to be hypnotically regressed to get a fuller picture of what happened to them. I believe he main reason many of these women will not attempt to acquire full recall of missing time and abduction is that they fear finding out that they were impregnated and then harvested. They could not stand the thought of knowing for sure that they have children, even possible alien hybrid children, somewhere that they would never be allowed to see. Most will not start down that rabbit hole and who can blame them? This begs the question what kind of creatures could harvest a human female in that way and then have no remorse about never allowing the mother to have contact with the child?

Real evil always starts with coercion. Anything that countermands our free will is inherently negative. In a true Extra-Dimensional abduction, no one gives their consent, although sometimes they might act foolishly, e.g.: flashing lights at an Extra-Dimensional craft or rushing to confront Grey entities that happen to be carrying on some activity in a remote area.

Abductees tend to have very high IQ's, above average intelligence (perhaps these are qualifiers for Extra-Dimensional abduction) have very good jobs/positions which they do not wish to endanger by going all the way down the rabbit hole of Extra-Dimensional abduction experience.

The general steps that occur during true Extra-Dimensional abductions are:

1. The Taking - The Abductee is taken without consent from Earthly surroundings to apparent alien surroundings.
2. Examination - Invasive medical or scientific procedures are performed on the Abductee. This is often the most terrifying part of the abduction.
3. Communication - The Abductors speak to the Abductee only to try to calm them down. Sometimes the Greys appear confused at extreme displays of emotion. They also appear to be able to read emotions of the subject (this can give the appearance of being able to read thoughts)
4. Tour - The Abductees are sometimes given a tour of their captors' supposed vessel.
5. Loss of Time - Abductees memories of the event are erased and sometimes replaced with false memories.
6. Return - The Abductees are returned to earth often with clothing askew (like shirts put on backwards) or with injuries they cannot explain.
7. Epiphany–Sometimes the Abductee will realize a mystical experience very much like the Contactees of the 50's and 60's who were touched by wonderful messages of oneness with God and the universe. Over time, the negative part of the experience will fade while this positive part will grow in strength and intensity in the mind of the Abductee.

Here are some investigative conclusions I have reached with true ED abductions:

• Although there do seem to be exceptions, every abduction situation begins with some action on the part of the Abductee that *could be* interpreted as consent for the situation to happen—arms raised up, lights flashed or physical pursuit of the captors.

• Females seem to be taken more often than men or it could just be that the men just aren't returned to tell the tale. Again, roughly 30,000 people are reported missing every year in the United States alone. Many of these are returned but a good portion of those who disappear are never heard from again and no resolution is ever found. If you want to be shocked, go look at the Missing person bulletin boards on the Internet for your state for *just this year.* There is no greater desperation and fear than that of loved ones of those who disappear without a trace for no apparent reason anyone can decipher.

• Greys are the type of Extra-Dimensional variety most often associated with abductions such as these. There is a great deal of machine-like efficiency during this process. There is no "*let's sit down and commune together*" which was experienced by the Nordic Contactees of the 50's and 60's. Because of their behavior patterns during these experiences, the most likely conclusion is that Greys are robotic, sentient, pre-programmed, bio-units that lack any emotion or empathy but are just carrying out behavior constructs that have been instilled into them by the superior alien races that created them.

44

MARTHA X

Martha X was in her twenties when she joined an ED outreach program. It was conducted by a very well known "guru" in the field of ufology. Martha had very negative experiences with mainstream religions throughout her young life, so it was refreshing for her to find fellowship with people who were very spiritual but unconstrained by the tyranny of organized religions. The group guru regaled her with stories of the wonderful adventures experienced by the group. The group, both male and females, reinforced the stories told by the guru. She entered into many ET outreach experiences over several years. During this period, she was sexually involved with the group guru as were most other females in the group and some of the males as well. She described the guru as "sexually voracious" but that did not bother her as she considered it a natural outgrowth of "group dynamics."

Later, Martha described mild negative side effects that she attributed to the outreach experiences like headaches, nightmares and horrible visions that would come upon her without warning. At times, these side effects seemed to be triggered by any discussion of Extra-terrestrial life. When her problems were made known to the guru, she was told that her human body is going through a period of adjustment to a "trans-human, positive evolution"—that what she perceives as negative side effects were just the quirks of her primitive humanity working themselves out as her biology progresses to a higher stage.

Over several meetings, I told Martha I wanted to know her most intense abduction experience. She told me like most Abductees, she only relates edited versions of her abduction experiences. Some parts of her experiences are so shocking and graphic that even true believers might judge her in a negative way. Even Martha herself often feels that she must have been responsible, at least in part, for the horror she had to endure because she had literally asked for it. She told me she had never even spoken of this one experience out loud (Martha calls this her "unspeakable experience") but that if I thought I had the constitution to withstand it and would keep her identity always confidential, she would tell me.

One night she was preparing for group-based ED outreach as she did every Sunday evening. She heard a clear voice speak to her. It was in her head but not through her ears. It told her that she was not to go to ED outreach that night and that instead she had an appointment for direct contact with those who called themselves her "Inter-Dimensional brothers." She was told to await the appearance of a "portal" which would bring her to her destination. Martha was instructed to take a vigorous shower, to scrub away any earthly chemicals that might be on her body. Martha had understood that she was not to have any perfume, makeup, fingernail polish or any Earth-produced substance on her body. Then, she was told to lay naked, facedown on her bed. Earthly clothing would also bring contamination to their world. She was somewhat frightened but she followed their directions. She lay on her bed for several hours but no one came. Martha fell asleep in the face down position. Several hours later, she was roused by a bright green light emanating from a pulsating source in what she thought was still her bedroom. She tried to move her head to see but found that she could not move.

She felt a tingling energy throughout her body that seemed to relax her muscles. The green misty light seemed to bubble with an effervescent, peaceful energy and it traveled through her body. She felt waves of peace and euphoria. Martha was not in her bedroom. Instead, Martha found herself on a *metallic-seeming* table that somehow had a yielding texture that contoured to her body. The metal seemed to light up and came alive wherever her body was in contact with it. Martha felt more comfortable than if she had been ensconced in a soft mattress bed.

She was in a dark room in which she felt several beings shuffling about. They had thin, dark appendages for legs but their feet were not visible under some type of slippers they wore. The room was brightly lit but it was gray with no discernible lines or corners. Then she heard metallic sounds like tools in a toolbox being laid on a metallic table. There were no soothing words or three-fingered stroking of her skin. The effects of the green energy began to wear off. Terror struck a cold chill through her. She tried to tell them she wanted to leave, that she didn't agree to this, that this wasn't what she thought it would be, that she wanted to go home. Instead, all she emitted was a pitiful groan. They approached within a few feet of the table/bed/thing she was on. She felt living tentacles examining her body. They felt wet like dog's noses as they sniff. She got a strong mental impression that somehow these appendages were seeing, smelling, tasting and measuring her vibration of emotional energy as they examined every crevice of her body. There were at least six of them coming at her from different angles—each as thick as a grown man's wrist.

They weren't coming from the creatures standing around but from some device. By now her body had been roughly arranged into a position on all fours—with only her knees and hands supporting her weight. Every part of her body was pushed into the position they wanted her—back arched sharply and posterior high in the air. She received more mental images of cows. *Human cows*...she didn't know what that meant...if they were insulting her or referring to some hybrid. They were struggling to hold steady a device several feet above her that was the source of the tentacles. It was suspended in the air and they had to keep it in a centralized juxtaposition above her back. The tentacles seemed to be testing the immediate spikes in her stress levels whenever they came close to her vaginal and rectal areas. Martha clenched as much as she could as the "sniffing" increased in intensity at her orifices, including her mouth. Martha had heard from other Abductees that the Greys had a liquid they would throw on subjects to make them "sexually receptive" whether they were men or women. She received no such courtesy. Martha deadpanned: "I was terrified. I knew what was going to happen and *I was dry as a bone.*" Martha would finish with a strange grin each time she tried to shock me as if that was an accomplishment to her.

The tentacles were apparently self-lubricated but that still didn't make the penetrations comfortable. Martha was penetrated in several places. Something even jammed down her throat so her breathing was blocked off. She lost her breath and couldn't get it back. She gasped and began to lose consciousness but then perceived a phrase from those that stood around the table:

Relax and breathing will be done...

Martha felt her body sprayed from above (it might have been some type of nozzle or another tentacle) with some sort of liquid. She felt the greenish tingly relaxation energy spread through her body again. This time, however, the energy did not dissipate. It seemed to intensify in waves throughout her body. She stopped struggling and *somehow she felt her body breathing.* The breathing was not through her throat that was fully occupied by the eel-tentacle that blocked her windpipe. Martha's entire body relaxed as the eels continued their work, penetrating her. Then she perceived another phrase.

This one may survive...

Instead of being frightened, she only felt the waves of the greenish energy cascading through her body and increasing in intensity. The energy transmogrified into euphoria all along her skin and she even felt it coalesce wherever the appendages thrust into her. At this point in the story, Martha looked at me and with a wry smile stated: "Then, after that, *it wasn't bad at all.*"

She scanned my face for signs of judgment and found none. Martha was done with the story. She would say nothing else except to add that the ones who took her did not mean to frighten her. She excused them by saying that they are limited in their interactive protocols. How she could know such a thing? I did not think to ask at that moment.

Martha advised that shortly after her ED abduction experience she was also abducted by government forces and implanted with several devices that she still has in her body today. At that time she stopped participating in alien outreach. She resigned from the group without explanation. They never attempted to follow up with her or check on her condition. Today she is unable to hold a conventional job or maintain normal relationships. Fortunately, since she is a very talented and well-known artist, she maintains a very good living in her field. The raw emotion of her shattered condition seems to add to the visceral power of her art. Today, she is completely convinced that her ED contact experience had nothing to do with the negative psychological and physical side effects she is suffering today. No amount of discussion can convince her otherwise.

Martha testifies that it was the government, which sabotaged her outreach experiences. She believes that the government found out she was participating in the outreach and then put her on a list to be surveiled, implanted and made a constant victim or black ops technology that most people don't even know exists. She advises that the government has MIB following her constantly—that they abducted her and implanted her with devices in her skull, neck and thigh. She becomes fuzzy on the reasons why she hasn't attempted to have these devices removed. People have suggested to her that she should look at possible alternative reasons why she suffers these symptoms. During a workshop, several participants suggested to her that she should consider seeing a priest or a shaman about possible negative spiritual entities that could be attached to her. Martha brushes these recommendations aside as she focuses only on numerous instances of government agents following her everywhere. She has hours upon hours of stories of government agent abuses against her and technological device harassment of her psyche for anyone who will listen. No matter how much anyone tries to help her, she remains dogmatically faithful to her interpretation of events and will not consider hypnosis or any method to remove possible screen memories. The last time I sat with her she had to visibly pause what she was saying every few minutes. Her face would tighten into a grimace and she would freeze for moments at a time.

"They (the government) are buzzing some signals into my skull." She would whisper through clenched teeth. Her shoulders and neck would tighten and I could see the fine hairs on her arms standing up. It was quite real but I don't believe it's the government or technological devices. Watching this up close is quite disturbing. Again, she continues to brush off any suggestions that she could have *Extra-Dimensional* negative attachments or implants. She insists that she's proven many times that it's the government that has been doing this to her for over twenty years.

Martha X chose the paradigm she currently lives and she will remain loyal to it until her dying day. We as a species will soon have to make similar choices and the consequences will be even greater. Like Martha, we will make a choice. We will either cooperate and welcome or reject and resist the taking of human sovereignty.

§

Here is the greatest reveal of this work: coming soon— The End Game. Look for entire city blocks of people, buildings full of people, entire sections of people, all disappearing in a flash without any explanation, followed by a transparent government attempts to cover it up, explain it away or to confuse the issue with disinformation, e.g.: responsibility taken by some new terrorist group that says it now possesses "the disappearance bomb."

Then, look for *entire towns, cities and regions of people, animals, anything alive,* to disappear the same way—without warning or a trace left behind. I don't expect them to reappear any time soon but if they do—they will have no memory whatsoever of what occurred and they will have missing time for the entire period they were gone.

Extra-Dimensional abductions of humans have not stopped but the average mainstream person has become so acutely dumbed down by cultural conditioning that it has become a simple matter for authorities to ignore this phenomena without any consequences. Very soon they won't be able to ignore it any longer.

45

THE TRANSDIMENSIONAL ADDENDUM

What could you possibly have that's more precious than gold?

It *isn't* your temporary physical life. It's not your house, your stocks or any material thing that the EPIC (Elite Powers In Control) can get their hands on. It's your eternal soul and the permanent spiritual connection it has back to Creator-Source. Zecharia Sitchin related to us, after enormous scholarship into ancient prehistoric documents, his final investigative conclusion that the human race was created as a slave race by alien masters called "Annunaki." Ultimately, he elaborated, the Annunaki wanted the human race to mine all the gold out of the planet Earth and that they are coming back to finish the job. Although I do not agree that anyone created humanity except Creator-Source; there are aspects of his theory that resonate in truth.

There are beings here on Earth with us who are caretakers and they are also our "conditioners" assigned to make us believe that all things are material and that we have nothing that is precious that they cannot take. That is the assignment of the Globocrats assigned to lord over us—the EPIC. They are the directors and rulers who issue orders through the Bankster class and the political class that sit astride the national populations of the earth.

The political "leadership" throughout the Western world does the bidding of the Overseer Bankster class who manage and "ordain them." They are the presidents, prime ministers and parliaments who, receiving marching orders issued from the Banking Overlords; send our people into manufactured wars, manipulated crises and created disasters. These political minions encourage us to separate into artificial racial, ethnic, political, and religious groups; so that we constantly attack each other and live at each other's throats. The political minions are good at little except to pretend that they are actually in charge of the nations they occupy. These political figures join together with the Global Media to create false global crises with pithy, noble titles like "The War on Drugs," "the War On Poverty," or "War On Terrorism." These are distractions to keep us trapped in the materialist fantasy that makes us much more open to the future endeavors that the EPIC is preparing for us. There are two types of control the EPIC has used more than any other to convince us that we have no gold, nothing precious and nothing of any value.

The two are: control of our language and control of *what we think of as real.*

Albert Einstein said: *you cannot solve a problem with the same mind that created it.* This is a profound statement addressing the priority of imagination over intellect. We must be able to perform this shift when pondering the great mind-traps. We must shift sideways from the limited thinking that created a crisis in order to resolve that crisis. How can we address the tragedy of global chem-trails with the same attitude of obsequiousness to national governments, which helped create this devastating plague? We cannot. We must enter a mind-frame of non-cooperation with those who seek to do us harm. Only then can we begin to seek solutions that have any long-term value.

The Transdimensional Addendum*: you cannot remedy problems that were created trans-dimensionally, while remaining confined to single dimensional thinking.*

How can the Awakened or even the unawakened mainstream masses hope to effectively resist the plans of EPIC when they do not understand their origins, composure or even their true motivations?

You can't just stay on that flat, two-dimensional map if you expect to find escape from prisons that were set up originally, thousands of years ago—from across other dimensions of reality and near-reality. The Extra-Dimensionals come and go from our extremely limited physical reality to other dimensions as do many other beings associated with and created by them. They do not abide in our time and space for long periods for the same reasons that we don't swim in sub-zero freezing water for very long—it becomes unpleasant and potentially fatal. Yet there have been periods during man's existence when the Extra-Dimensionals were able to stay in our dimension of time and space for extended periods because they achieved fully physical incarnations somehow. Currently, they are working to create that situation again and *very soon* they will, once again, achieve that goal.

The term "UFO" was an attempt to address a transdimensional conundrum by addressing it as a purely physical phenomenon, existing in our time/space dimension. What did you see? What happened when you touched it? Did you get pictures and videos? Will the military try to shoot them down? These are all the questions of the single reality thinker and they will never get us anywhere while investigating the Extra-Dimensionals. This fact is well known to global controllers of our society, EPIC— simply because they *also* were put into place over our society *trans-dimensionally.* The EPIC are also multi-dimensional, so they are quite tickled as they watch us after six decades continue to play the game of *"prove it's a supernatural UFO."*

"NWO" is also part of the old language the awakened need to leave behind. The EPIC delights in such language because it serves two purposes. It's used as a code word label for those resisting EPIC to self-identify so that they are easy to find when the hour of global registration and accounting arrives. Also, the description is so inaccurate that it leads us in all the wrong directions in trying to identify the Elite Powers In Control. The EPIC is not a "New World Order." The EPIC is not "New." It is very ancient. It was put into place right after the beginnings of the world as several human bloodlines were established in dominance of the global human pyramid. These bloodlines travel through thousands of years of our history always in the same position at the top of the pyramid. The bloodlines transmogrify and re-invent themselves into slightly different cultural identities each time a new world empire enters into dominance over the globe but they always maintain their position at the top of the pyramid. They have no loyalty to nations, to humanity or even to each other—they only value power.

Also the EPIC is not, strictly speaking, of this world. And finally it has almost nothing to do with "Order." The EPIC is only about subjugation and control. The only "Order" involved is the order of oppressive institutions meant to enforce and regulate control. Its true aim is *chaos* and then control. This type of "order" is akin to the horrific brand of order enforced as the Nazi officer uses his left hand to direct weaker prisoners to go into the gas chambers while using his right hand to direct healthier workers into the slave camp to labor and live a bit longer for the benefit of the ruling class.

We can never hope to fully comprehend EPIC, how it functions, maintains control of the national governments of the world without understanding transdimensional realities. We face the exact same challenge with the Extra-Dimensionals that have visited and co-inhabited our planet since before recorded history. The question of who exactly rules this world and how they do it; can be answered by looking to a system and structure that was originally placed into dominance over humanity by ancient bloodlines utilizing transdimensional modalities. Similarly, the question of who the Extra-Dimensionals are and what they want can also only be answered by looking beyond the physical confines of our present illusion/prison of time, space and physical reality.

Here is the final Investigative Conclusion of this section. The main roles served by EPIC is to convince as many humans as possible that we are only material beings—not ensouled, eternal spirit creatures wrapped in a temporary bio-suit. Only in this way can they make us vulnerable for whatever plans the Extra-Dimensionals have for us in the very near future

46

P.L.A.S.M.A.S.

The EPIC maintains control over mainstream culture largely through linguistic devices—code language that creates a reflexive response in those who are trained and controlled to represent what EPIC calls "the common herd." These linguistic controls are so deeply ingrained into the culturally conditioned minds of the herd that they don't even know they are acting in accordance with their training. Mental reflex makes the herd designate anyone on whom the trigger labels are pinned as: obtuse, ridiculous, untrustworthy, mentally unstable—lunatics whose opinions can be dismissed with no loss to the intellectual discourse of society:

conspiracy theorist
conspiracy believer
Bigfoot believers
Ghosts-hunters
Poltergeist-seekers
Aura-readers
Psychics
New World Order Resisters
Illuminati
Clear-Hearers
Seers
Shamans
Paranormal Believers

Certain labels have been so linguistically developed and instilled into the mainstream population as to elicit a biological response from the human amygdale. This is the organ at the base of the human brain that produces fear, anger, suspicion, distrust and hatred. The trigger of a dismissive attitude is only the first level of response. Setting off the fear response is the real aim of cultural conditioning. Fear-response-code-language has been cultivated only to target people participating in legal, protected activities. The national governments can't arrest them but they can still target them for their EPIC masters. The proxies of EPIC in the media always color these people and associates as: borderline criminals, liars or putatively dangerous to ordinary members of society. The agents of mainstream culture will pontificate on such groups for long hours just for the precious seconds needed to unleash those trigger labels/code-words on the culturally conditioned mainstream audience:

anti-government
militia-members
potential terrorists
fundamentalists
extremists
marijuana-users
believers in the supernatural
UFO believers

These labels are the pulsating neon collars they wish to wrap around our necks. They are so ingrained into our mentality that not only do we accept their usage by the agents of the mainstream without taking umbrage—we, The Awakened, actually continue to use them *on each other*. This is like prisoners, during their private time together at the prison, referring to each other by their prison numbers instead of by their given names.

"Hey 95045-87, how you living today?"

"I'm living easy baby, but 83874-09 has been hassling me to pay up those stamps I owe him so he can pay 94353-43."

Could there be anything more self-degrading than that? Prisoners would never submit to such degradation, yet this is exactly what we are doing when we voluntarily used labels like "Conspiracy, UFOs" or even "Extra-Terrestrials."

This archaic language designed by jailers for prisoners is highly destructive of liberty, freedom and self-respect. These are code-phrases for recognition and control. Over many years they have shaped these phrases to elicit the images and opinions they wish to inculcate in the hearers of these phrases. Once these labels have been unleashed, the agent of the mainstream has done his/her work. They know *very few* awakened exist in any general audience. By dropping these all-important phrases, they have triggered the dismissal/fear reflex in 95 percent of the audience, thereby guaranteeing prevention of any further awakening. This is what EPIC demands.

When we use these phrases among ourselves it is like placing neon dog collars around each other's necks. They can be spotted from a mile away, *even at night*. They make us easy to find, identify and re-corral back to the pen.

We are hopefully at the end of the road for the phrase "UFO." The phrase UFO doesn't really say anything or help anyone in any positive way. It means nothing more than an object flying that no one can identify at that moment. It's term made up by an Air Force pilot *in the 1950's* and people in the Awakened Community still use it as if it means something. It is also associated to another antiquated wildly inappropriate term "Flying Saucer." What sort of images does that term conjure up? These terms mean nothing more than we are still playing into the hands of those who dictate our language and place those verbal collars around our necks. The only real purpose the phrases "UFO" and "UFO believer" really serve is that they immediately elicit, in the culturally conditioned mind: images of people who exist on the fringes of society, adult males in their 30's who live in their mothers' basements and who watch too many science fiction movies, hillbilly's living in the outback hills who still think helicopters in whisper-mode are alien craft and sky-watchers who don't know what Chinese lanterns, military grade flares or the planet Venus look like on a moon-less night.

This trained response should have been undone by the last several decades of former government officials, astronauts, Generals, pilots, politicians and many high government officials with nothing to gain and everything to lose; coming forward in public to give personal testimony as to the reality of unexplainable, paranormal, supernatural objects. The huge disconnect between the paranormal suspicions of yesteryear and modern paranormal reality should have eviscerated the mainstream reflex responses and the power of the old code words. You would think so but *you'd be wrong.*

Once cultural conditioning takes hold, it requires shocking, bold action to break it. It cannot be undone by polite alternative education for the tiny awakening minority that exists today. It requires linguistic rebellion against the code words of the previous paradigm. It requires jarring non-compliance with the masters of mainstream language in public, in private and wherever ideas can spread. It requires bold new speech patterns—backed up by the belief and commitment that we will *not* wait for the mainstream to accept our ideas. Instead, we will boldly seize: the initiative, the inspiration and create our own language—a language that rejects fear and embraces the infinite.

Mainstream repeaters will always confront such rebellion with umbrage, ridicule, laughter; which are disguised forms of fear—fear that they might be wrong in everything they believe, fear that they have invested in the wrong paradigm and fear that as we discard these neon collars, they may be left behind.

The phrase "UFO" carries an enormous amount of negative baggage. The majority of society don't even read books on a regular basis and aren't aware of the developments outside of mainstream culture in the last couple of decades. They aren't even aware that the scientific community has been dragged kicking and screaming into the reality that the Earth is constantly being visited by Non-Terrestrial beings. Yet, mainstream media's highest mission remains the same—to suppress any chance of the sleepers awakening and escaping from the control matrix—*and they do it very well.*

As we replace the phrase "New World Order" with Elite Powers In Control (EPIC) and "Conspiracy Theorist" with Truth-Seeker, we must now replace the ancient, outmoded and obsolete term "UFO." These labels and many others are just self-identifiers than allow the national governments to target (data-mine) and find potential troublemakers (or worse, possible Awakening Thinkers). We must discard these collars. The time has arrived.

The replacement for UFO is the acronym **PLASMAS**:

Paranormal—having supernatural qualities such that no terrestrial explanation or natural explanation can be provided for this particular craft in the physical/material iteration

Living—a living creature, sentient, intelligent but also programmable like a computer

Aura-Reading—able to read the auras and emotions of living creatures, especially humans

Soul-Printing—able to record, collect and store a blueprint of a human soul for later reference

Mobile—able to move through physical or non-physical media and even able to dematerialize

Aerial—most likely in the air when it wishes to be seen by as many humans as possible

Scanners—unoccupied scanners constantly roving to carry out their programming—to collect soul-prints of as many "interested" humans as possible

SUPERNATURAL PLASMAS

The likely material that genuine Paranormal Extra-Dimensional craft are made of is some sort of plasma in a fluid flux state. Plasma is electrically neutral, highly ionized gas composed of positive ions, negative electrons, and neutral particles. The plasma state is a phase of matter distinct from solids, liquids, and normal gases. Objects that have the ability to materialize as solid and then disappear again out of the visible spectrum of light probably have to shift the presence of charge carriers to respond strongly to electromagnetic fields. Like gas, plasma does not have a definite shape or a definite volume unless enclosed in a container. Plasmic state, therefore, is an appropriate state of matter/energy for *shape-shifting objects*.

Plasmas are hot gases containing a significant number of electrically charged particles, and are on display in nature, especially its shape-shifting properties: in lightning, the Sun's core and the Aurora Borealis. Plasmas also are depicted in devices such as fluorescent light bulbs, fusion reactors, and even plasma televisions albeit on a tiny scale compared to the weather related variety. Plasma was originally referred to as "radiant matter."

There is much anecdotal and even photographic evidence that these paranormal objects do shift through the plasmic state. Creation of craft out of anything resembling plasma is far beyond the technological reach of any human technology by not just centuries but probably by eons. It is both paranormal and supernatural.

These paranormal objects we see in the skies, the oceans, disappearing into the earth, the volcanoes and mountains may not literally be "made" of plasma—but our understanding of what plasma is—is probably the closest we can come to describing the high intensity vibrating, phasing and shifting energy particles that make up these supernatural vehicles/entities.

LIVING

We are jumping to conclusions when we see PLASMAS and assume they are craft carrying beings inside of them. We are anthropomorphizing Alien Visitors into our own version of human space travelers. Because *humans* would need craft to protect us in intergalactic space travel, we imagine they are also cramming themselves physically into little spacecraft as humans would need to do. Their technology is likely thousands of solar years ahead of that need.

Coincidentally, in the majority of anecdotes about both Contactees and Abductees seeing PLASMAS and then coming into contact with ED beings almost never do the witnesses actually seen anything emerge from any craft. The Alien Visitors usually appear in the immediate vicinity, in closer proximity to the witnesses than to the supposed vehicle craft. The witnesses never see a moment like from the 50's movies where the silver ship dramatically opens its portal and the beings emerge in a geyser of mysterious vapors. I don't believe any of the Alien Visitors are really in those ships at all.

I have concluded that the various craft that accompany the appearance of these ED creatures: Grey, Nordic or Reptilian, are like "familiars" in sorcery. These PLASMAS are similar to trained cats or dogs that travel alongside their owners for a limited and specific purpose: to scan and collect information about the subjects of the visitors attentions—*us*.

Here is the account in the Bible that appears to refer to the typical PLASMAS that are in the popular consciousness today.

Ezequiel 1:16 to Ezequiel 1:21

> *This was the appearance and structure of the wheels: They sparkled like chrysolite, and all four looked alike. Each appeared to be made like a wheel intersecting a wheel. As they moved, they would go in any one of the four directions the creatures faced; the wheels did not turn about as the creatures went. When the living creatures moved, the wheels beside them moved; and when the living creatures rose from the ground, the wheels also rose. Wherever the spirit would go, they would go, and the wheels would rise along with them, because the spirit of the living creatures was in the wheels. When the creatures*

moved, they also moved; when the creatures stood still, they also stood still; and when the creatures rose from the ground, the wheels rose along with them, because the spirit of the living creatures was in the wheels.

This sounds similar to remote control of unmanned guided vehicle technology, except far more advanced. Yet the most essential idea expressed is this: ***the spirit of the living creatures was in the wheels.***

The Plasmas are not vehicles for anyone inside but are actually sentient life. They are guided/navigated by spiritual creatures both existing outside them nearby but also giving them a portion of their life force as well. Later in the same passage they are called *"the whirling wheels"* when they are called into dynamic action

Any study of Contactee and Abductee and even near-Contactee cases releases a torrent of anecdotes about the many ways that people arrived at the conclusion that the PLASMAS are: alive, sentient, intelligent and that there is *no one and nothing* crammed inside of them.

"Skinwalker Ranch," is a property located on approximately 480 acres southeast of Ballard, Utah. It is the site of numerous PLASMAS sightings and contacts. One rancher on this property was patrolling his property at night when he was "stalked" by something he called a "black manta craft." He hid in a planted field, as the enormous craft passed over his position. The rancher crouched among tall corn crops in his field. The enormous silent vehicle was scanning from about 500 feet above his head in the night sky. Blue spotlights came close to his position. He held his breath. The floating behemoth passed by his position. The rancher exhaled and shifted his weight. He cracked a twig under his boot. The craft stopped and turned toward his position. The beaming blue lights came down squarely on his position, edging closer to him. As the spotlight hit him—an explosion of furious black wings ejected through the spotlight. It was two young turkeys. The blue spotlights followed the birds as they flew, ran and crashed through the far side of the field. Then, the spotlights cut off and the manta craft continued on its way. The Manta let the birds go but the rancher didn't feel he would have been as fortunate.

After that experience, the rancher advised paranormal researchers on his land to treat the phenomenon as if it were *a wild animal.*

The annals of past ufology are replete with numerous examples of evidence that these craft are not craft at all but are living, sentient creatures. The preponderance of these anecdotes and witness testimony attesting these Extra-Dimensional "craft" are alive could easily serve as the subject for another work all on its own.

So if they are sentient life—what is their purpose? It is primarily to hunt down and retrieve (that's right like a dog) human data and bring it back to the ones who programmed them. How do I know this?

Because it happened to me.

AURA READING/SOUL PRINTING

When I was a child nearing my ninth birthday in New York City, my family took me to a wedding reception party at a rented hall where I had a wonderful time playing with other children in my age group. At some point during the late night, myself and about six other children ran out into the streets as the hour approached midnight on this particular Saturday night. Our group of unruly kids left behind the bright lights and the echoing Spanish meringue music of the joyous festival and ran out into the urban landscape. A dynamic game of tag degenerated into boys running and attacking each other in the streets. One boy I was sparring with was a little big for me. He was a rough-hewn character, big and strong but slow as molasses on a winter day. I tagged him with ease several times, avoiding his attempts to reciprocate. But with a puncher's luck, he caught me with a vicious uppercut to my stomach. I went down flat on my back on the concrete sidewalk. One of the kids screamed something about me being badly hurt—so they took off. They disappeared back in the direction of the rented hall several blocks away.

I was on the cement sidewalk lying on my back, trying to catch my breath. A sharp pain in my stomach subsided as my breath, thankfully, came back. As I sucked in the cool night air, I finally noticed where I was. Although I was only several blocks away from the rental hall where two hundred people were dancing and partying, I might as well have been miles away. The streets were deserted, there was no sound and I was alone in one of the most dangerous places on earth. I was in "The Projects."

Projects were the high-rise apartment buildings built by the Federal government to warehouse poor people and welfare recipients from the 1960's to the 1980's; when they were, mercifully, all torn down. Governments thought these were the perfect solution to provide low cost housing for urban poor on massive scale. The poor grudgingly accepted the benefit of living in these projects but their extreme resentment expressed itself, as they destroyed every one of these projects: graffiti, vandalism and crime made all the projects unlivable until they all had to be destroyed by the same governments that eagerly put them up thirty years previous.

Yet, despite the danger of where I was, something kept me rooted to that spot. Instead of running back to the elegant rented hall, I kept staring up between the two tallest buildings I had ever seen (they were each about twenty stories tall). Something began to swirl and materialize just above the two buildings. It appeared to be a black cloud that roiled, expanded and contracted like a living thing. It reminded of the "Jacque Cousteau's Mysterious Oceans," when they would show the black ink cloud used by an angry squid to escape Jacque's probing hand. The cloud far above my head looked just like that black ink cloud given off by the squid—except, times a thousand. There was no moon and the sky was pitch black so the cloud blended perfectly with the night so as to be invisible—nearly. Something was disturbing the cloud, causing it to throw off tendrils of black and puffs of inky smoke. Then, from the bottom of the cloud something emerged. It was a large circular silverish thing like a (forgive the language) "flying saucer." At that age my only frame of reference for such a thing was a television show called "Lost In Space" that regularly depicted such things. The thing in the sky just above those buildings resembled the pretend saucers on Lost In Space. From the bottom of the "whirling wheel" there were lights that appeared to be spinning in a circle at the bottom.

I was now on my feet and staring straight up toward the "whirling wheel" emerging from the inky black cloud. I felt a hypnotic fascination as it appeared to descend lower. I was transfixed as the thing lowered down closer. A bluish spotlight struck me and I knew something life changing was about to happen. Suddenly, from my left, two teenage black girls appeared. They were trying hang on to each other and look up at the same time. Their eyes were wide with fear as they whispered curse words over and over as the glowing lights of the floating craft reflected on their frightened faces. One of them looked over at me and shrieked.

"You better run home to your Mama, little boy. The world might be ending!"

The spell was broken. I jumped in place and shifted my feet. The girls were gone as if in a puff of smoke. The saucer just above me abruptly reversed course. It began elevating back into the inky black cloud. It disappeared along with the cloud, like the cartoon characters that jump down a hole and then pull the hole in after themselves.

As I looked back from my full gallop and saw that saucer disappear that night, I couldn't help feeling it had "read me." Beyond just reading me, I intuited that it had recorded something about me that told the scanner everything there was to know about me. It had *"soul printed"* me for future reference. This was long before I knew anything about what auras were or what "soul printing" was but I knew that whatever information the saucer acquired about me; it did not like. That may be why I was not taken that night.

AERIAL/MOBILE

Whether we see them materializing or dematerializing in our skies, rising from the oceans, disappearing into the earth, egressing volcanoes and the mountains; they are often moving to places where they garner massive attention. In the air is the most likely place to find them but they will go anywhere that human attention can be attracted so they can do their work and complete their program. That program, once again, is to scan humans, read our auras to determine receptiveness, collect a soul-print (which may also include a genetic chromosome blueprint as well) and return all this data back to their masters.

SCANNERS

There is a new hobby spreading throughout the Awakened Community. It involves getting the latest generation infrared night vision goggles. Then, the person has to find a spot out in the high desert (or any area away from city lights) and set up camp until real darkness falls. It is best to plan it on a moonless night so there is a minimum of light pollution/ambient light to interfere with the night vision. Any extra light coming toward your position from any source around you will corrupt the device's ability to pierce far out into the night sky. With these devices you can perceive bands of light that are not normally visible to the human eye. You'll see things that otherwise can't be seen at all. You may even know intuitively that these things are up there but even with that intrinsic belief, the naked eye still can't see them. However, with these devices over your eyes and under the conditions I described if you maintain your visual acuity, focus and faith; you will see something *that will astound you.*

Eventually, among the stars, satellites and planes you will begin to see PLASMAS— ships that move, maneuver, appear and disappear in ways that human-created ships cannot. You'll see them jump, skip, do hard 90 degree pivots/turns, do complete stops, do total reversals in a fraction of a second, you'll see them jump around each other (not bumping or crashing into one another but coming close). Anyone who has any familiarity with physics at all knows that human craft that maneuver in this way would smash their human occupants into red jelly due to the reality on our physical plane of "G-force." Supposing for a moment that these were human- made, unoccupied, *remote controlled vehicles* (human made but *without human occupants*)—no such maneuvers could be executed because they would lose control over almost all such unmanned vehicles, due to the hazards of executing such risky maneuvers. Also, remote pilots from the ground would never be permitted by the military establishment to execute such risky maneuvers for any reason.

The craft described here are not of human origin and are not occupied by humans. Amazingly, you'll even occasionally see them shoot beams of light at each other. This goes on over our heads every night and, consequently, some in the Awakened Community have sounded the alarm that an intergalactic war is going on in our skies. They say that the governments know what is happening but refuse to tell us so as not to induce a panic.

After having observed these antics in the night sky myself, I have reached a different conclusion. The movements, the cadence, the rhythms of the ships, semi-circling around each other, breaking off suddenly, running at each other, stopping, running back and circling back around—it all reminded me of an earthly scene I'd observed before many times. If you are a dog lover you already know what I'm going say. Watching these Extra-Dimensional ships over our atmosphere during many months reminded me of something that was in my consciousness but it took me a long time to recall. Have you ever been in a dog park and watched several dogs that may or may not know each other, play with other until they get over excited? They will run at each other, bark, growl, break off at the last possible second before a collision, run around, circle and come in for another pass at the other dogs; until things get out of hand and one dog will finally nip at another. Then the masters will call a halt until things calm down and they can begin the whole cycle over again.

There is no war or even a serious battle going on above us. If there were, with the technology that the Extra-Dimensionals have available to them, the destructive results would be felt throughout the Earth, both in the skies and on the ground. That is not happening. Once in a while during these observations we may even see one ship emit a beam of light towards another. Soon afterwards, both ships usually dematerialize. I believe these sentient, plasmic, living, mobile/aerial scanners—these PLASMAS—are playing with each other like dogs would…running around each other and barking like dogs do. During this play, when we see a beam of light shot from one PLASMA to the other it is because they are attempting to steal data from each other—like a dog attempting to snatch a bone from another dog. What is that data? It's us. They are scanners after all and that is their business—scanning, collecting and soul printing. Once the beams start shooting I believe their masters recall them from the dog park in our night skies. They usually disappear once the beams start.

Here are the Investigative Conclusions of this section. The PLASMA's are sentient, intelligent, programmable life. They live, scan and collect our information. They are like familiars for their masters that accompany them from and to the other dimensions. Their masters do not ride them like horses or wagons. They simply accompany the masters they are assigned to and do their utmost to collect information for them—information *about us.*

47

THE PRIMROSE PATH

We are being led down the primrose path.

The "primrose path" originated as an idiom from ancient England wherein the most wonderful path a person could be led on was strewn with the best of the "first roses" of the season also known as "prima rosas." How wonderful to be led by someone sincere onto a road that is splattered with beautiful, lush, red roses. Yet, often such paths are not as rosy as they appear.

Here is a story that has persisted in the consciousness of Western Europe since the Middle Ages. There were a group of knights charged with providing escort for a captured fugitive—the most vicious and powerful enemy their kingdom had ever known—a man so dangerous that an entire retinue of knights were required to provide security and insulation so that the prisoner could not communicate his lies to anyone. A vow of no contact and no communication had been imposed upon the knights before undertaking the arduous journey to bring the man to judgment. They had been regaled with many tales of the man's merciless butchery of helpless children before he ravished their mothers and then killed them as well. They were told the man was the chief of a band of vicious killers who considered wholesale slaughter of entire towns as a sport, and he also engaged in the ritualistic eating of human flesh to honor his dark gods. They were told the man's followers had fought unto the death and that only the accidental flat of a soldier's blade to the cranium had allowed the Chief to be taken—unconscious but alive. Because the man was such a dangerous enemy of the kingdom—he was being brought back alive for identification by the King himself and (presumably) summary execution.

The knights had been instructed by their nobles to maintain utter secrecy and security as this fugitive would no doubt attempt to escape from the rolling carriage cage that kept him secure during the journey. But far more than security, it was the vow silence that was emphasized to the knights as evidenced by the heavy tarp that was kept over the rolling cage at all times. They were told never to directly observe the fugitive, as he was also an Enchanter who had been given the power by his dark god to enchant anyone into a stupor with just a baleful glare.

They provided him food and amenities through a slit in the tarp and a food slot in the bars. Only the eventual tossing back out of the empty bowl confirmed that the prisoner was still alive in there. One bright morning, half way through the arduous journey, the "senior knight" roused the others to attend the rolling cage. He stated that knights of the King *had to know* whom they were transporting. Senior Knight stated he would drop the tarp for all to observe the savage "Cannibal Chieftain." The other knights intervened but could not stop him before he cut the tarp free.

Instead of the monstrous Cannibal Chief they expected; they were confronted with a wide-eyed young boy gnawing on a mutton bone. The boy couldn't have been more than eighteen years old. Rather than wearing belts made of human ears and other body parts; he had on a simple vest with the seal of the King and wore a ring with the King's bloodline seal and signet. The knights, shocked, regarded each other to confirm if they were all seeing the same thing.

This was the King's sibling.

There had been legends that the King had a younger brother taken and hidden by monks many years ago; so he would not be slaughtered to guarantee the ascension of the King's firstborn son. The knights pieced together that there had been a slaughter at a neighboring monastery; but it was *not* of a band of cannibals—instead the holy monks had been wholesale-murdered by the King's troops. These were Holy men whose only crime was sheltering a helpless child for eighteen summers. The boy would be identified by the King himself (for who else would know for certain) charged with high treason and then be executed.

The knights fell into argument about what was the right thing to do. The argument was quelled from inside the carriage-cage by a commanding voice.
"*Good Knights! Your duty to King and Country are clear. You must deliver your cargo and fulfill your vows.*" The mature man's voice had come from the man-child now standing erect at his full height.

The knights united and stopped their squabbling and set themselves to the grim task. The second half of the journey was much more difficult than the first. There was a flash flood as they passed through a valley that cost many knights their lives. Then, an attack by bandits was fought off with more casualties. Then, serious illness struck their party and reduced their number even further. By the time they were within sight of the King's Castle, there were only three Knights left from the original thirty.

Senior Knight and his two loyal protégées thanked young prisoner for all his help during the harrowing journey. The royal prisoner had shouted for the three to clamber up to the top of the prison cage to survive the rampaging waters in the valley. The boy keeping his own head above the waters rushing into his cage shouted encouragement to them: "*hang on good knights; remember you shall be greatly rewarded by your King once you deliver me.*"

Bandits attacked during the night while the posted guard had fallen asleep. It was the prisoner who yelled alarm and probably saved half their number. Later, during the sickness, the boy provided herbs he had on his person to the final three—herbs that the monks had taught him to use for curative effects. The bewildered surviving three knights asked the boy why he was so anxious to save their lives so they could pull him to his execution. The boy would thrust his chin forward and he would reply: "*Justice had to be done in accordance with the King's will.*"

The next day, Senior Knight, before entering the city saluted the boy for the final time—all three did. They told the boy he was the most honorable man they had ever known. They asked for the boy's absolution for what they were about to do. They knelt before his cage. The prisoner reached through the bars and gently touched each of their heads. The boy forgave each of them for what they were about to do and wished God's grace upon them. The final three, exhausted and relieved, finally entered the city with their cargo. The heavy guard around the city did not question them. Their arrival was expected. Inside the city gates, the town was noisy and busy but they could see the final destination.

The gates opened and a royal escort met them just outside. Without daring to open the canopy that covered the prisoner, the General Agent unfurled a scroll declaring that the prisoner's trial had already been held by a duly appointed Justiciar of the King's Court. The prisoner had been found Guilty En Abscencia of High Treason and would be summarily executed. Then it was pronounced that they were relieving the good knights who were now dismissed from the completion of their sacred assignment. Before handing over a heavy sack of coins, the King's General Agent lifted the tarp to lay his eyes upon the prize.

There was nothing there.

All the men were agog, transfixed, as if staring at the empty space hard enough would force the prisoner to materialize. The General Agent shouted orders to his retinue to spread out, search the city...*leave no place unsearched—no stone unturned.*

The General Agent shouted threats to the Knights. The protégées shifted and looked at their mentor. Senior Knight could not hear the General Agent because he was lost in bewilderment. Blocking out everything else, he approached/focused upon the cage lock mumbling how none of this is possible. The General Agent continued to shout hysterically as Senior Knight examined the lock.

No force marks, no tool marks, and the lock had been turn-keyed into the open position. *There could only be one answer...*

"*He had the key the entire time.*"

Senior Knight experienced a rush of images. Things the boy said came back.

"...your duty to King and Country are clear."

"justice has to be done in accordance with the King's will"

"you three shall be greatly rewarded by your King once you deliver me."

A buzzing, clanging noise at the periphery of hearing increased as the General Agent approached to strike Senior Knight for turning his back on him.

"You fool...I'll see you lose everything for this. You've lost him and the King will never forgive you." The Senior Knight caught the Agent's gauntleted right hand and laughed.

"You're the fool for we've lost no one! I know exactly where he is." Everything stopped. The two protégées thought their mentor had lost his mind. He continued.
"You sent your squadron in the wrong direction. *He's in there."* Senior Knight pointed at the King's Castle. The General Agent snorted at the Senior Knight.

"You are mad. He escaped just to go to the place where his doom awaits?" The senior Knight accorded no submission.
"No. You're wrong. Only his kingdom awaits. *Listen."*
A clamor and clash of arms could be heard from inside the Castle. The Agent turned pale and sent a rider to call back his military retinue immediately. During those precious minutes a cry went up that the King was dead. A look of ashen horror came over the General Agent's face and he galloped away from the castle along with his personal guard.

Later that evening, in the new King's court, the three knights were kneeling before the new King they had previously known only as a disheveled boy-prisoner. Senior Knight chuckled as he regarded the gold-crowned Monarch of his country in purple and gold-lace robes. This day had been planned for a very long time. His troops had been in place in and around the castle. The army had been secured for the Boy-King and the final ingredient of the rebellion was to get the Boy-King inside the city walls and even inside the castle to put his treacherous Elder brother to the sword. Only a King should dispatch a King. The Knights stood before the Boy-King and Senior Knight leaned forward.

You led us down the primrose path your Majesty.

The Boy-King smiled.

"Yes, good knight but it was a necessary part of a great plan. Had you, against such long odds, not fulfilled your oath to deliver me personally to this place, my men at arms could not have carried forth the rebellion they desired against the villainous usurper of my throne. I have generals, military officers and nobles who have awaited my return for years but I have *never* known such brave and determined men as you three. I will keep good on my promises. You have done your duty for King and Country. The villain is dead. His line is cut off and my beloved monks have been avenged. Justice has been done in accordance with my will. Now you three will be rewarded in accordance with your valor, loyalty and trust by your true and righteous King.

All three men received estates, titles and high offices as counselors to the King. They served as his most trusted advisors during his long and prosperous reign.

§

We are also being led down the primrose path. We trek along a long and arduous journey that may be strewn with the first roses of the season or may be a path to our own destruction. We have a mission like the knights, to grow, become better, reach enlightenment, love and help one another, attain spiritual increase and ultimately connect into the Mind of Creator-Source. Like the three knights, we have many parties interested in our progress, in our mission and in our success or failure. We do not know for certain which actors wish us ill or wish us success—but we had better learn fast.

Just as the young prisoner gave his captors a script to follow in congruence with their natural tendencies (honor, integrity, duty) for his own secret purposes; humanity is also being given a script which is contoured and tweaked to appeal to our natural human tendencies (desire for security, longing for salvation and the need to worship things higher than ourselves). Like the story of the three Knights, the story of humanity can easily go either way. We must seize upon any advantage to sort out the conundrum of which Extra-Dimensional beings are for us and which are against us. It is very apparent to the Awakened Community that both types are constantly communicating with us and sending us messages—we have only to listen and exercise wisdom and integrity.

Imagine if the three knights had mistreated and abused their young prisoner instead of treating him with dignity and respect—their story would have had a much darker ending. In order for our human story to take a turn toward the wonderful ending, we must keep moving forward and looking for methods to distinguish between that malevolent King who oppresses and murders his own people and the benevolent "Boy King" who might sacrifice to save us all.

48

THE SIX PERCENT
RESOLUTION

One method for receiving Extra-Dimensional messages is the phenomena known as "Crop Formations or Crop Circles." These are patterns of extraordinary size that are created by flattening out of certain crops such as cornstalks, wheat, barley, rye and many others. Some of these crops are notoriously difficult to flatten through ordinary physical means and even harder to fasten into an arrangement that would keep them in a flat position. This phenomenon has steadily increased around the world since the 1970s. The simplistic name: "crop circle" is a misnomer because these formations run the gamut of complexity from graphic illustrations of geometric cascading patterns to mathematical formulas for building Non-human machines and devices. They carry a variety of codes, images and data that often are quite difficult, if not impossible for human beings to decipher.

They appear in every major nation around the earth and are not restricted to places where crops cover large areas. They also are spontaneously produced against natural stone floors (like the Nazca Lines in Peru) and have appeared in even in permafrost ground in the Antarctica. Against these backgrounds, they consist of ingrained demarcations, visible from high above the Earth, created with an unknown technology that conventional means cannot reproduce.

England gets the largest portion of the most complex, intricate and significant Crop Circles every year. Scientific-Materialists will say that's because England has one of the highest rates of unemployment among youth in the Western world. I opine that the very high amounts of supernatural crop circles that occur in England are due to facts of ancient history. England had the largest population of Shamanic Holy-men in the Western world that were all murdered in the same short period by the rising Roman Empire. The Druids and other lesser-known offshoots were the practitioners of multi-dimensional magicks and many sacred ancient arts that kept people in harmony with the Earth and in touch with the Mind of the Creator-Source. Rome, as part of their campaign to "civilize" the world, committed wholesale slaughter against them so that the people would have no spiritual resistance to Roman forms of organized religion and other spiritual oppression. This is a blueprint for domination that has been carried out all over the planet wherever there existed natural resources to be conquered and exploited long term by EPIC. It is said that because of the commingling of the blood of the Druids/Shamanic Holy men and the soil of England, multi-dimensional portals were opened in the soil of the Earth to *"somewhere else."*

Whatever is in that somewhere else is trying to: reach us, to warn us, to help us and even to help save us. However, it may also be trying to trick us and deceive us. Yet both varieties are attempting to imbue us with an understanding that they exist in other dimensions and will be here soon—all too soon. These messages may seem contradictory but they are not because many realities are revealed from the other side of those "crop circles."

Some crop circles *are* frauds. There have been numerous tricksters who have stepped forward to demonstrate how they make the patterns (although they always leave out how they would do them at night without creating enough light to alert the Queen herself). There is also the question of how anyone could flatten and lace cornstalks in such a way as to keep them from rising back up since this is humanly impossible to do. Anyone who has worked with corn crops can tell you so. Admittedly, some crop circles appear amateurish and can be seen to be frauds prima facie—at first glance—on their appearance alone. Yet, in the business of debunking, usually it's *the sheer volume* of genuine paranormal phenomena that defeats debunkery.

The Six Percent Resolution: In paranormal areas, approximately 94 percent of reported incidents are those in which there are natural, physical or even fraudulent explanations ultimately provided or proven. This resolution still leaves an average of six percent of reported paranormal phenomena, which are genuinely paranormal or supernatural in origin.

There are hundreds of these Crop formations around the world every year and when we apply the Six-Percent Resolution: it still leaves an average of many dozens of annual reported crop circles that are supernatural. That's an enormous number of formations around the globe that have no earthly explanation.

Here is one that falls well within that six percent of genuine supernatural crop formations. There was a crop circle with a binary code message in England that appeared overnight over a space of several acres of land. The entire crop circle was 120 meters large, 80 meters wide—covering almost two football fields of territory. The "2002 Chilbolton Crop Circle ET Face and Disk Message" appeared in wheat on August 15, 2002, Crabwood, Hampshire United Kingdom. It was monumental in artistry and complexity, far above what human instruments could have made in the dark, in a single night, over several football fields of wheat. It had a partial face of what we know as a Grey Alien and a binary code that would take inordinate labor to decipher. Eventually, several experts cooperated to the reveal the binary code and it was translated into English.

"Beware the bearers of the False presence
and broken promises...
Much pain but there is still time
Believe there is still good out there
We oppose deceit
The conduit is closing"

While rationalists and debunkers waste their energy and time arguing over whether this particular crop formation is a fraud, I will let the reader in on a secret known to all Awakened Investigators. Every claim of fraud or charlatans afoot must coincide with human nature in order to merit serious consideration. Any investigation into the breath-taking complexity and artistry of most of these formations depicts that if a cadre of human artists were making these intricate patterns *they would claim well-earned credit* and then go on to become famous artists in some more practical venue. Also, humans would not create these masterpieces at night but would instead create them in full daylight in front of television cameras with throngs of adoring fans looking on. People, especially artists, want to be recognized for their hard work, not so much for ego-gratification, although that is a consideration, but to expand their opportunities to spread their art. *That's just human nature.*

However, I don't believe *human* nature is involved in this formation at all, since it appears to be genuinely paranormal and authentic. In binary code or plain English, we should take this message as truth and respond accordingly. We should agree worldwide to upload a response to computer databases, SETI transmissions, distribute as a prayer/meditation and create as a Crop Circle; a message back to the Extra-Dimensionals. Here is the message we, The Awakened, should put forward:

"We have received your message. We will be wary
of false promises and deception. We shall remain
open to truth and love. We shall hold on to our
gifts and will not worship any except God. We
welcome love and accept no substitute. We will
not be a resource for consumption or slaves.
God is with us always.

49

TAKE-AWAYS

We used to call this bullet points. In this new twitterific, hash-tagged, faced-booked enterprise-tech, multi-media uploaded reality we live in; pithy statements of important ideas serve as more than just bullets. They are dynamically evolving missiles that travel, multiply geometrically and even regenerate themselves until they spread across the Earth to explode in resonance with the masses that believe as the sender does. Here is a review of the most transcendent concepts in this work.

Everything Must Change—Even the Awakened Community has been stuck in paradigms that have kept their reality filter essentially the same for the six decades. By changing just one single thing—the way we think, we will actually be evolving our reality filter—we will be switching from the predigested pap filter that bears the stench of the mainstream and EPIC. In elevating our reality filter we will infuse a new, better reality with the power of our conscious manifestation. We will empower a better reality. Then, we will find, *everything has changed*.

Awakened Investigative Skills Are Key—These are the abilities we must develop to pierce EPIC's veil of deception—No deception, artifice, dissemblance, distraction, elaborate super-structure of lies upon lies; can long survive true Awakened Investigative skills. This is why Awakened Investigators have been so persecuted under the current system—see the author's book—"The Para-Investigators."

Understanding Extra-Dimensionality Is Vital—By comprehending Extra-Dimensionality, we will be opening up our consciousness to much greater spiritual truths. It is our natural Cosmic Birthright to intuitively understand existence outside the opaque veil of limited time and space. We are headed there anyway…eventually. What better opportunity do we have to begin to grasp multi-dimensional reality, other than the fact that multi-dimensional beings are constantly visiting us? Once we understand where they are coming from and going to, then other greater truths will open up to us.

The National Governments Have Nothing For Us—For the Awakened

Community—they have nothing—no disclosure, no remedies or solutions. They follow orders—period. Their great art is to appear spontaneous, embattled, conflicted, and engaged in society's needs; all while they simply carry out the "theater of the pretend dialectic." At this point, professional wrestling should be more convincing to you.

They Need Us—We Don't Need Them—Here is the central heresy that jettisons this work forward into undiscovered country. The Extra-Dimensionals are consumed with a need to contact and engage with humanity. There is voluminous evidence of this fact but even more than engage us—they need to capture our fascination and wonder. They need us to be enraptured with them but conversely also require that we be in fearful dread of them at the same time.

However, we don't *need* them, because we are already ensouled, eternal, spiritual beings who need nothing more to return to Creator-Source. Yet, we must still engage them in order to better protect ourselves from possible interference with our Cosmic Destiny.

Changing Our Language Is The First Step To Changing How We Think—by throwing off all the old cultural trigger language labels: UFOs, Conspiracy Theory, Channelers, Hallucinogens and the rest; in favor of Awakened language: PLASMAS, Truth-Seekers, Clear-Hearers and Entheogenics; we serve everyone. We make it harder for EPIC to keep track of us. Not only should we desist from using the old prisoner language; we must eschew and avoid forums and platforms that continue to use the old language. Only in this way will we proclaim independence from code language distributed by EPIC to an obedient mainstream population. Then, we will strengthen the bonds among the Awakened Community and we begin to change the perception of these concepts even among those who are not yet awakened.

PLASMAS Are Not Controlled By EPIC but the responses are—Whether we are talking about Giants, discs, submergibles or just orbs; all the aftermath to all these events is carefully orchestrated by EPIC institutions. Whether the response is denial, subterfuge, disinformation operations or all three; this response is calculated and executed at the level of the Elite Powers In Control of national institutions.

Para-Normal Is The New Normal—mainstream normality is the last place you want to be standing when the current paradigm tears asunder. Those people will have nothing except panic then terror and finally self-destruction. The good news there is that you are *already paranormal*. You are a glorious, supernatural and eternal entity temporarily shrouded in a gossamer veneer of physicality. You have paranormal abilities whether you know it or not. You only need to decide that this is true and then find out what they are and how to use them.

We are at a saturation point. Like a sponge that is holding more than its capacity of liquid and cannot soak up even a drop more of liquid, we are filled past the brim with sightings, contacts, abductions, Extra-Dimensional (ED) outreach, ED channelings and ED encounters of every possible description (plus many more variants which are kept on the down-low). Genuine sightings of PLASMAS and Extra-Dimensionals are increasing past the point where it is even possible to catalogue (much less analyze) them all—and yet they *still* continue to increase all around the planet.

The stakes have been raised. The wonderment that Extra-Dimensionals instill in human beings is something they cannot afford to lose but thanks, in large part, to innumerable pioneers of the Awakened Community, we are getting very close to a world that accepts the presence of Extra-Dimensional beings as nearly "mainstream knowledge." This will put us in a highly dangerous situation. Out of all the positive and negative developments that have occurred over the eons of ED visitation, I foresee a new epiphenomenon that has more to do with humans than with the Extra-Dimensionals. It is the diminishment of the extreme levels of wonder, astonishment and awe that has traditionally been experienced by humans confronted with the reality of the Extra-Dimensionals in whatever venue. This blasé attitude has already taken hold in the Awakened Community, which has already become very accustomed to E.D. events. In Awakened Circles, E.D. visitations are not just known fact but are even commonly *manifestable* phenomena. Believers congregate in morphogenic energy areas and *actually conjure up* contact episodes with E.D. visitations! If you doubt the truth of this just peruse publicly available video databases to see that it is true (search words: "summoning UFOs").

We are approaching the time when even mainstream people might look up at the sky and say: *"Another UFO? Interesting, but not the best I've seen."* Once the mainstream begins to reflect the same casual attitudes towards our ED Visitors that the Awakened Community exhibits; we will be in mortal danger.

There are two things the Extra-Dimensionals cannot tolerate:

1. Humans actually knowing who they really are and why they are really here.
2. The loss of awe and wonder on the part of the humans who observe them.

Once the Extra-Dimensionals are faced with these two factors, it will mean they will have "to step up their game." They will undertake far more extreme measures to inculcate the awe and wonder they require from humans. It will not matter that these measures also create terror and panic in the targets. Additionally, they will manifest new levels of obfuscation to confuse the issue of who the Extra-Dimensionals are. Like the Roswell crash, designed and executed so long ago for the purpose of disinformation and distraction—there will be multiple Extra-Dimensional operations unfolding across the Earth, to show those who think they have resolved the ED mystery; *they ain't seen nothing yet.*

Here are just a few of the daunting scenarios that could confront humanity shortly:

- City-sized PLASMAS simply set in place above our cities—not moving, not responding, not communicating—how maddening would that be after a year or two.

- Moon bases, which have lain dormant for eons, energized and brought to life and opening up all those underground bases on the "dark side" that NASA has worked so furiously for the last fifty years to cover up—coming to life and sending numerous machines, vehicles and biological creatures to Earth. This would begin a furor against the agencies that were supposed to monitor space for such things.

- Arrival of planet-sized PLASMAS that approach the Earth and maintain a short distance away with no contact. The frenzy of resultant panic, neurosis and sudden rampant religiosity on this planet would lead to chaos.

- Activation of new, menacing, behemoth-like life forms from the center of our own Earth—suddenly proving that hollow Earth is a reality. This would be an attack upon humanity from the Earth itself.

- The rising from our oceans and from beneath the earth of massive bio-machine creatures that will shake our cities all over the globe. This could be ED invasion from an inexhaustible supply of creatures that are fully expendable since they are not truly alive.

- The changing of the DNA genome structure of many segments of human society to morph them into creatures that display strange abilities and may themselves morph into Extra-Dimensional familiars of some sort. This would be E.D. invasion from our own people.

Yet these scenarios, as implausible as they might seem, could be imagined and perhaps even illustrated by Hollywood moviemakers. These hypothetical situations could be entered into war-game computer simulations for generations of possible responses. Yet, I also believe they will be only the beginning, precisely because *they can be imagined*. Far more important are future scenarios that are currently beyond our present imagination.

50

TEOTWAWKI

I am here to suggest the unthinkable.

That isn't just grandiose hyperbole—it's the natural conclusion of Extra-Dimensional truth. Unthinkable in this context means: not within the realm of what humanity can conceive under the current regime of thought and reality—what is beyond our *present imagination* so that we don't have mental framework for it or even have the proper language to describe the possibility.

The nations of the Earth do war-game scenarios for every imaginable hostile event in order to generate defense contingencies for protecting against all possible forms of aggression. This is precisely why humanity can never prepare for a true Out of Context Event. Such an event is something so unthinkable, so outside our human way of thinking, so unimaginable that it would be something that humanity has no frame of reference for—it is *unthinkable*.

I propose this is exactly what humanity will be facing. A tepid descriptor for this type of situation is the "Black Swan event." Since we all know that all swans are brilliant, fluffy white, if we were to see a black swan, we may not even know what we are looking at. Our brain might have trouble acknowledging the reality that such a thing exists; but eventually we would accept it as an extreme anomaly.

A more appropriate descriptor for the Earth-shaking, Out Of Context Event would be a "TEOTWAWKI" event. This is a term that has used among various groups in the Awakened Community for many years. It stands for: The End Of The World As We Know It—the end of the previous world-view, the end of the previous system of understanding, the end of the ways thing were—that's TEOTWAWKI.

In ancient days, the Aztec empire was a very powerful and even technologically advanced human empire. They could defend against and repel any invader, conquer and dominate neighboring nations and even extend their influence to lands far beyond their borders. Although they could conquer any threat in the ancient world, they were not prepared for the TEOTWAWKI event that arrived: the Conquistadores. The Spanish invaders arrived on gigantic wooden ships that represented technology so alien to the Aztecs as to be completely outside their imagination. The Aztecs could not conceive: the enormous floating fortresses the Spaniards rode the oceans in (ships of the Spanish Armada), metallic armor worn like skin over the body, humanoid creatures (the Spaniards) with pale white skin or the giant, four-legged creatures the Conquistadores rode on (Spanish horses).

Since the Aztecs had no mental frame of reference for these things but were still seeing them, they had to adapt whatever mental construct seemed closest to the reality they saw—it was the context of their gods and prophecies. The invaders learned of the Aztec prophecies and with a view toward representing themselves as gods—contoured their behavior to fit many elements of the Aztec "end time prophecies." What began as an Out of Context Event ultimately became a TEOTWAWKI event for the Aztec Empire and Aztec civilization.

Humans face entry through portals into "the paranormal" on a continual basis in this physical existence regardless of what they believe or don't believe. We enter through gateways into dimensions that cannot be explained by scientific materialism during two very common events: *death and dreams*. What occurs to our consciousness and spirit during those times cannot be properly comprehended nor articulated by those still trapped inside the physical/materialist paradigm. When scientists and psychologists attempt to explain what happens to us during death or dreams it sounds like machinery running that someone forgot to turn off. It's just rote prattle that has no connection or effect on we who are not locked in the same the materialist prison with those attempt to explain what they cannot know.

During dreams, we are firmly within the paranormal/supernatural state. Shamans and hyper-spiritualized individuals have the most resonating articulations of what happens to our consciousness and spirits during this nightly journey. Since every human being must sleep and dream, then each human being enters a paranormal state every single night.

If and when any overt, dominance-minded, Extra-Dimensional invasion of this Earth does occur—it may not be (at first) through any of the confrontational, physical, military vs. superior alien hardware scenarios that are played out in national military war-games and in Hollywood movies. It may be in a manner that bears with the central theme of this work—Extra-Dimensionality and all its implications.

Here is the final Grand Reveal of this book: any Extra-Dimensional invasion of Earth; will represent the ultimate TEOTWAWKI event. *It will occur in a commonly shared, world wide dream-state.*

The methodology and implications of this are beyond what can currently be conceived by human beings. That's exactly why it would work. Ninety nine percent of humanity has no abilities or skills in the dream state. Most people don't know how to "lucid dream" or what that really means. Because the mainstream is still frozen in the materialist-scientific paradigm, they don't even comprehend (or really even care) what the dream state really is. A multi-dimensional civilization advancing against humanity in this realm will do an effective end-run around all the human military, social and continuous resistance that might await them on the physical plane. They could appear and operate in a continuous, shared-dream common throughout humanity that would be without many of the restrictions of physical space and time. Yet, because the multi-dimensional nature of the Extra-Dimensionals, they will have great facility in moving about in this state, manipulating it, bending and commanding the "laws of dream physics" in this continuous, planet-wide dream. This dream-invasion will be an irresistible supplement to any physical action taken against humanity. During the ongoing dream state, many advances against humanity can be manipulated in order to affect the waking state of humankind. In that way effective resistance could be stamped out *before* it is even conceived in the physical world.

Humanity would face TEOTWAWKI in a world that they didn't understand even when it was simple. The Extra-Dimensionals could be everywhere at once and yet nowhere if they chose to be. In the "dream state offensive," they could create new civilizations blanketing the Earth in a moment while erasing the previous human matrix with barely a thought. They could raise E.D. Mega-Cities that, instead of buildings, would be made up of mountainous semi-biological protuberances that soar thousands of feet into a permanent red-haze sky. They could control absolutely every aspect of human movement, commerce and communication from this "dream dimension." They could make the shared, common dream state longer and *more real* than the physical world we wake up to. They could reduce the physical reality state to shorter and shorter periods. Those diminishing periods would be punctuated by blind terror and scheming for ways to stay awake—all to no avail and the moment that slumber overtakes us—they would be waiting on the other side to continue the dominance process they started. The dream-state reality would become our more vivid reality—like lucid dreaming but without any power in the human dreamer. In contrast, our physical—waking state would become a listless, gray, hazy sleepwalk through a shrinking (*in realness*) existence.

51

THEY ARE COMING

For those of you who are more concrete thinkers, who may have a difficult time grasping the reveal about "dream-state invasion," I have yet another reveal. It is purely rock solid and material in nature and I call it simply: *They Are Coming.*

The sad factor about this reveal is that it is commonly known information or at least it should be since it is publicly available for the cost of a few minutes of cyber-research. Surrounding the upper atmosphere of the Earth, there are numerous sentries keeping watch in the space directly around the Earth. These sentries consist of what appear to be ships of a wild diversity of shapes and sizes. These ships are not connected to anything remotely human. Many of these ships range in size from several miles wide or long, depending on the shape to *possibly hundreds of miles long.* These craft never appear to require fuel, sustenance of any sort or contact with any living creatures. These craft often tend to be of such massive sizes that they would be utterly impractical for humans even if we were moving the entire human race to another planet. They just circle and move around the Earth, just above the atmosphere, as if on guard duty in a tower. One of the most well known such craft is commonly referred to as "The Black Knight Satellite." It has been photographed and recorded in our upper atmosphere in various spots around the Earth for many decades now. It appears to be in the shape of a black metallic chess piece except it has no right angles—it was designed never to land on any surface. It was made to be perpetually out in space without any intention for it to ever land anywhere. It is sixteen miles long/tall and its age is estimated at about 30,000 years old—long before recorded human history ever began.

Could this craft carry the records of Atlantis or Lemuria? Could it hold other races that evacuated from Gateway Earth long ago? Left to human devices we will never know because NASA instead of investigating this structure was busily misnaming it as "a satellite," as if it was created and put into the atmosphere by humans. It is not a satellite. It is a non-terrestrial structure that has nothing to do with human origination. Five minutes of cyber research would reveal these same conclusions to anyone. These are not hidden facts. They are public and available to anyone.

Yet, the sixteen mile long Black Knight is only a small part of the innumerable army of sentries that presently surround this planet. There are many types of ships in space just beyond our upper atmosphere that are on patrol looking for anomalies in human space interaction. Again, none of this is the least bit secret. "The Tether Incident" was in February 1996 when NASA captured video of the International Space Station suffering an unforeseen incident. A twelve-mile long "unbreakable" tether was deployed which could conduct electricity in space. The tether was holding and preparing a satellite to be deployed from the Space Station until it unexpectedly snapped. The satellite floated away but that was not the most unforeseen part of the events. As the tether stood out from the Space Station in a straight line into space— *dozens* of PLAMAS swarmed into view checking out the tether, the satellite and what had gone wrong. One shocked NASA technician exclaimed: "I see the tether sticking straight out and many things swimming in the foreground." Another NASA speaker tried to put the numerous unknown vehicles off as "debris." They were clearly not debris. They were various unknown craft of different shapes and sizes (mostly disc shaped) that were intensely curious about an event in the outer atmosphere of space above the Earth. Something had clearly gone wrong in *their territory* and they were intent to find out what it was.

The video of this bizarre incident is still available for anyone to study. It clearly shows what appear to be numerous crafts. One of the disc-like objects is estimated to be *a hundred miles in diameter*. No one needs to trust NASA's descriptions. Any truth-seeker can see for themselves that there are dozens of vehicles speeding through the scene of the broken tether. Some of the craft pause only long enough to check the nature of the tether. Others simply speed through the scene of the Tether Incident. It seems that the Tether break was somehow sensed by these numerous sentries who left their usual posts around the Earth to check on the activities that created such an expected ripple in the space continuum. The only thing all the craft have in common is that clearly NASA knows nothing about any of them. NASA tries to disavow any knowledge of what they are. Later, it is revealed that none of the nations have any involvement or knowledge of what they are. How is it that these things are not detected from the Earth but can clearly be seen from the camera of the space station? It is because they somehow massively broke their cover (cloaking or invisibility) to investigate the Tether incident.

These are only two of innumerable incidents during the last thirty years during which PLASMAs are recorded checking on extraordinary human activities in our upper or lower atmosphere—such as the launching of a new rocket, launching of a space shuttle, launching of a missile, space travel and many other human phenomenon that entail travel in outer space. Even though NASA quickly shuts down and erases such video evidence, the viral nature of such things ensures truth-seekers will always have access to what really happened during these many incidents.

Here is *another* reveal of this section. These innumerable, gigantic sentries continue to patrol around the Earth, whether we can see them or not, *they are up there*. And they are waiting. They are waiting for some extraordinary signal to descend and establish their supremacy over the airspace just above the cities of the Earth.

The Hollywood depiction of unknowable alien ships coming in over our major cities and settling into fixed immobility over the great mega-cities of the Earth are largely accurate foreshadowing of future events. They will simply fall into place above the urban centers of humanity and they will NOT communicate or directly contact humanity—in the sense that no on will emerge from those ships. They will just hover there. Ships from several miles wide to ships one hundred miles wide will just hang over our cities—over our Earth. Imagine that for a moment. *Men's hearts will fail them for fear of things coming upon the Earth.*

This physical invasion will happen much sooner than we think and it will change everything. Beings we assume are inside these ships will not show themselves. I don't believe there will be actually anyone inside those ships. Instead of producing Extra-Dimensional beings, the ships will direct us to communicate with their representatives who are already here. These representatives will be said to be in constant communication with the beings inside these ships but we will have to take their word for that assertion.

Again, we are surrounded and *they are coming.*

The question that remains is what will be the trigger for this particular black swan event? I believe it will be any of the following: the detonation of nuclear bombs upon the Earth, world wide catastrophic Earth changes on such a scale that it will effect global disaster or, most likely, it will be an event mentioned earlier: the mass disappearance of entire cities, towns or a significant percentage of the human global population. Regardless of what the final trigger will be, the one thing I do know is this.

*They Are Coming…*and we are not ready.

As we get closer to this TEOTWAWKI event, I am reminded of the following story.

When I was twelve years old, my father would take me to my grandfather's farm for vacation. It was a working farm with chickens and horses. My grandfather had a teenage maid who would come around after school to help around the farm. She was about fifteen years old. Sometimes she would have some fun at my expense by bringing me out to the chicken coop with the announcement that it was time to slaughter a chicken for a special dinner. This was a chore that was done about once a month. She wanted to give me *the honor* of picking and delivering the animal for her to take to the slaughter area. I didn't have to see or participate in the slaughter but I considered it a fun assignment to collect the sacrificial animal. I would chase and grab at any chicken. Everything was a blur of white feathers, angry clucking and flapping resistance. Those chickens were so fast and angry it amazed me. Even when I got a hold of a wing, a head—even a tail—the hens would just flap, scratch and get free. After much running, fighting and even falling in chicken-poop—I emerged on several occasions from the coop scratched, humiliated and *chicken-less*. The girl shook with laughter.

For next time I had a plan ready. During the following weeks, I carefully spied the teen maid while she handled the chickens. I took mental notes. I was ready for the next time she asked me to help with the ritual at the coop. She did so with her usual smirk but was surprised when I volunteered and raced to the coop. She sat on her comfortable laughing bench and waited. I'm no good with livestock but I am good at imitating people. Just as I saw her do, instead of grappling with the bodies of the chickens, I snatched out the two legs of the slowest moving chicken and flipped it upside down. I held the legs in one hand and swung it along like a handbag. This was just as I had seen her do. The teenage maid was astonished. The kid was victorious. Once the chicken is held upside down they stop struggling—they're beat and they know it, no more flapping, scratching or fighting.

People who live only for the physical/material life we temporarily inhabit are like the hens, having a grand old time running around in and out of the coop. But the moment some force takes them outside that realm and holds them upside down—they become helpless. They give up.

Learn about what's on the other side. Don't wait any longer. It's not that hard. It just begins with a decision.

Be the kid—not the chicken.

The hour grows short. Recalling the debacle over the apocryphal date setting of 12/21/2012, we know that nothing really happened on that date. Yet, despite the fact that nothing happened on that anticipated date—everything that matters is actually happening.

We now pass the year 2015 *and beyond*; we see the true beginning of The Age of Mass Awakening. Date setting always takes away people's power. EPIC knows this full well so they will soon come up with another date to implant into the popular culture—another awaited "date that will change everything." When that one fails, another will be contrived and so on. People who are focused on dates don't focus on their own abilities and gifts to change the world they live in. Dates take away our power but Ages empower us. The Age of Mass Awakening could be five years or fifty but what really matters is that the Age carries with it no specific time-trigger for people to latch onto. *The trigger is you.*

The Age of Mass Awakening only opens doors and gateways that were previously shut. Individuals who boldly enter that Awakening Process must still step through the gateway and become the real change that engenders further awakening. They must withdraw their support from the EPIC systems that have kept them enslaved for so long. Then, they must go forward and create new alternative systems that will empower and lead humanity toward real liberty on levels never before seen on our planet.

52

THE AWAKENING RESOLUTION

So now what?

There is so much innovative thinking in the Awakened Community but what good is it if it doesn't lead us toward some sort of solution we can implement right now to prepare us for what is to come?

The answer to this very legitimate objection is to arrive at an inviolable resolve that we must unite in ways that will empower us to deal with the Extra-Dimensionals in the very near future, whether this will be amicably or not. Governments, national or global won't be doing it for us. They are busily preparing underground cities to hide in when the necessity arrives. We are on our own. If we don't help each other—we will be S.O.L.

The Awakening Resolution: *We, the Paranormal Believers, and all the Awakened Communities who can see beyond the frailty of this false reality, resolve to prepare for what is to come by coalescing into associations that utilize our paranormal talents and abilities; in this way we shall support, strengthen and meld together into partnerships that will help us to attend to the betterment of humanity.*

Here is the short version: *form tribes.*

I am not just talking about just any tribes but only those tribes that are anathema to the current mainstream reality paradigm and that are based upon the paranormal/spiritual abilities of those who form them.

I'm not talking about the tribes that drain and use up your energy as a means to keep you enslaved in a system that simply feeds you lies or tribes that make you watch bread and circuses so that you forget to look up and wonder what's behind it all. I don't mean: the struggle for power between the political right or left, the military struggle between Muslim nations and the Western world or involvement in any tribal wars declared by national governments. I'm not talking about the latest "EPIC created struggle" manufactured to keep prisoners occupied so they can't think of escape. I'm not referring to the tribal struggle for or against Global Climate Change, the tribal struggle to save the (insert endangered species here), the struggle to reform the prison system or even the struggle to change things in the mainstream establishment through mechanisms set up by *the mainstream establishment*. Mainstream institutions made these devices precisely to siphon and dissipate our potential energy for change.

If you see the mainstream lapdogs welcoming a new tribe—you must run away from it as fast as you can. If the corporate media cannot ridicule an Awake and Aware tribe out of existence, their masters have them use more direct methods such as character assassination and disinformation operations. When you see these moving forward, it is the crucial moment to support and assist those tribes.

There are many tribes being formed and strengthened among the groups in the Awakened Community to attend to our physical and survival needs: some are called preppers, survivalists, off-the-grid communities, micro-nations, and self-sustaining associations. Paranormal Believers have meet-up clubs, associations and conferences that constantly come together and support each other but these groups must prepare themselves for an influx—actually *a deluge* of interest and new membership as we go forward in the Age of Mass Awakening.

Paranormal Believers need to form elder-younger alliances for the organization, distribution and marketing of new materials. Seasoned Believers tend to have a great deal of personal history in the supernatural, a dearth of experience and knowledge that does little good to the wider Awakened Community of the planet if they lack skill in cyber-transmission of this wisdom out to the world. In academic and social venues, younger people crave to be immersed in such knowledge but they don't have the opportunity often enough. Whenever, such alternative education is made available to younger people; it tends to be wildly popular. That's why it is never allowed to go on for very long. The last thing mainstream University Academia needs is to be implicated in fomenting some sort of Mass Awakening among the very people they are trying so hard to put into a permanent mental slumber.

Yet these young people are exactly the segment of the population that Paranormal Believers must reach out to more than any other. These younger Awakening Believers are the ones who possess the skills that are absolutely required to effect wide scale distribution of paranormal education and truth. Teach a community college class, create a new booth at a paranormal convention, volunteer with younger people in any helpful capacity—but reach out to them and teach them that the version of reality being sold to them every day is a false veneer and that they deserve better.

One of the greatest scholars alive today is a man named Joseph P. Farrell. He is a PhD. refugee from university academia who writes about the hidden true history of cosmic wars and humankind that will never be allowed in the mainstream. Farrell wrote "Genes, Giants, Monsters, and Men: The Surviving Elites of the Cosmic War and Their Hidden Agenda." He has also given us "The Cosmic War: Interplanetary Warfare, Modern Physics and Ancient Texts." He is probably most well known for "Giza Death Star" series of books in which he explains what the Giza pyramids really are and why they were created. He is one of the most brilliant alternative scholars I have ever had the pleasure of listening to, reading and seeing. He has an extraordinary followship among young people.

Many years ago, while he was still a university professor treading carefully between the mainstream and the truthstream, he was encouraged by young Awakening Believers, who urged him to strike out on his own, away from the restrictions of mainstream universities. He was even encouraged by university students who aided him with the cyber-distribution and marketing of his work. Otherwise, his work might not be as widely known as it is today. The same is true for virtually every great alternative thinker. The moment they took their expertise from that small circle of devoted followers and expanded it through outreach, with help from those younger, tech-savvy people—their Awakening Movement went from being a cult to being a global movement.

No matter how much knowledge and or intellectual dominance an alternative researcher/thinker might have in any given area of truth-seeking; that intersection with "cyber-skilled" youngsters is what sparks inspiration and distribution at new levels they might never reach otherwise. Without this intersection being reached, all that knowledge and understanding can simply become "stove-piped" among a small circle of loyal followers.

That might have been fine twenty years ago when the gatekeepers of EPIC guarded every ingress and egress of information distribution but today the situation has radically altered. The major publishing houses of New York City that had an ironclad grip on the world of book publishing; are now just shuffling cadavers animated with a semblance of life but possessing none of its substance. The great "legacy" publishing companies have now begun disintegrating even as they amble along; keeping themselves barely alive on a respirator filled with the noxious fumes of empty celebrity and spiritless repetition of ideas from decades past. The greatest writers of tomorrow are already appearing from outside the ancient ruins of the establishment publishing system.

Another badly kept secret about the former Gate-Keepers of EPIC is that today, all the effects-filled Hollywood movies can be easily duplicated, almost completely, with a humble home-based computer studio utilizing software programs with commercially available retail OTS technology (Off The Shelf—not custom made software but commonly available software). A movie that used to cost several hundred millions of U.S. dollars to make, can now be duplicated by a couple of tech-nerds with some digital camera equipment, gritty determination and a few friends (yes, tech-nerds have friends even if it's just from their gaming ring) for grand total production costs of just a few thousands of dollars. The only thing they don't have that Hollywood movies have are establishment name actors.

Again, the only respirator keeping Establishment Hollywood alive is the empty celebrity factor of famous actors and actresses who crave the security and instant recognition of working with the big Hollywood Establishment. This system also is dying on its feet as more and more people realize it isn't actually that hard to find reasonably attractive people who can read, memorize lines and learn to emote. Joining that realization with the reality of gritty tech-nerds making movies in defiance of Hollywood establishment; is already making major inroads against the old Hollywood gatekeeper system. That's what "The Matrix" movies were—a major guerilla battle against Establishment Hollywood and the guerillas won.

Today there is a steady stream of high-end, technologically sophisticated special effects "blockbuster type" movies coming from independent American, Indian and Asian movie makers. This is especially happening in many other nations around the world where the local movie establishment isn't as strong or traditional as Hollywood is in the United States.

The Awakened Community, Paranormal Believers and all Alternative Thinkers must continue to storm the gates. The old establishment gatekeepers are dying but *they ain't dead yet.* As I write these words, physical newspapers (that carry news that is at least 48 hours old from the moment they are printed in an age when everyone can get cyber-feeds of up-to-the-second news) actually still exist and are bought in some places—who buys them and for what purpose I still haven't figured out. I shouldn't be that shocked—*horse and buggies also still exist.*

Just because horrific anachronisms still sputter red foam and agonize in their public death throes doesn't mean we should still pretend they are relevant. We must take every opportunity to withdraw support from their systems and funnel every support possible toward alternatives outside the mainstream. In the Awakened Communities, the elder-younger alliances will prove to be the most important new proliferation of tribes that will help spark Mass Awakening and the global spread of original ideas from the Awakened Community across the entire Multi-Verse.

For the practical considerations of creating and amplifying any type of tribe, I recommend the books of marketing genius, now turned bestselling author: Seth Godin; especially "Tribes: We Need You To Lead Us" and "Linchpin: Are You Indispensable?" He elucidates the mysteries of tribal formation, tribal maintenance and the punctuation of positive tribal rituals with products and global marketing. Godin is an inspirational writer/marketer who provides the absolute requirements and even the obscure subtleties of global distribution and viral marketing. Whether the product is paranormal related merchandise or just supernatural ideology; Godin is one of master-teachers at whose feet we need to learn.

As the old gatekeepers of EPIC finally die off, the new global direct-to-market paradigm requires that all in the Community of Awakened Paranormal Believers be humble, open-minded and gracious as we coalesce into dynamic new tribes for the magnification of human consciousness and our liberty.

One of the break through realizations of Awakening is this: *You Are Paranormal.*

The most important rising groups that need to assemble right now—forthwith—are those who possess paranormal abilities, which really means: anyone who finds themselves drawn to paranormal topics. Here's one of the great secrets I'm releasing here: you are not drawn to paranormal topics by some coincidence or happenstance of fate or luck—you are drawn to paranormal topics because, in part, *you are paranormal.*

Whether you display the abilities right now or are repressing them, they are there waiting to be revealed, used and employed for the betterment of humanity and Creator-Source's glory. The revelation of this secret is awful news to those who entire existence and advancement depends upon you continuing to believe that you are less than a miracle—that you are powerless and empty—just meat. To them, it will be a terrible day of reckoning when you finally stop the endless chase after the material goods they hold out in front of you and instead go inside yourself to find out that Christ told us the truth: *the kingdom of heaven is within you.*

It's all in there. The only question is which abilities will you display when the moment arrives to confront or welcome the Extra-Dimensionals?

Here are some current rising tribes in the Awakened Community.

The Out-Reachers—those who reach out to the Extra-Dimensionals—not the way it's being done now—recklessly. These are careful meditators who wrap themselves in prayers of protection to Creator-Source before they venture out on a quest into dangerous fields. They also use circles of light and other Shamanistic devices of light protection. Every little bit helps. There are astral predators out there in the Ekashic wilderness stalking about and seeking prey. Many adventurers who have boldly reached out without proper preparation and protection have come back with some nasty attachments.

The Out-Reachers prepare carefully and prayerfully. They also rid themselves of all human anthropomorphic tendencies (the inclination to humanize everything) and reach out to positive Extra-Dimensional beings of light for truth and understanding. Nothing negative can touch them, much less attach because the golden light of Creator Source's love covers them at all times.

True Death Returnees (TDE's)—Replace the old term "Near Death Experience." That is old paradigm language that must itself "die." These people have not been "near" anything. They died and yet they came back. Most often, they come back different and better…much, much better. They tend to come back with insights and abilities that you can only achieve by standing "in the Breath of God." They display a higher power of love. They detach from the materialist fantasy that this life matters (except in the aspect of providing opportunities to serve others). They often exult in supernatural abilities to continue higher forms of communication with positive forces of light. These forces from behind the veil tend to stay in contact with them for the rest of their material existence. The time to study these people like lab rats is past. We must sit at their feet and revel in the teachings they can bring us about what they have been shown. Human language is a poor vehicle to express such wondrous things but we can come close only through open minds and hearts.

How would you treat someone who went into a time machine and spent an hour with Buddha or Gandhi, upon the return to our time? Would you hand them over to old world scientists to be poked and prodded and interrogated? Would you sit with them and try to learn what they know? I would urge the latter. True Death Returnees have experienced Creator-Source Itself.

Clear-Hearers—Individuals also called Clairaudients have the abilities to perceive the words of a clear Voice of Authority that assists, protects and magnifies the perceiver during moments of crisis and turmoil—physical, spiritual or emotional. The Great Voice that comes to them often alters their destiny for the better and yet does not interfere with their personal free will. With practice, Clear-Hearers can contact the Great Voice at will for guidance, support and strength in any endeavor.

The Para-Investigators—are conventional investigators such as police officers, detectives, Federal Agents, private investigators and even *civilian truth-seekers*; who uncover and connect: clues and evidence utilizing rational investigative methods initially but then utilize intuitive paranormal mechanisms in order to reach their Para-Investigative conclusions. In a world filled with deception and subterfuge that is built into all major cultural systems; Para-Investigators are vital for separating truth from illusion.

Angel-Speakers—an entire subculture is now being composed around Angel-Speakers. These are people who have developed the ability to speak with, commune with and summon the assistance of angels. They develop a familiarity and intimate method of communication so that a constant dialogue exists between the particular type of angel (because each of them serve different purposes for Creator-Source) that helps the Speaker with their highest purpose, whatever that might be. Again, the purpose must serve light, not darkness—it must be for the benefit and betterment of humanity.

The Christ Based Transcendents—here is the tribe for all those Christ-Followers who have been chased out of "mainstream Christianity" which has little to do with true Christ followship anymore. This group of refugees is a massive worldwide movement that finds true spirituality and faith among others who believe as they do and who celebrate the paranormal as part of God's plan.

Ekashic Seers/Travelers—this rising tribe is composed of those who find truth through lucid dreaming, Out of body experiences and deep meditation—in other words, any of us could be in this group. The only question is what will we do with the insights we gain from the Ekashic Field?

Medical Intuitives—someday, I pray, medical personnel can someday all be in this category—openly. Currently, there are covert Medical Intuitives who are physicians, nurses, ambulance attendants and in every phase of the health industry. These are people with a supernatural detection and healing gift from God. I've seen them work and *it is amazing*. They can lay hands on a person or even an animal and they feel every rhythm and function of the biological system—through their hands. They then can assess and determine the deficit in the body and they act to correct it by natural means or by supernatural means when necessary. The only problem is that they must hide their abilities because we still labor under the old tyrannical paradigm of "*they're just meat so drug them with pharmaceuticals.*"

....and there are many more that we can discover together.

INVITATION

I fully expect for the ideas and suggestions from this work to be copied and spread virally. For this reason, I request that you do spread this book—share it with friends—with those with open minds and to believers and even with fence-sitters. Please give attribution to the Author and Publisher. Give encouragement to others that they may break from old paradigms as effectively as you have.

Always dare to seek out others who believe as you do. Seek fellowship among others who suspect what may be coming soon. If you have stories of contact with Extra-Dimensionals or of new concepts and truths in this area, reach out to us to share them. (Do not compromise any ongoing investigations.) Visit johntamabooks.com. God Bless you and may you always be a light for the Awakening of others.

John DeSouza

THE AGE OF MASS AWAKENING— TAMA LEXICON

False labels are in place to limit discussion and imagination, not to encourage it. Ludicrous descriptors are invitations to ridicule anyone who opens a paranormal topic for discussion. Breaking from this "control language" is the purpose of the New TAMA Lexicon. Discarding the old labels and refusing to support them any longer will be our first step down the long road to reclaiming our ideas, our thoughts and our truth.

The Extra-Dimensionals—non-terrestrial, intelligent life forms who are visiting our dimension of time and space as transitory beings *from outside* our plane of physical time and space—e.g.: from outside our material existence and who return to outside this physical existence.

PLASMAS—The TAMA lexicon replacement for the old mainstream trigger word: "UFO." This term is an acronym PLASMAS which stands for the following words:

Paranormal—Living—Aura-Reading—Soul-Printing—Mobile—Aerial—Scanners.

Paranormal—having supernatural qualities such that no terrestrial explanation or can be provided for this particular craft in the physical/material iteration of time and space.
Living—a living creature, sentient, intelligent but also programmable like a computer
Aura-Reading—able to read the auras and emotions of living creatures, especially humans
Soul-Printing—able to record, collect and store a blueprint of a human soul for later reference
Mobile—able to move through physical or non-physical media and even able to dematerialize
Aerial—most likely to be in the air because it wishes to be seen by as many humans as possible

Scanners—these are unoccupied scanners constantly roving to carry out their programming—to collect soul-prints of as many "interested" humans as possible

Warning: Don't start slinging around TAMA terms among mainstream repeaters unless you have complete command of this language because they will attack the user in keeping with their mind control training.

Decompensation—when an integrated system that has important biological functions can no longer compensate for defects or minor deviations in form and substance because it has grown exhausted, sick or overstressed.

The Six Percent Resolution: In paranormal areas, approximately 94 percent of reported incidents are those in which there are natural, physical or even fraudulent explanations ultimately provided or proven. This resolution still leaves an average of six percent of reported paranormal phenomena, which are genuinely paranormal or supernatural in origin.

TEOTWAWKI—The End Of The World As We Know It—the end of the previous world-view, the end of the previous system of understanding, the end of the ways thing were.

The Awakened Investigative Rule of Evidence: the true value of evidence is in the depth of its connection to human consciousness. The connection between evidence and human consciousness is formed by truth, faith and authenticity. It is only by making this determination that we can decide the true value of evidence.

Carpet Stain Syndrome—a collection of National government behaviors and responses expressed through: agencies, bureaus, military structures and various government actors aka: Carpet Stain Monitors; wherein governmental authority is used to secure the jurisdictional territory and responsibilities assigned to the monitor and reinforce the monitor's purpose: jurisdiction over his governmental carpet stain.

The Doctrine of Diminishing Returns: the return of liberty to the people for the sacrifice made by the Whistle-Blower is, in most cases, far out of proportion to make the sacrifice worth it. Due to the institutional and global power of EPIC, the modern lack of any independent investigative media and EPIC's willingness to abuse that power, Whistle-Blowers, in most cases, should forego that exchange in favor of joining Awakening Movements that will provide greater benefits to human liberty in the long run.

The Carpet Stain Doctrine: *Carpet Stain Monitors all over the world, in every national government, far prefer that the public think the worst of them: that they are lazy, indifferent, or part of a global conspiracy against humanity; rather than believe that they do not control their Carpet Stain.*

EPIC—The Elite Powers In Charge of the world that come from the ancient bloodline families that have ruled humanity since the very first world empire came to power. These same bloodlines have persisted at the tops of the pyramids of humanity through every successive world empire right up until today. They are not in charge of us as free and sovereign individuals but they are only directly in charge of the global institutions which tell our political leaders what they must do from day to day. Individuals accept EPIC power over their lives whenever they accept EPIC institutional conveniences.

The Persistent Consciousness Corollary—Since the basis of all reality is actually consciousness—not time, space and matter, things come into existence and remain in existence because we give them our energy in the form of attention, belief and our consciousness. We do not give them our energy because they exist. They exist because someone, somewhere has given them energy in the form of consciousness.

The Extra-Dimensional Corollary: given that Extra-Dimensional visitors to our planet are from outside the physical universe; it therefore follows that: there is no complex biological life (similar to ourselves) outside of Earth (at least on this physical plane of existence) and that our Earth is the sole origination point, entry point and transit point; for all biological and Extra-Dimensional life in our physical universe.

The Awakened Community—the disparate tribes that are awakening from the false paradigm of mainstream control institutions and searching for ways to break free: paranormal believers, political/religious institutional refugees and even cultural dissidents.

Hollywood CRAPOLA—The movie-making Establishment's regular practice of "Confiscation, Reshaping And Promotion Of Limiting Attitudes" in any area of paranormal concepts in order to redefine and reshape new contours of allowable thought on any supernatural topic.

MIB Reality Doctrine: The facts have clearly demonstrated around the world that the real Men In Black are contemptuous, abusive and disdainful of human civilians—in direct contradiction to Hollywood's portrayal which depicts them as heroes looking out for human interests.

The Second Extra-Dimensional Corollary: the passage of Extra-Dimensional Visitors into our dimension creates temporary "quantum-flux gate" portals that can be accessed by other energetic entities to enter our time and space. These entities (ghosts, orbs, crypto-creatures) vibrate at a similar resonance as the ED's they follow but may have nothing else in common with the ED's except for the actual transition point they use.

The Transdimensional Addendum: the assertion that no one can comprehend or begin to remedy problems that were created trans-dimensionally, while remaining confined to single dimensional thinking.

The Awakening Resolution: We, the Paranormal Believers, and all the Awakened

Communities who can see beyond the frailty of this false reality, resolve to prepare for what is to come by coalescing into associations that utilize our paranormal talents and abilities; in this way we shall support, strengthen and meld together into partnerships that will help us to attend to the betterment of humanity.

The Out-Reachers—those who reach out to the Extra-Dimensionals—not the way it's being done now—recklessly. These are careful meditators who wrap themselves in prayers of protection to Creator-Source before they venture out on a quest into dangerous Ekashic fields.

True Death Returnees (TDE's)—this is the replacement for the old paradigm language, "Near Death Experience." These individuals actually died and yet they came back to this life. They often come back different and better…much, much better. They tend to come back with insights and abilities that you can only achieve by standing "in the Breath of God."

Clear-Hearers—Individuals also called Clairaudients who have the abilities to perceive the words of a clear Voice of Authority that assists, protects and magnifies the perceiver during moments of crisis and turmoil—physical, spiritual or emotional.

The Para-Investigators—are conventional investigators such as police officers, detectives, Federal Agents, private investigators and even civilian truth-seekers; who uncover and connect: clues and evidence utilizing rational investigative methods initially but then utilize intuitive paranormal mechanisms in order to reach their Para-investigative conclusions. In a world filled with deception and subterfuge that is built into all major cultural systems; Para-Investigators are vital for separating truth from illusion.

Angel-Speakers—These are people who have developed the ability to speak with, commune with and summon the assistance of angels. They develop a familiarity and intimate method of communication so that a constant dialogue exists between the particular type of angel (because each of them serve different purposes for God) that helps the Speaker with their highest purpose, whatever that might be.

The Christ Based Transcendents—this is the tribe for all those Christ-Followers who have been chased out of "mainstream Christianity" which has little to do with true Christ followship anymore. This group of refugees is a massive worldwide movement that finds true spirituality and faith among others who believe as they do and who celebrate the paranormal as part of God's plan.

Ekashic Seers/Travelers—this rising tribe is composed of those who find truth through lucid dreaming, Out-Of-Body-Experiences and deep meditation—in other words, any of us could be in this group. These are those who enter the Ekashic Field to glean the truth of mysteries, deceptions and every hidden thing in the multi-verses.

Medical Intuitives— these are covert Medical Intuitives who are physicians, nurses, naturopaths and even non-professional caregivers. These are people with a supernatural perception and healing gift from God. I've seen them work and it is amazing. They can lay hands on a person or even an animal and they feel every rhythm and function of the biological system—through their hands. They then can assess and determine the deficit in the body and they act to correct it by natural means or by supernatural means when necessary.

BIBLIOGRAPHY–
ADDITIONAL RECOMMENDED READING

BIBLE QUOTATIONS

All Bible quotations are from the King James Version of the Old English Bible first published in 1611. Public Domain usage applies.

OLD PARADIGMS DECOMPOSE

THE PARA-INVESTIGATORS by John DeSouza

I begin this section with a shameless plug for one of my own books only because I have never seen any other work that defines and illustrates what an Awakened Investigator really is and what they can do. This non-fiction book is a collection of "X-file type," true stories about conventional investigators and even civilian truth-seekers that happen to have paranormal abilities. These tales recount how and why they employ these abilities to solve investigations and protect the public.

FIRE IN THE SKY: THE WALTON EXPERIENCE
by Travis Walton (Author)
FIRE IN THE SKY: THE WALTON EXPERIENCE; THE BEST
DOCUMENTED CASE OF ALIEN ABDUCTION EVER RECORDED
HARDCOVER by Travis Walton

Travis' trauma, recovery and even new insights in his own words in new editions and please buy his books directly from Travis Walton so he can continue to travel around the country and share his truth with others who have had similar experiences.

SIGNATURE KILLERS by Robert D. Kepple
SERIAL VIOLENCE: ANALYSIS OF MODUS OPERANDI AND
SIGNATURE CHARACTERISTICS OF KILLERS by Robert D. Kepple
RIVERMAN; TED BUNDY AND I HUNT FOR THE GREEN RIVER

KILLER
by Robert D. Kepple

These are the seminal nonfiction examinations of what serial killers are and how they function in a world that is dedicated to catching them and stopping them at any cost.

CAPTURED! THE BETTY AND BARNEY HILL UFO EXPERIENCE:
THE TRUE STORY OF THE WORLD'S FIRST DOCUMENTED
ALIEN ABDUCTION
by Stanton T. Friedman and Kathleen Marden

Stanton Friedman is the terrestrial gold standard of former old-world scientists turned Quantum Truth-Seekers and the universe is a better place for his courage.

MYTHS TO LIFE by Joseph Campbell

This book is an excellent examination of the driving forces that often make myths far more important to the development of a society than "solid facts" and about the ways in which myths actually tell more truth than facts and "provable empirical-based knowledge."

EXTRA-DIMENSIONALITY RISING

CONTACTEES: A HISTORY OF ALIEN-HUMAN INTERACTION
by Nick Redfern

Nick Redfern is among the most dedicated and professional journalists turned Truth-Finder in the Awakened Community today. His books cover every paranormal topic with meticulous attention to detail and great respect for the subject matter. Anyone who needs a solid background in paranormal history and supernatural reality should start with all his books.

A.D. AFTER DISCLOSURE: WHEN THE GOVERNMENT FINALLY
REVEALS THE TRUTH ABOUT ALIEN CONTACT
by Richard Dolan and Bruce Zabel

The case for unavoidable Disclosure is laid out by the most brilliant mind in the Awakened Community. Dr. Richard Dolan takes us step by step through the history of national government malfeasance, omission and obedience to powers far above them.

GREY ALIENS AND THE HARVESTING OF SOULS; THE
CONSPIRACY TO GENETICALLY TAMPER WITH HUMANITY
by Nigel Kerner

Kerner is exactly the type of innovative thinker that is so desperately needed in the Awakened Community to move forward after so many decades of being trapped in the old fallacies and conundrums of the EPIC systems. He is unafraid to breach the forbidden barrier between ufology and spirituality especially since this is the only way to get to the truth.

PRESENT EXTRA-DIMENSIONALITY

DECLASSIFIED H.P. ROBERTSON PANEL PROCEEDINGS AND REPORT OF SCIENTIFIC ADVISORY PANEL ON UNIDENTIFIED FLYING OBJECTS CONVENED BY OFFICE OF SCIENTIFIC INTELLIGENCE, CIA, January 14 - 18, 1953 (Document Credit: Government Document/Public Domain)

Facts reported in this typical Government Commission are mostly true but the conclusions are disinformation and fakery.

ALIEN AGENDA by Jim Marrs

Marrs is another former mainstream journalist who courageously departed from the mainstream for the truthstream. No one exposes cooperation between high government minions and the ruling class quite like Jim Marrs.

UFOS: GENERALS, PILOTS AND GOVERNMENT OFFICIALS GO ON THE RECORD by Leslie Kean B003JZDXFM

This work is the final authoritative and ultimate documentation of the fact that people with the most credibility and also the most to lose by telling the truth, are now telling the rest of us that Extra-Terrestrial beings have been visiting us for a very long time; despite the best efforts of the national governments to deny and obfuscate this truth.

THE PHOENIX LIGHTS: A SKEPTICS DISCOVERY THAT WE ARE NOT ALONE by Lynne D Kitei

An excellent case made for undeniable truth, paranormal reality and illustration of ruthless government disinformation.

THE EXTRA-DIMENSIONAL AGENDA

THE REAL MEN IN BLACK: EVIDENCE, FAMOUS CASES, AND TRUE STORIES OF THESE MYSTERIOUS MEN AND THEIR CONNECTION TO UFO PHENOMENA by Nicholas Redfern

Again, Redfern is the most reliable and consistent researcher/journalist in the

Awakened Community today. His documentation is outstanding and his research is impeccable.

FINAL EVENTS by Nick Redfern

This is Redfern's fascinating foray into the mind of spiritualistic/UFO believers and it is pretty shocking stuff. While Nick makes it clear repeatedly that he doesn't necessarily believe most of the assertions in this particular book, I can't help feeling he had a very good time regaling us with the fevered, apocalyptic passions in this work.

Books by Zecharia Sitchin:

> *TWELFTH PLANET: BOOK I OF THE EARTH CHRONICLES*
> *(THE EARTH CHRONICLES)*
> *THE LOST BOOK OF ENKI: MEMOIRS AND PROPHECIES OF AN*
> *EXTRATERRESTRIAL GOD*
> *THE STAIRWAY TO HEAVEN: BOOK II OF THE EARTH*
> *CHRONICLES (THE EARTH CHRONICLES)*
> *THERE WERE GIANTS UPON THE EARTH: GODS, DEMIGODS,*
> *AND HUMAN ANCESTRY: THE EVIDENCE OF ALIEN DNA*
> *(EARTH CHRONICLES)*
> *THE END OF DAYS: ARMAGEDDON AND PROPHECIES OF THE*
> *RETURN (THE EARTH CHRONICLES)*
> *THE WARS OF GODS AND MEN: BOOK III OF THE EARTH*
> *CHRONICLES (THE EARTH CHRONICLES)*
> *THE LOST REALMS: BOOK IV OF THE EARTH CHRONICLES*
> *(THE EARTH CHRONICLES)*
> *WHEN TIME BEGAN: BOOK V OF THE EARTH CHRONICLES*
> *(THE EARTH CHRONICLES)*
> *COSMIC CODE: BOOK VI OF THE EARTH CHRONICLES*
> *DIVINE ENCOUNTERS: A GUIDE TO VISIONS, ANGELS, AND*
> *OTHER EMISSARIES*
> *THE EARTH CHRONICLES HANDBOOK: A COMPREHENSIVE*
> *GUIDE TO THE SEVEN BOOKS OF THE EARTH CHRONICLES*

Sitchin was our greatest authority on Alien Hybrids and many other ancient alien mysteries. This is just a portion of his books. Amazing to see how much power innovative scholarship can have.

FINAL WARNINGS

> *THE ALIENS AND THE SCALPEL by Dr. Roger Leir*
> *CASE BOOK-ALIEN IMPLANTS by Dr. Roger Leir*
> *"IMPLANTS AND ALIEN AGENDAS" by Dr. Roger Leir*
> *OVNIS AND IMPLANTS by Dr. Roger Leir*

THE NEW ROSWELL by Dr. Roger Leir

There aren't many certified medical physicians who are willing to enter the arena of Extra-Dimensional implants and help those who so desperately need medical help. Having spent time with such individuals over the last two decades, I can express on their behalf: a thousand times a thousand times, "thank God for Dr. Roger Leir."

SECRET LIFE: FIRSTHAND, DOCUMENTED ACCOUNTS OF UFO ABDUCTIONS by David M. Jacobs

The desperation and helplessness of many Abductees is captured and presented by the world's foremost authority on Alien Abduction. Dr. Jacobs has dedicated himself to helping the most ignored victims of ET phenomena.

HUMAN RACE, GET OFF YOUR KNEES by David Icke

Icke is one the great Truth-Sayers of our generation and in this book he elucidates what our true value is and how the entire universe fabricated around us by our EPIC overlords is designed mainly to keep us away from that crucial understanding of our own true preciousness as eternal human souls.

HUNT FOR THE SKINWALKER: SCIENCE CONFRONTS THE UNEXPLAINED AT A REMOTE RANCH IN UTAH by Colm A. Kelleher and George Knapp

There are allegations constantly swirling around this place of eerie, non-terrestrial visitations, contacts, exchanges, and unspeakable rituals. I'm not sure how much of it is true but I'll see you there soon.

OPENING MINDS: A JOURNEY OF EXTRAORDINARY ENCOUNTERS, CROP CIRCLES, AND RESONANCE by Simeon Hein

Crop formations are one of the most important mysteries on Earth and we must find out their source in order to fully grasp their value to humanity and to the Earth

Books by Dr. Joseph P. Farrell:
GENES, GIANTS, MONSTERS, AND MEN: THE SURVIVING ELITES OF THE COSMIC WAR AND THEIR HIDDEN AGENDA
THE COSMIC WAR: INTERPLANETARY WARFARE, MODERN PHYSICS AND ANCIENT TEXTS
THE GIZA DEATH STAR
SAUCERS, SWASTIKAS AND PSYOPS: A HISTORY OF

A BREAKAWAY CIVILIZATION: HIDDEN AEROSPACE
TECHNOLOGIES AND PSYCHOLOGICAL OPERATIONS

In the paranormal there is far too much retreading of old ideas that just spin around and around for about sixty years or so. Farrell is an explosive thinker who has come to change all that. If you don't believe me just crack open one of his books but beware— this is not the usual whiney *"flying saucers are real, please believe us"* fare.

LYNCHPIN, ARE YOU INDISPENSABLE? by Seth Godin
TRIBES, WE NEED YOU TO LEAD US by Seth Godin

I never would have guessed that the Awakened Paranormal community would be led into the future by a marketing guru but I guess stranger things happen every day.

AUTHOR BIOGRAPHY

JOHN DESOUZA was an FBI Special Agent for over 20 years and collector of the real life "X-Files." The author has researched and uncovered paranormal experiences as they have been revealed to him. Trained as an attorney and investigating official of the U.S. government, John DeSouza unravels mysteries that elude investigators restricted to the purely material world. The author devotes himself to his companies and to writing books on spiritual and paranormal topics. He can be reached through his website www.johntamabooks.com or his email johntamabooks@gmail.com.

ACKNOWLEDGEMENTS

Many thanks go out to my assistant Goldie Serrano who has advised and counseled throughout the fruition of this project and to Scarlett Rugers who made it all look great. Also gratitude and respect to the iconoclasts at TAMA Publishing. Eternal gratitude also goes out to all those referred to in this work that gave testimony, interviews and encouragement that many would be helped by what this work had to say.

Made in the USA
Coppell, TX
22 March 2023

14625940R00128